'Ian Law has written an excellent book. It provides a wide-ranging overview of ideas and concepts, illustrated with reference to some illuminating historical and contemporary examples. It is all the more accessible to students through the specification of clear learning objectives at the beginning and references at the end of each chapter, the use of photographic and other illustrations etc., and the signposting of some of the key figures in the history of the study of ethnicity and racism. An ideal textbook for undergraduate students.'

John Gabriel, Professor of Sociology and Head of Department of Applied Social Sciences, London Metropolitan University

'This book is a highly valuable toolbox to understand the dynamics of racism, ethnicity and migration in the globalized world. It is clearly written and organized, exhaustive and theoretically sound. A must read, not only for the British academic public but also for students across the planet.'

Marco Martiniello, Research Director, FRS-FNRS, Professor of Sociology and Politics, University of Liège and Director of the Centre d'Étude de l'Ethnicité et des Migrations (CEDEM-ULg)

'*Racism and Ethnicity: Global Debates, Dilemmas, Directions* provides a thorough and perceptive analysis of some of the most critical issues facing the world in the twenty-first century. Concise, balanced and incorporating a genuinely global perspective, Law's timely book should be compulsory reading for every student wishing to understand this complex, dynamic and vitally important subject.'

John Stone, Professor of Sociology, Boston University and Founder Editor of 'Ethnic and Racial Studies'

Racism and Ethnicity

Racism and Ethnicity
Global Debates, Dilemmas, Directions

IAN LAW
University of Leeds

Longman
is an imprint of

Harlow, England • London • New York • Boston • San Francisco • Toronto • Sydney • Singapore • Hong Kong
Tokyo • Seoul • Taipei • New Delhi • Cape Town • Madrid • Mexico City • Amsterdam • Munich • Paris • Milan

Pearson Education Limited
Edinburgh Gate
Harlow
Essex CM20 2JE
England

and Associated Companies throughout the world

Visit us on the World Wide Web at:
www.pearsoned.co.uk

First published 2010

ISBN: 978-1-4058-5912-7

British Library Cataloguing-in-Publication Data
A catalogue record for this book is available from the British Library

Library of Congress Cataloging-in-Publication Data
Law, Ian.
  Racism and ethnicity : global debates, dilemmas, directions / Ian Law.
        p. cm.
  Includes bibliographical references and index.
  ISBN 978-1-4058-5912-7 (pbk.)
 1. Racism. 2. Ethnicity. 3. Race discrimination. I. Title.
  HT1521.L37 2010
  305.8--dc22

                                                2009042475

10 9 8 7 6 5 4 3 2 1
13 12 11 10 09

Typeset in 9.5/13pt Stone Serif by 30
Printed and bound by Ashford Colour Press, Gosport

The publisher's policy is to use paper manufactured from sustainable forests.

Brief contents

Contents

Acknowledgements

Firstly, this book is dedicated to my father Geoffrey Law, who died in April 2009. If there was one thing he really taught me it was how to look after your family, and his core values of care, fairness and positivity have been fundamental in shaping my outlook on the world. Huge thanks also to my family: Jude, Seb and Alex. Their unswerving support, help, criticism and advice has been crucial to the successful completion of this project. All three spent much time reading, discussing and giving critical comments on draft chapters for which I am particularly grateful.

Secondly, I would like to thank my many colleagues for their critical engagement, and I would like to single out Bobby Sayyid for his friendship and intellectual vivacity which have been a vital ingredient in pushing my ideas forward and in my enjoying the writing process.

Thirdly, many thanks to Andrew Taylor, Catherine Morrissey and Philippa Fiszzon, my editorial team at Pearson, for their tremendous support, encouragement and advice throughout this project, together with the many readers who provided valuable comment from start to finish.

Fourthly, the primary research on which this book draws received funding from a variety of sources, for which I am grateful; these include the European Union FP7 programme, the European Monitoring Centre for Racism and Xenophobia, the Commission for Racial Equality and Leeds City Council.

Fifthly, thanks to all those many ordinary people, particularly from racialised groups, who gave their time and input to the various research projects drawn on in this book.

Publisher's acknowledgements

We are grateful to all the reviewers who participated during the writing of this book for their time and scholarly advice.

We are grateful to the following for permission to reproduce copyright material:

Figures

Figure 6.1 from Report entitled 'Unfavourable view of Jews and Muslims on the increase in Europe' 9/17/08 from the Pew Global Attitudes Project, a project of the Pew Research Center, http://pewglobal.org/reports/display.php?ReportID=262

Text

Extract on page 10 from Race should be discussed and understood across the globe, *Anthropology News* (Takezawa, Y.), Feb/March 2006, Reproduced by permission of Professor Yasuko Takezawa and the American Anthropological Association from *Anthropology News* Volume 47(3), pp. 6–7, 2006. Not for sale or further reproduction; Box on page 17 from http://africawithin.com/bios/edward_blyden.htm, from the Biography Resource Center, 2001; Extract on page 42, African Ancestry Traces DNA Roots, The Washington Post 05/28/2003, permission from Steve Sailer; Article on page 46 from Culture24, Sarah Morley 12/05/2006, http://www.culture24.org.uk/places+to+go/east+of+england/ norwich/art37392; Extract on pages 48–9 from Caumartin, C. (2005) Working Paper No. 11: 'Racism, Violence, and Inequality: An Overview of the Guatemalan Case', Oxford: CRISE; Extract on pages 80–1 from Human Rights Watch. Human Rights Watch and Fédération Internationale des Ligues des Droits de l'Homme, *Leave None to Tell the Story: Genocide in Rwanda*, © 1999 by Human Rights Watch; Box on pages 146–7 from *2008 Hate Crime Survey: Antisemitism*, http://www.humanrightsfirst.org/discrimination/reports.aspx?s=antisemitism&p=index; Box on page 150 from 'The Political Breakthrough of the BNP: the case of Burnley', *British Politics*, 4, 1 (Rhodes, J. 2009), Reprinted by permission from Macmillan Publishers Ltd: British Politics (4, 1), copyright (2009) published by Palgrave Macmillan; Extract on pages 172–3 adapted from http://www.errc.org/cikk.php?cikk=2602; Box on page 188 from IRU (International Roma Union) (2009) Romani Nation Building Action Plan, London: IRU, author Floarea Maria (Florina) Zoltan and co-author Bajram Haliti; Box on page 231 from Documenting A Democracy website, copyright Commonwealth of Australia, 2005, http://www.foundingdocs.gov.au/item.asp?dID=64, Reproduced courtesy of the National Archives of Australia – originally published in *Documenting a Democracy* at http://foundingdocs.gov.au/; Extract on pages 225–6 from Lattimer, Mark (2008) 'Peoples Under Threat', in Minority Rights Group (eds) *State of the World's Minorities*, London: MRG.

Photographs

Corbis: Annie Griffiths Belt 91; Jim Young/Reuters 222; Rafiqur Rahman/Reuters 229; **Getty Images:** AFP/Getty Images 165; **Panos Pictures:** Justin Jin 199; **Print and Picture Collection, Free Library of Philadelphia:** 16; **Reuters:** 143; **Stefano Montesi:** 144; **University of North Carolina at Chapel Hill:** North Carolina Collection, Used with Permission of Documenting the American South, The University of North Carolina at Chapel Hill Libraries 56.

In some instances we have been unable to trace the owners of copyright material, and we would appreciate any information that would enable us to do so.

Other books by Ian Law

Racism, Postcolonialism and Europe, Liverpool: Liverpool University Press, 2009, edited with G. Huggan.

Institutional Racism in Higher Education, Stoke-on-Trent: Trentham Press, 2004, edited with L. Turney and D. Phillips.

Race in the News, Basingstoke: Palgrave, 2002.

Racism, Ethnicity and Social Policy, Hemel Hempstead: Prentice Hall/ Harvester Wheatsheaf, 1996.

Local Government and Thatcherism, London: Routledge, 1990, with Butcher, H., Leach, R., and Mullard, M.

The Local Politics of Race, London: Macmillan, 1986, with Ben-Tovim, G., Gabriel, J., and Stredder, K.

Race and Housing in Liverpool, London: Commission for Racial Equality, 1984.

A History of Race and Racism in Liverpool, 1660–1950, Liverpool: Merseyside Community Relations Council, 1981, with Henfrey, J.

1 Historical groundings: the global formation of racism

Key issues in this chapter:

- Race as a social and political construct
- The development of pre-modern race ideas
- The many different forms of race thinking
- The centrality of race to the formation of modernity
- Colonial genocide and race
- The development of resistance to racial oppression and the development of black consciousness

At the end of this chapter you should be able to:

- Understand the origins of race thinking
- Discuss the significance of historical contexts for race thinking
- Recognise genocide and its importance in colonial relations
- Understand the ways in which resistance to racial oppression has developed
- Discuss the contribution made by key black voices including W.E.B. Dubois and Frantz Fanon to the sociology of racism and ethnicity

Introduction

'We recognize and affirm that, at the outset of the third millennium, a global fight against racism, racial discrimination, xenophobia and related intolerance and all their abhorrent and evolving forms and manifestations is a matter of priority for the international community, and that [there is] a unique and historic opportunity for assessing and identifying all dimensions of those devastating evils of humanity with a view to their total elimination.

(World Conference Against Racism 2001: 9)

This book seeks to inspire a response to this planetary challenge. The most recent attempt to recognise all the many and varied forms of racism across the globe was at the World Conference Against Racism, held in Durban in 2001. Over 4000 non-governmental organisations and over 250 nations were represented, and all were concerned to address the operation of race and racism in their specific regional, national and local contexts. Inevitably conflict and discord arose with competing claims for recognition and reparations, for example for Atlantic slavery and over exploitation of indigenous peoples. But this event illustrated the huge complexity and variety of ways in which ideas of race and racism operate across the globe. In order to understand why and how racism has become such a critical source of global concern we need to examine the historical ways in which it has come into being.

The complex origins and the ongoing power and durability of race provide a central focus for this chapter. Race ideas have taken many different forms in different places and have been mobilised both to implement imperial conquest and domination and to voice narratives of emancipation and liberation. This chapter consists of three sections introducing the origins of race thinking, its mobilisation in mass violence and its use in strategies of opposition and resistance.

Firstly, this chapter will consider the development of archives of race thinking and notions of racial origins and ancestry to name and label perceived divisions between groups of people. Early pre-capitalist sources, or archives of knowledge, and contexts for race thinking will be discussed with attention to differing forms of white, black, yellow, Islamic, Semitic and gypsy racial categorisation. Particular consideration will be given to the development of both European forms of race thinking and racial systems of thought emerging from other regional contexts such as China and Japan.

Secondly, the links between colonialism, genocide, mercantile capitalism and plantation slavery will be examined. The intertwining of race with imperial expansion, the rise of nation states and the formation of racialised modernity will be identified. Genocidal strategies in Africa and Australia will provide case study material.

Thirdly, the progressive power of race to mobilise groups in the context of struggles of resistance, emancipation and liberation will be examined, for example opposition to slavery, African nationalism, Pan-Africanism and Négritude. The contribution of Edward Blyden, W.E.B. Du Bois and Frantz Fanon to these debates will be highlighted. This chapter will then provide a historical grounding in the global formation of race introducing the complexity of race thinking and its power to inspire both mass violence and mass resistance.

Origins: the complex global roots of race

[Across the world as civilisations and societies emerged, ideas of race have had practical adequacy for people in helping them make sense of their social and cultural position] The history and origins, or etymology, of the notion of race reveals a wealth of differing meanings (see Hannaford 2004: 5), from which emerged the central understanding that it refers to a 'rhetoric of descent'.

Key concepts: Race

The social and cultural significance assigned to a group of people who are recognised as sharing common physical or physiognomic characteristics and/or a common lineage of descent, hence for Goldberg (1993) race refers to a 'rhetoric of descent' resulting from cultural choices in naming a set of markers of difference between human beings.

Key sources: Ivan Hannaford (1996) *Race, the history of an idea in the West*, London: John Hopkins University Press; David Goldberg (1993) *Racist Culture, Philosophy and the Politics of Meaning*, Oxford: Blackwell; and (2002) *The Racial State*, Oxford: Blackwell.

[Naming, categorising and frequently mis-recognising people's characteristics, levels of civilisation, mental and physical abilities, cultures, sexual mores and/or biological kinship are required to construct racial differences] They involve the construction of myths of many forms. The ability of natural science to determine the truth or accuracy of these myths has often been highly questionable, as Chapter 2 explores in more detail. Racial myths have often been treated as self-evident truths in many societies.

Race ideas comprise many differing forms, elements and discursive strategies. This chapter is concerned to open up the ways in which some of these processes operate. Race ideas have often been intertwined with other notions of blood and kinship ties, descent, lineage and genealogy, and have been used by societies in the representation and making of both internal and external hierarchies of difference and belonging. Emerging constructions of colour and race in highly varying forms have been identified in many pre-modern societies including the Greco-Roman empire and in East Asia. The purpose of this section is to examine the durability and pervasive nature of elements of race-thinking over millennia, and particularly evidence prior to the development of mercantile capitalism. The many different ways in which race has been coupled with negative associations and linked to social action is at the core of understanding how racism works:

Key concepts: Racism

Racism comprises two core elements in all historical and geographical situations, it presupposes that some concept of race is being mobilised and involves negative attribution of a specified racial group. Identifying how race is being utilised and represented and how negative attribution is being articulated in particular situations are the two central problems that social scientists face in establishing the existence of racism across the globe.

Key source: Paul Spickard (ed.) (2005) *Race and Nation, ethnic systems in the modern world*, London: Routledge.

The formation of race thinking in Europe and the Middle East

Classical racism

The development of Western mercantile capitalism inaugurated the development of major international circuits of racialised human relations, for example Atlantic slavery. But, race thinking has deeper roots and the importance of recognising pre-capitalist, 'pre-modern racism' in Europe and elsewhere has also been strongly advocated (Delacampagne 1983, 1990). Here, modern racist discourse is seen as drawing upon and requiring elements of older discourses which are identified in the writings of ancient philosophers and medieval theologians and scholars. Delacampagne argues that the naturalised superiority of Hellenic culture in relation to both external 'barbarians' and naturalised internal divisions between propertied Greek adult males and women and slaves both involved the derivation of the cultural characteristics of a group from its biological characteristics. In addition, Aristotle discussed the nature of both the Hellenic race and other peoples, and there was strong evidence of colour symbolism in ancient Greek and Roman cultures, with whiteness being associated with positive values and blackness with death and the underworld. It has been argued that the reductionist move of inferring people's culture from their physical characteristics was not specifically racial in character, as it was applied to many different groups that were not defined in racial terms (Goldberg 1993). But not only is a focus on minority and migrant culture differences a constituent element of many forms of contemporary racist discourse today, but the denial of racism in the Greco-Roman empire has also been strongly rejected in recent scholarship. Benjamin Isaac's (2004) book entitled *The Invention of Racism in Classical Antiquity* makes a number of key claims. He identifies 'proto-racism' as the linking together of the character of entire peoples being determined by geography, with hierarchies determined by blood ties or lineage (autochthony) which is exemplified in the writings of Ptolemy of Alexandria. He also identifies assumptions that mixed descent would corrupt human qualities and argues that eugenics originated in the writings of Plato and Aristotle where it was seen as necessary for the upper class to maintain racial superiority. This work was drawn upon in the popularisation of eugenics in the nineteenth and twentieth centuries. Classification of peoples according to external physical features and derivation of characters and destiny from these, physiognomics, was shown to be highly popular. For example, Pliny the Elder provided an account of 'monstrous races' in the first century AD (Jahoda 1999: 3–4). Comparison of foreign people to animals and other forms of xenophobia and ethnic hatred are identified as becoming more hostile and aggressive in the context of imperialist and expansionist moments. Strong anti-Oriental attitudes emerged in accounts of Persians and here Isaac identifies a direct determinate link between imperialism and the inferiorisation of Asiatics. Proto-racism is also identified in Roman views of subject peoples, the idea of collective natural slavery was intertwined with patterns of conquest, subjugation and governance. This linking of proto racism and imperialist ideology is exemplified in the work of Tacitus in presenting Roman views on Germans (Isaac 2004: 515). Far from being irrational and nonsensical, then, these ideas were seen in many cases as a core element in the specification, delineation and political construction of these civilisations and societies.

Anti-Judaism and anti-semitism

Also in the Roman empire anti-Judaism became established. For example, there were anti-Jewish pogroms and riots in Alexandria at the time of Emperor Caligula and both Romans and Greeks refused to grant Jews citizenship rights

(Laquer 2006: 41). By the fifth century Jews had spread throughout the Roman empire. They subsequently became the object of demonisation and hostility driven by the Christian church, blamed for the death of Jesus Christ, and were subject to mass violence by the Crusaders across Europe and mass expulsions from English territories 1288–90, and notably in Spain, Portugal, Bohemia and Italy in the late Middle Ages (Poliakov 1975). By 1500 a well-established Jewish presence had disappeared from large areas of Western Europe (Edwards 1994). Religious anti-Judaism developed with a range of stereotypes, hostility and discrimination that later transformed into secular anti-semitism, which vilified Jewishness in the context of modernity and emerging nationalisms and highlighted ideas of racial difference (Bauman 1989) (also see sections on racial Palestinianisation in Chapter 5 and contemporary anti-semitism in Chapter 6).

Middle-Eastern racism

Ancient Hebrews thought interbreeding between different natural kinds abhorrent and saw it as leading to the development of a race of wild giants which is more clearly articulated in the Curse of Ham. (The story of Noah's son Ham is told in Genesis 9:18–25.) This biblical story involved God cursing black Africans with eternal slavery and has been used as the single greatest justification for slavery for millennia (Goldenberg 2003). Here Hebrews fused notions of blackness with ideas of bondage, pagan idolatry and accursedness. Use of the colour black as a metaphor for evil is found in all periods of Jewish literature and as David Goldenberg argues categorisation of humans by skin colour is found in Jewish, Christian and Muslim biblical texts from the seventh century onwards. Noah's sons are seen as representing the three skin colours of the world's population, with black indicating inferiority. Bernard Lewis (1971) confirms the existence of colour-coded identities and related forms of discrimination in the pre-modern Middle East, which became more fixed in the context of Islamic conquests of Asia and Africa and related processes of enslavement. This argument fits with that of historians such as Frank Snowdon (1970) who finds no evidence of anti-black racism prior to the sixth century, and Alistair Bonnett (2000) who emphasises the prevalence of whiteness in the formation of social identities in non-European and pre-modern societies and also the complex variation of positive and negative connotations.

Christian European racism

Following the rise of Islam and the Arab conquest of North Africa, notions of anti-blackness and Islamophobia became fused in the term 'Moors', with later became detached into 'white Moors' and 'Blackamoors' (Jahoda 1999: 27). The Jewish and Moorish presence in Spain which lasted for a millennium and their subsequent decimation and explusion is seen as a critical moment in the making of the race idea in Western civilisation. This involved the setting of Jews and Muslims outside the political community, the end of multi-faith civility, legitimised violence, and racial distinctions determined by a test of purity of blood to assess Spanish descent from those who had resisted the Moorish invasion in the eighth century and those who did not (Hannaford 1996). In confronting Islam, the symbolism of the black demon was transferred to Muslims, as Jan Nederveen Piertese (1994) notes; in early medieval paintings black Saracens are represented torturing Christ. A key thread to the making of a Christian Europe was opposition and denigration of Muslims as barbaric heathens, illegitimately occupying the Holy Land, and showing excessive violence and uncivilised morals and sexuality. These ideas and associated discourses constituted an archive of Orientalism which was central to the making of European culture. Edward Said (1985: 3) shows that,

> European culture gained in strength and identity by setting itself off against the Orient as a sort of surrogate and even underground self.

Classical knowledge is identified as a key archive from which representations of other peoples and other places outside the West were drawn (Hall 1992a). These ideas together with those from other key archives, including religious and biblical sources, mythology, travellers' tales and early ethnography, were reworked and assimilated into medieval European literature and other forms of cultural representation and knowledge. White/black dualism developed which involved religious associations with whiteness being linked to goodness and chastity, and these ideas influenced Western secular culture. Key ideas of nobility, colour, Christianity and superiority were linked together in Spain and other parts of Europe and forged into a 'colonial discourse of white superiority' (Bonnett 2000: 17).

European cultural hybridity

Denying the importance of external cultures to European civilisation helped allow the construction of white superiority. This intellectual stratagem has been highly influential on the development of Western knowledge, as Martin Bernal (1987) claims in relation to classical and archaeological scholarship. The interaction of peoples and cultures has been central to the making of Europe, for example the influence of Semitic and African cultures in the making of Greek classical civilisation. But the denial and 'forgetting' of this process in classical and archaeological scholarship in the nineteenth and twentieth centuries involved the construction of an 'Aryan model', which saw Greek culture as self-generated, fitting with colonial hierarchical and cultural racisms (Young 1994). This is a process that Bernal (1987) calls the 'fabrication of Ancient Greece' as the untainted cradle of European civilisation. This argument is developed more generally by Piertese : (1994: 146)

> each of the celebrated stations of Europe – Greece, Rome, Christianity, Renaissance, Enlightenment – turns out to be a moment of cultural mixing...the most celebrated European philosophies, political principles, forms of knowledge, technologies, arts and styles turn out upon closer inspection to be multicultural in character, origin and composition.

The hybridity of European culture, its borrowing, adapting and transforming ideas and influences from other regions did not necessarily involve recognition (as opposed to misrecognition) of difference and a decline in the racialisation of culture. Western culture was delimited and often constructed through race, for example in the development of Western aesthetics and morals, including ideas of virtue, sin and rights (Goldberg 1993: 39). This Eurocentrism revolves around assessment of others in relation to European social, economic and cultural norms, both inside and outside Europe. The next section considers forms of racialisation that developed within Europe.

The internal civilisation and racialisation of Europe and anti-gypsyism

The 'colonial' paradigm for explaining racism only through the operation of Atlantic slavery and European colonialism *outside* of Europe ignores the internal processes of civilisation and racialisation *inside* Europe that preceded colonialism, for example anti-gypsyism (Miles 1993). The political and social project of civilisation in Europe is documented by Norbert Elias (1982). Here, the development of codes of manners and behaviour by the feudal aristocracy were part of a process where they attempted to civilise themselves and then impose their civilisation on other classes inside Europe prior to colonial ventures and subsequent forms of domination. This process involved the racialisation of both 'superior' and 'inferior' classes and the subsequent civilising mission became a theme for European colonialism. The French aristocracy for example, as with the Spanish nobility, were seen as a race differentiated by blood ties and descent, from the lower classes, and with differing capacities for art, culture and civilisation. The formation of multiple racisms within Europe, such as anti-semitism and long-established anti-gypsy hostility, whose targets were internal groups also confirms the need to interrogate intra-national forms of governance and social control.

The contemporary vilification, discrimination and hostility faced by the Roma in Europe and their selection for total annihilation along with Jews in the Nazi Holocaust arise from their positioning as a racial threat to national stability. The Roma people arrived in Europe in the 1400s, having moved from India in a succession of migrations due to Islamic invasion of Asia during the Ghaznavid Empire. The historical roots of anti-gypsyism can be traced from this period and some key causes for this specific form of racism have been identified by Ian Hancock (1997). These include early associations between Roma and an Islamic threat with terms such as heathen, Saracen, Tatars and Gypsies being used and the equation of Roma skin colour with darkness, sin, dirt and evil, and accusations that they were spies, carriers of the plague and traitors to Christendom. Exclusivist Roma culture with restrictions on contact with non-Roma, combined with their positioning as outside the state and lacking protective territorial, military or economic strength, has facilitated their treatment as vulnerable scapegoats. This treatment included mass murder, enslavement and removal of children from families, for example in Germany from 1400 to 1800. By the early 1800s Roma were referred to as 'the excrement of humanity' and the 'refuse of the human race' (Hancock 1997: 7). (For further information see www.radoc.net, and sections on 'Who are the Roma' in Chapter 2, and also Chapter 7 on contemporary evidence of Roma exclusion and discrimination in Europe).

The formation of race thinking outside the West: China and Japan

A key concern of this book is to examine the formation of ideas of race across a range of continental contexts and to challenge theories which see race and racism as entirely bound up with the West, Atlantic slavery, European colonialism and globalised anti-blackness. Such accounts not only forget the longevity and variety of global race thinking but also fail to provide an adequate basis to understand and analyse the contemporary contexts in which racism operates and also the hybridity of European culture itself, drawing as it does on core influences from Africa and the East. The key point here is the need to recognise both the differentiated and highly varied forms of race thinking and racialised governance that developed within different societies, and the interaction and mixing of ideas about race and culture between different societies.

The necessity of recognising that the social construction of racial identities should be understood as a global process being produced by many societies outside the West is exemplified effectively in examination of the cases of China and Japan. The development of racial theories and race ideas in East Asia, particularly China and Japan, has been established by a growing group of scholars including Frank Dikotter (1992, 1997), Michael Weiner (1997, 2004), Kai-Wing Chow (1997) and Kazuki Sato (1997). The centrality of the race idea in the development of both Chinese and Japanese societies has drawn on notions of blood, barbarism, skin colour, lineage, purity, pollution and pseudo-scientific classifications such as ideas based on differences in hair and odour. Beyond the development of racist cultures, myths both of descent and of the origin of peoples have played a key part in the construction of nation states, whether referring to the invention of the Han race and associated biological descent from the 'Yellow Emperor' of China or the identification of the pure 'Yamato race' in Japan. The largest national group in China is Hanzu, or 'Han race lineage', who have a sense of affective belonging to the 'yellow race'. There are many other minority groups in China and conflict and policy regarding these groups and relations with Tibet will be examined in Chapter 5 and also Chapter 9. In both countries nationalist movements have presented imagined biological groups as having unified political and territorial claims.

Race in China

From antiquity China's pre-modern elite developed the notion of colour consciousness and a white–black dualism, with white complexion being identified as beautiful and highly valued and dark complexions being negatively valued. This colour consciousness inscribed class differentiation between the elite and peasants or slaves, and reflected widespread cultural aesthetics. Early sources equated Africans with blackness, slavery and the lowest social standing and this 'existed well before Westerners established themselves at the frontiers of Empire' (Dikotter 1992: 17). Westerners' 'ash-white' complexions were seen as physically defective. Sources from the tenth century onwards increasingly referred to the symbolic value of yellow, with its attached meanings of superiority, progress and nobility, and to China as the 'yellow centre' (*huangzhong*) as distinct from barbarians who lived elsewhere and had different cultures and customs. In the context of increasing interaction with the West, Chinese people abandoned their claim to be 'White' as they and Europeans came to refer to them as 'yellows' and this was a firmly positive form of identification with deep symbolic roots in Chinese culture. The idea of a yellow race developed rapidly in Europe with the French scientist Bernier distinguishing four races including the 'yellows' in 1688 (Dikotter 1992: 55). Racial consciousness developed rapidly from areas that were having increasing contact with Westerners and others, such as Canton, spreading to the rest of the country. In China, 'the discourse of race has shown singular resilience throughout recent history and has tended to drift towards the centre in periods of instability' (Dikotter 1992: 195). By the late nineteenth century China was undergoing major social transformation with reformers challenging the traditional elite. One of these reformers, Yan Fu, introduced an elaborated discourse of racial hierarchy, and identified the white, yellow, brown and black races, with the black race as the lowest. Domination of the world by the white race was seen as the key threat, which necessitated a military and economic challenge to foreign trade and intervention which the yellow race had to engage in to survive. Here, Charles Darwin's ideas of racial evolution were integrated with the Chinese notion of *zhong* ('race', 'breed', 'seed' or 'type') (Chow 1997: 36). In addition, representation of Jews and the language of anti-semitism was also appropriated and used to legitimise Chinese racial discourse' (Xun 1997: 56). A warning note on Dikotter's account is sounded by Bonnett (2000: 8–14), who urges care in reading pre-modern sources from a modern perspective and overstating the development of race categories. For example, through the application of modern meanings in the translation of earlier concepts, for example 'zu', which carries a general meaning for a group of people linked by descent rather than a more clearly delineated idea of 'race'. But he does argue for the need to recognise the existence of pre-modern white identities confirming that Chinese people employed the category white to define which social group they belonged to. He also expands this point to suggest that whiteness was a widely used identity construct in non-European and pre-modern societies including those in South America and Africa, which facilitated, but did not determine, the formation of modern ideas of race and racism (for further information see section on China and Tibet in Chapter 5).

Race in Japan

In the case of Japan, racial discourse similarly developed through the grafting together of emerging ways of understanding relations between the Japanese and others, including Shinto beliefs in divine ancestry and Confucian ideas of social hierarchy, with emerging European ideas of racial categories, typologies and hierarchies, for example notions of black inferiority (Weiner 1997, Young 1997). The development of Japanese colonialism was articulated through racialised language and 'levels of civilisation', legitimating aggressive modernising Japanese expansion in the face of backward, inferior colonial subjects. In the face of Western imperialism, the 'white peril', the Japanese integrated European ideas of racial fear (yellow peril) and racial mission (the white man's burden) (Young 1997: 161).

Contemporary evidence of the durability of racism has been identified in both the stereotyping and infantilisation of 'Blacks' in political discourse and advertising campaigns, and widespread publication and sale of virulently anti-semitic material (Weiner 2004: 8). Seeing racism as a Western invention and hence only referring to European domestic and colonial contexts has worrying political implications in that it has provided a rhetorical strategy for countries in East Asia to resist attempts by the United Nations to promote elimination of racial discrimination (Dikotter 1997: 2). Japan belatedly signed up to the UN Convention on Racial Discrimination in 1996. Notions of Japanese racial and ethnic purity have underlain reactions to both migrants and other minorities. The position of the Burakumin group exemplifies some of these arguments:

The Burakumin in Japan and minorities in other non-European contexts

Burakumin people were officially designated as outcastes in the Tokugawa, or early modern period in Japan, although caste systems were abolished a few years after the Meiji Restoration in 1867. Burakumin are, in reality, physically identical to other Japanese, and the only distinct markers have been location in specific residential districts and stigmatised occupations such as those dealing with death including leather workers and undertakers, these workers are also called '*eta*'. For centuries, and among some even today, many in Japan assume the burakumin have an alien racial origin, despite no scientific evidence for this. Such beliefs can be traced all the way back to medieval literature. For example, one document in the early eighteenth century states, 'They are polluted due to being different in species (race) origin [from us].' At the same time there are medieval sources that show the institutionalised discrimination through codified laws. A law in the mid-sixteenth century even stated that anyone who associated with *eta* would be 'punished by stones being piled on top of them'. So, clearly both ideas about alien racial origin and practices of institutionalised discrimination already existed in the pre-modern period in a society outside the West, namely Japan, though they were later greatly transformed in the modern period.

There are many other cross-cultural, ethnographic examples of groups that have certain features in common with the burakumin: for instance, the pekuchon of Korea, quho of Sichuan Province in China, and the low caste people of the Toba Batak of Southeast Asia, the Yap of Micronesia, and the untouchables of India, Nepal and Sri Lanka. All of these groups have been socially stigmatised, discriminated against and ranked low in social hierarchy based on a folk belief that they are 'impure', and each is then recognised by both themselves and others as having different descent. Further, the discrimination against them is institutionalised, involving how land and other kinds of resources are distributed.

Many of these groups have traditionally been recognised by state and international governments only as religious minorities or former outcastes. At least that is the justification the Indian government used when it refused a proposal to include the historically discriminated against Dalits, in the past known as 'untouchables', in the agenda of the 2001 UN World Conference Against Racism held in Durban, South Africa. The Japanese government has also taken the same position in the past, acknowledging the discrimination, but not racism, the burakumin have suffered. Because these groups do not fit the established concept of race primarily defined by Western scholars, it allows governments and policymakers an excuse not to recognise them as having experienced racism, and thus to keep them from participating in global discussions to address social injustice.

Source: extracts from 'Race should be discussed and understood across the globe', *Anthropology News* (Takezawa, Y.), Feb/March 2006, Reproduced by permission of Professor Yasuko Takezawa and the American Anthropological Association from *Anthropology News* Volume 47(3), pp. 6–7, 2006. Not for sale or further reproduction.

A recent report by the UN Commission on Human Rights on racism in Japan concluded that there is racial discrimination and xenophobia in Japan, and that it affects three groups: the national minorities – the Buraku people, the Ainu and the people of Okinawa; people and descendants of former Japanese colonies – Koreans and Chinese; foreigners and migrants from other Asian countries and from the rest of the world. It said that

'all surveys show that minorities live in a situation of marginalisation in their access to education, employment, health, housing, etc. Secondly, the discrimination is of a political nature: the national minorities are invisible in State institutions. Finally, there is profound discrimination of a cultural and historical nature, which affects principally the national minorities and the descendants of former Japanese colonies. This is mainly reflected in the poor recognition and transmission of the history of those communities and in the perpetuation of discriminatory images of those groups.

(UNHCR, 2006: 2)

Race, colonialism and genocide

[The history of race is not just about the development of a set of ideas, it is also about the operation of systems of domination and governance and in many cases mass killing.]The power dynamics that construct racial differences across many societies have operated in the context of colonialism and empire, as has been argued in the cases of China, Japan, Europe and the Middle East.] There have been many types of colonialism and they have invariably resulted in the construction of racialised hierarchies (Memmi 1967). For example:

> The British in South Africa and India, the French in North Africa, the Germans in Southwest Africa, Euro-Americans in California and Hawai'i, Soviet Russians in Central Asia and Italians in Eritrea. In each of these places the colonisers created a language of racial order with themselves at the top and local peoples arrayed below.
>
> (Spickard 2005: 14)

[Colonialism is the 'conquest and control of other people's land and goods] (Loomba 2005) and it has been a pervasive feature of modern historical social relations often involving a process of escalating domination. Iberian expulsion and persecution of Jews and Muslims, and English treatment and domination of the Irish provided lessons in state governance which were drawn upon by Spain, Portugal and England in the development of European expansionism in the Americas. Howard Winant (2001: 41) refers to this as a 'proto-racial rehearsal for broader imperial efforts'. The elaboration of racial distinctions as a means of exercising colonial power involved the stripping away of prior tribal and kinship identities and the social death of those who were subjugated. The English colonised Ireland from the mid-sixteenth century, subduing the native Irish through this process and establishing plantations.

Close parallels in such processes of racialised governance of the Irish have been drawn with Native Americans and African slaves by Theodore Allen (1994), with enormous variation in the nature and intensity of racism across different colonial contexts and historical moments (Thomas 1994). A relatively simple division has been identified between those contexts where colonial relations with indigenous people involved land dispossession and genocidal extinction, and colonial relations based on control of trade, with marked variations in stereotypes and imagery (Hulme 1986). The rich cultural and state reservoirs of race thinking, imagery and oppressive practices provided European nations with a repertoire of ideological positions and arguments which were used to construct patterns of social interaction as global international trade and colonial settlement developed. Race was exploited for the benefit of Empire. Key elements of settler colonialism discourse included denial of native people's rights to land on which they lived, seeing conquest as justified by religion where native souls were saved, and seeing extermination of 'primitive' people as a natural part of modern progress (Jones 2006: 68). Mis-recognition of differences between Europeans and indigenous peoples, whether physical or in patterns of sexual morality, systems of trade, religion or governance, was a central component in the formation of Western notions of superiority and colonial conquest.

One-sided mass killing of vulnerable social minorities primarily by states, or other official actors, characterises the phenomenon of genocide. Many of the historical and contemporary examples of such international crimes involve forms of racialisation as in the case of the Roma, with the most recent example being persecution in Kosovo during 1998–99. The rise of race as a central feature of the modern world system from the 1400s onwards has been etched into our memory and understanding of the world by key forms of genocide. These include mass killing of indigenous peoples in the Americas and Australia in the context of settler colonialism, and Atlantic slavery which, despite its impulse to exploit labour, constituted one of the worst examples in human history, involving 15–20 million deaths (Jones 2006: 23). Forms of bondage and slavery were present across Africa, and in particular Islamic Africa, before Atlantic slavery became established. Major differences between these earlier forms and the system instituted by European states in terms of scale and institutional character is clear, although this question is the subject of fierce debate (Walvin 1992: 8).

Key concepts: Genocide

To murder in whole or substantial part any national, ethnic, racial, religious, political, social, gender or economic group.

(Jones 2006: 22)

Genocide is a 'crime under international law', and includes acts such as:

Killing members of the group,

Causing serious bodily or mental harm to members of the group,

→

Deliberately inflicting on the group conditions of life calculated to bring about its physical destruction in whole or in part,

Imposing measures intended to prevent births within the group,

Forcibly transferring children of the group to another group.

(UN Convention on Genocide 1947, Articles I and II)

Key source: A. Jones (2006), *Genocide: a comprehensive introduction*, Abingdon: Routledge)

- In the *Caribbean* an early territory to be conquered was Hispaniola (now Haiti and the Dominican Republic), here Spanish slaughter over 30 years reduced the indigenous population from 8 million to 20,000
- In *Canada and the USA* the local native population was reduced over five centuries from about 10 million to 237,000 involving state sanctioned mass killing, disease epidemics, death marches to reservations, vigilante killing, starvation, elimination of food sources such as buffalo and bison, and removal of children into residential institutions.
- In *Australia*, from 1788 to 1911, the aboriginal population was reduced from about 750,000 to 31,000 by massacre, disease, starvation, campaigns of extermination and removal of children from their families into white-run institutions (Jones 2006: 70–85).

These examples indicate the sheer scale of death that arose from the establishment of settler colonial societies. Colonial genocide accompanied exploitation of land, minerals and human resources and was therefore central to the development of European capitalism. Huge tracts of land were seized, native populations were destroyed, plantation production was established and Atlantic slavery brought Africans to labour in the New World. The growth of genocidal settler colonies, where developing democracy went hand in hand with mass killing provided the imperial context for Spanish, Portuguese, Dutch, British and French plantation slavery.

Plantation slavery developed from its beginnings in mid-sixteenth-century Brazil and by the late seventeenth century hierarchies of racial distinction were integral to class relations across colonial societies. The periodisation of Atlantic slavery has been defined as:

- *implantation* (1492–1650) involving exploration, settlement and conquest;
- *maturity* (1650–1770) with the growth of colonial governmental institutions; systems of trade and economic production and social hierarchies;
- *transition* (1770–1888), a period of revolution, rebellion and abolition, which came lastly to Brazil in 1888 (Karras and McNeill 1992).

These periods have inscribed race into the foundation of modern nation states and the establishment of the international economy placing race at the centre of the making of modernity.

Michael Mann examines the specific case of genocidal democracies in the New World and suggests that here settler democracies, for example in the United States, Mexico and Australia, illustrate the most direct relationship between democractic regimes and mass murder of all the examples he studied, 'the more settlers controlled colonial institutions, the more murderous the cleansing' (Mann 2005: 4). The nature of racialised hierarchies and levels of violence is seen here as being dependent on the nature of economic, political, military and ideological power relations established between colonisers and colonised. Mann distinguishes an ascending level of violence between settlers and natives across a typology of economic relations:

- trading colonies where little settlement took place and where little conquest and little violence and murder took place and initial entry with reliance on local elites and more ambivalent construction of racial difference;
- plunder and tribute-taking, for example Spanish incursions into America;
- plantation colonies, pioneered by the Portuguese, where local people were worked to death;
- settlements not requiring native labour where indigenous people were subject to mass murder show an increasing level of violence.

The last of these colonial situations is well exemplified by the Tasmanian case. Here, settlers had extensive powers, a de facto settler democracy, but no desire to utilise native labour and genocide ensued:

> About 4,500 aborigines lived on the island [Tasmania] when they arrived in 1804. Every full-blooded aborigine was wiped out inside 80 years. The last man died in 1869 and the last woman in 1876. A few of mixed blood survived. Shooting on sight, 'hunting parties' and poisoning flour were more common here ... the last aborigines were transported to a small island and crowded together with little food.
>
> (Mann 2005: 83)

The recent BBC4 series, *Racism: a short history* (2006) provided coverage of this case and interviews with some of the last aborigines remaining. This series also highlighted a more recent example, the genocide of the Herero and the Nama in South West Africa by German modern military means. In Namibia by 1911 only 16,000 of the Herero population, which numbered up to 80,000 in 1903, were left alive. This was the first genocide of the twentieth century and through its use of concentration camps, the idea of complete annihilation (*vernichting*) and racial supremacy it has been argued to provide an important precursor to both the Armenian genocide and the Nazi holocaust (Madley 2005, Mann 2005, Jones 2006).

Mobilising race: blackness

Slavery, colonialism and genocide which have sought to establish the system and sub-systems of a 'global racial order' have everywhere spawned resistance and this has taken many different forms. In examining resistance to Atlantic slavery

Winant (2001) provides a valuable account of some of these struggles including sabotage, subversion, escape, revolt, revolution, abolition and maroonage. Maroonage is a common feature of many slave systems and is the formation of communities of escaped slaves. Brazil, Surinam and Colombia are some examples of places where this process has been examined. Later forms of resistance include anti-colonial, national liberation and anti-racist movements. The construction of black identities across the globe revolve around three forms of thinking and reflection or reflexivity (this is where self-conscious evaluation of one's specific social context informs action to change that social situation):

- an anti-*slavery* reflexivity which is concerned with restoring humanity and integrity to black people;
- an anti-*colonial* reflexivity that makes claims for black people's 'lives, livelihoods and cultural heritage' in the context of national sovereignty;
- an anti-*racist* reflexivity which challenges racialised inequalities in material and political conditions in Western societies (Hesse 1999).

Key theme: The Double Use of Race Ideas

Race has not only been used to structure and carry through colonialism and imperial domination, it has also been inverted and used to mobilise and champion resistance.

In this section we look at the social and political construction of blackness and the contribution to the understanding of race by Edward Blyden, W.E.B. Du Bois and Frantz Fanon.

There are many places in the world where racial dynamics are fundamental to understanding the operation of society and where 'Blackness (far from being the master narrative) is a non-issue' (Spickard 2005: 21), for example Japan, Turkmenistan or Cambodia. But across many regions of the world where people called 'Black' live, the political idea of blackness has provided a powerful motif for the development of individual consciousness and collective narratives of emancipation and liberation. During the late eighteenth century, resistance to Atlantic slavery took many forms including armed struggle and the development of the political movement of Pan-Africanism.

Toussaint L'Ouverture: the racialised image of a revolutionary

Black revolutionary: Toussaint L'Overture

In the French colony of St Domingue, Toussaint L'Overture led the largest slave revolt in history which began in 1791. This eliminated France as a major slaveholding power and led to the founding of independent Haiti in 1804. For this challenge to European racial colonialism he was routinely vilified and this is also evident in representations of his body. The French considered Toussaint 'a villain ... this serpent which France has warmed in her bosom,' and representations of him by French artists reflected this perspective. In 1832, a new image lithographed by Nicolas Eustache Maurin appeared in *Iconographie des contemporains*, with a facsimile of Toussaint's signature below. No doubt influenced by three decades of vilification of Toussaint, the portrait's ape-like profile was widely accepted as an authentic likeness, and it became the most frequently reproduced image of Toussaint.

Source: This and further discussion can be found at the *Africans in America* website, **www.pbs.org/wgbh/aia/home.html**.

Toussaint L'Ouverture
Source: Print and Picture Collection, The Free Library of Philadelphia.

The moves to build links between slave-led resistance struggles and leading activists and intellectuals across differing colonial contexts in Europe, North America, the Caribbean and Africa led to the early development of Pan-Africanism, a political movement which sought to emphasise the commonality of shared suffering and exploitation of black people. Quobna Cugoano, Olaudah Equiano and Ignatius Sancho, a group of African scholars who were all former slaves, produced key texts and campaigned for abolition. These works included Cugoano's *Thoughts and Sentiments on the Evil and Wicked Traffic of the Commerce of the Human Species*, the first directly abolitionist publication in English by an African, which was published in 1787 and addressed to the 'Sons of Africa by a Native'. Narratives of race, slavery and resistance were also to be found in an emerging genre of autobiographies, captivity stories and memoirs published by African-Americans, including one of the most widely read – *Narrative of the Life of Frederick Douglass, An American Slave*, published by the Boston Anti-Slavery Society in 1845. Broken bonds between mother and slave, the victimised/whipped female body and the struggle for education and freedom were key themes in this powerful anti-slavery text. The mobilisation of slaves, developing democratic movements and the rise of industrial capitalism facilitated the abolition of African slavery, but continuing racialisation of post-slavery societies and strengthening imperial governance brought new challenges. As Seymour Drescher (1990) reminds us in his account of the emergence of European scientific racism which began during this period, 'the entire abolitionist process altered the path of racism very little' (quoted in Smaje 2000: 160).

The mobilisation of black consciousness and its linking to modern Pan-Africanism can be clearly found in the writings of a group of black intellectuals working at the end of the ninteenth century which include Edward Blyden. He maintained that all races were equal, but advocated black 'race purity' as a mental buttress against European colonial domination (Law 1985, Lynch 1971). He also advocated the use of African names and dress and championed the establishment of educational and cultural institutions specifically designed to meet African needs and circumstances.

Black spokesman: Edward Blyden

Edward Wilmot Blyden (1832–1912) was the father of West African nationalism and, together with Henry Sylvester Williams, of Pan-Africanism. He was born in the Virgin Islands, went to the United States to become a clergyman but was denied a place at theological college because of his race. In January 1851 he emigrated to Liberia, an African-American colony which had become independent as a republic in 1847. He subsequently was appointed to become professor of classics at the newly opened Liberia College. He was also an accomplished historian and sociologist. From 1871 to 1873 Blyden edited *Negro*, the first explicitly pan-African journal in West Africa. He saw himself as a champion and defender of his race and in this role produced more than two dozen pamphlets and books, the most important of which are *A Voice from Bleeding Africa* (1856); *Liberia's Offering* (1862); *The Negro in Ancient History* (1869); *The West African University* (1872); *From West Africa to Palestine* (1873); *Christianity, Islam and the Negro Race* (1887), his major work; *The Jewish Question* (1898); *West Africa before Europe* (1905); and *Africa Life and Customs* (1908).

Edward Blyden
Source: Library of Congress Collection.

Blyden sought to prove that Africa and Africans have a worthy history and culture. He rejected the prevailing notion of the inferiority of the black man but accepted the view that each major race has a special contribution to make to world civilisation. He argued that Christianity has had a demoralising effect on blacks, while Islam has had a unifying and elevating influence. Blyden's political goals were the establishment of a major modern West African state which would protect and promote the interests of peoples of African descent everywhere. He initially saw Liberia as the nucleus of such a state and sought to extend its influence and jurisdiction by encouraging selective 'repatriation' from the Americas. He hoped, also in vain, that Liberia and adjacent Sierra Leone would unite as one nation. He was ambivalent about the establishment of European colonial rule; he thought that it would eventually result in modern independent nations in tropical Africa but was concerned about its damaging psychological impact. As a cultural nationalist, he pointed out that modernisation was not incompatible with respect for African customs and institutions.

Sources:

A full-length biography of Blyden can be found in Hollis R. Lynch (1967), *Edward Wilmot Blyden: Pan-Negro Patriot, 1832–1912*, Oxford: Oxford University Press (1967). Edith Holden (1960) *Blyden of Liberia: An Account of the Life and Labors of Edward Wilmot Blyden*, New York: Vantage Press, is an important source containing biographical details and excerpts from Blyden's letters and published writings. See also Hollis R. Lynch, (ed.) (1971) *Black Spokesman: Selected Published Writings of Edward Wilmot Blyden* New York: Humanities Press, the only representative anthology of his writings.

Web source:

www.africawithin.com

The first Pan-African Conference, organised by Henry Sylvester-Williams, was held in London in 1900 which brought together 'men and women of African blood and descent' from Africa, the USA and the Caribbean. This first conference was addressed by William E.B. Du Bois who, in his classic text *The Souls of Black Folks* (1903), sought to 'show the strange meaning of being black here in the dawning of the Twentieth Century' and made the classic statement 'the problem of the Twentieth Century is the problem of the color line' (Du Bois 1903: 2). An emotional, expressive sense of blackness is illustrated at the beginning of each chapter of this book, where Du Bois presents a verse from old 'Sorrow Songs' from which the 'soul of the black slave spoke':

> They are the music of an unhappy people, of the children of disappointment; they tell of death and suffering and unvoiced longing toward a truer world, of misty wanderings and hidden ways.
>
> (Du Bois 1903, Chapter 14: 1, see www.bartleby.com for an online version of this text, and also see the Introduction to this text by Donald Gibson in the Penguin 1996 edition)

This echoes Frederick Douglass' autobiography which also speaks of spirituals as revealing the souls of the slaves who sang them. This text seeks to reveal the soul of a race, the 'struggles of the massed millions of the black peasantry'. He recalls also his many personal encounters with whites who treat him as a problem not a person, and seeks to reveal both black humanity and the contribution of black people to society and culture. Du Bois calls for recognition, 'would America have been America without the Negro?', and he calls for a tearing down of the racial veil to let 'the prisoned ... go free'. Du Bois was the 'first sociologist of race' (Lewis 2000: 550). Race was for him the most social significant construct of modernity, as class was for Karl Marx (Zuckerman 2004: 4). For Du Bois, the 'history of the world is the history not of individuals, but of groups, not of nations, but of races', and that race is:

> a vast family of human beings, generally of common blood and language, always of common history, traditions and impulses, who are both voluntarily and involuntarily striving together for the accomplishment of certain more or less vividly conceived ideals of life.
>
> (Du Bois 1897: 6)

He also identifies in this paper, *The Conservation of Races*, which races exist across the planet:

> We find upon the world's stage today eight distinctly differentiated races, in the sense in which History tells us the word must be used. They are, the Slavs of eastern Europe, the Teutons of middle Europe, the English of Great Britain and America, the Romance nations of Southern and Western Europe, the Negroes of Africa and America, the Semitic people of Western Asia and Northern Africa, the Hindoos of Central Asia and the Mongolians of Eastern Asia. There are, of course, other minor race groups, as the American Indians, the Esquimaux and the South Sea Islanders; these larger races, too, are far from homogeneous; the Slav includes the Czech, the Magyar, the Pole and the Russian; the Teuton includes the German, the Scandinavian and the Dutch; the English include the Scotch, the Irish and the

conglomerate American. Under Romance nations the widely-differing Frenchman, Italian, Sicilian and Spaniard are comprehended. The term Negro is, perhaps, the most indefinite of all, combining the Mulattoes and Zamboes of America and the Egyptians, Bantus and Bushmen of Africa. Among the Hindoos are traces of widely differing nations, while the great Chinese, Tartar, Corean and Japanese families fall under the one designation – Mongolian. Du Bois (1897: 8)

So for Du Bois race was socially real, but it was not based on any essentialist biological or physical difference because, for scientists, the 'criteria of race [colour, hair, cranial measurements] are exasperatingly intermingled'. Criticisms of Du Bois include the 'residual primoridalism and naturalism' in his conceptualisation of race (Louis 2002, Appiah 1986). In other words his emphasis on the socio-historical construction of commonalities of racialised experiences for blacks and whites is tied to racial science (this is examined in detail in Chapter 2), here political and poetic expressive desire for black improvement is founded on racial anthropology and notions of common origin and descent (Louis 2002: 664). This unresolved tension between social and scientific understandings of race did not inhibit Du Bois' examination of emancipatory political strategies, but it did produce inherent weaknesses in the construction of his arguments, with idealisation and exaggeration of affinity, solidarity and mobilisation of black political constitutencies. The social construction of the Negro and blackness were a central concern in Du Bois' work and he pursued many different responses to the problem of racism including cultural and economic black separatism, integration, international communism and African solidarity. This last concept developed from the idea of the collective unity of African states to the collective unity of the black diaspora which arises from the forced and brutal dispersal of Africans to societies across the globe. He also developed a groundbreaking analysis of whiteness in an essay entitled *The Souls of White Folks*, published in *Darkwater* (1920). He examines the comic manifestations of whiteness in the strut of the American Southerner and the arrogance of the Englishman, the doctrine of the divine right of white people to steal lands, resources and people and the theory of human culture where everything great, good, efficient, fair and honourable is white, where everything mean and dishonourable is yellow and where the devil is always black. The division between white and black social worlds is encapsulated in his notion of the veil, a see-through curtain that separates but does not obstruct a racialised gaze. The analysis of racial dualism in Du Bois' writing explores the double-consciousness of being an American Negro in the context of post-slavery, pre-civil rights white supremacy. Grappling with the process of constructing racial identity while in a marginalised, subordinate, 'subaltern' position, and furthering black interests under dominant white rule were central challenges taken up in the output of Du Bois and many other diasporic intellectuals.

The 'first sociologist of race': William Edward Burghardt Du Bois

W.E.B. Du Bois (1868–1963) is one of the leading sociologists of race and racism, making a massive contribution to our understanding of race in a global context. He was born in Great Barrington, Massachusetts. He was a pioneering Pan-Africanist and died in Ghana where he had become a Ghanian citizen, director of the *Encyclopedia Africana* and a member of the Communist Party. He was the first African-American to receive a PhD at Harvard University and established the Department of Sociology at Atlanta University. He produced the first classic American study of urban sociology, *The Philadelphia Negro* (1899). He spent a year living amongst the black population of Philadelphia's seventh ward, personally interviewing thousands of people and assembling data on 10,000 people, examining patterns of poverty, education, family life, crime and race relations. The work on crime in this book was seminal, arguing that the effects of slavery, racism, Northern migration and poverty need to be taken into account in examining crime rates. He was also a pioneer of rural sociology with works including *The Negroes of Farmville, Virginia* (1898) and *The Negro*

W.E.B. Du Bois
Source: Library of Congress Collection.

Farmer (1904) where he examined the lasting impact of slavery, intimate relations, family structures, property and class relations in small Southern towns. He was also the first American sociologist of religion producing a key work on *The Negro Church* (1903). This collective endeavour inaugurated serious empirical research on blacks in America. His theoretical contribution to the understanding of race and racism included building linkages between racial and class analysis and developing an account of interlinked systems of oppression, although he failed to acknowledge the significance of gender. Unlike Marx, Weber or Durkheim he recognised that racial distinctions are central to how people experience the world. Lemmert (2000) argues that Du Bois was 'one of the first great decolonising thinkers' linking race, class and globalisation.

Sources: P. Zuckerman, (ed.) (2004) *The Social Theory of W.E.B. Du Bois*, London: Pine Forge; D.L. Lewis, (1993) *W.E.B. Du Bois: Biographer of a Race, 1868–1919*, New York: Henry Holt, D.L. Lewis, (1994) *W.E.B. Du Bois: a Reader*, New York: Holt; C. Lemmert, (2000) *Social Theory: The Multicultural and Classic Readings*, Boulder, Co: Westview, R. Dennis (2003) '*W.E.B Du Bois's concept of double consciousness*', in J. Stone and R. Dennis, *Race and Ethnicity, comparative and theoretical approaches*, Oxford: Blackwell, also see the discussion in Chapter 4 of P. Gilroy, (1993) *The Black Atlantic, modernity and double consciousness*, London: Verso.

Négritude and new black identities

The 'indigenist' military struggle led by Toussaint L'Overture in Haiti, and the work of Blyden and Du Bois which advocated the formation of black/African diasporic identity inspired a new conception which developed in the French Caribbean: Négritude (blackness). This term was coined by Martinican poet and statesman Aimé Césaire in Paris in the 1930s in discussion with fellow students Léopold Senghor and Léon Damas and elaborated in the magazine *L'Étudiant Noir*. They were inspired by the example of the Harlem Renaissance, which was the 'flowering of Negro literature' in the period 1919–35 centred in New York. Here writers such as Langston Hughes and Claude McKay extolled the value of black expressive culture seeing blackness not as a source of inferiority and stigma, but laid claim to it as a source of pride. Césaire's interpretation of this concept locates blackness in the context of Atlantic slavery whereas Senghor provided a more simplified and general account of global blackness. For him, Négritude was the totality of the 'values of civilisation' of 'the Black-African world ... the sense of communion ... and the gift of rhythm' (quoted in Gibson 2003: 45). The ontological state of being black arises here from the black soul, black nature, and has been characterised as an objective view of the black race, inspired in part by colonial ethnographers and racial scientists such as Arthur de Gobineau. Senghor, who became president of Senegal, found his interpretation was subject to heavy criticism. Césaire's more dynamic and contingent construction of Negritude has been highly influential in the development of black consciousness. Together these ideas espoused the virtues of mobilising a common black identity in the face of French colonial racism and domination, rejecting the idea of assimilation and reclaiming the term 'négre', which was used as a positive affirmation of identity. Jean-Paul Sartre's widely read account of the Négritude movement, *The Black Orpheus* (1948) describes Négritude as *racism antiraciste*, the opposite of colonial racism. Drawing on this earlier work Césaire went on to produce a classic text; *Discourse on Colonialism* (first published in France in 1955). This made a significant contribution to the intellectual inspiration of national liberation struggles in Africa, Latin America, and the Caribbean and subsequently provided inspiration for the American Civil Rights movement, Black Power, and other anti-war movements. Césaire's analysis critiques capitalism and colonialism, challenges Western conceptions of modernity and civilisation and reaffirms black/African diasporic identities in the course of arguing for a fundamental process of political, social and psychological decolonisation.

Trying to move beyond the polarities of a black and white colonial world was a task taken on by a leading humanist intellectual, Frantz Fanon. He yearned for liberation of both the self and the nation and advocated, often painful, self-reflection and collective violence as necessary means to achieve this goal. He contested the 'unconditional affirmation of African culture', challenged simplistic advocacy of Pan-Africanism, as well as Pan-Arabism and restrictive forms of nationalism, preferring to advocate Third Worldism as an oppositional space (Reed 2006). Challenging the reactive position of Negritude, Fanon examines the corrosive power of colonial racism which leads to the development of a split consciousness among the black elite. Arising for example through the French policy of assimilating a small black 'civilised' elite, and suppressing the mass population, which created a conflict of loyalties, this is the position of being in a black skin with a white mask (Fanon 1967).

The internalisation of another's idea of yourself expressed here fits closely with Du Bois, concept of a dualist racial identity. Fanon is dismissive of nostalgia for an idealised black culture embedded in its African past and argues for participation in violent action, a 'fighting culture' and a war of liberation, for example in Algeria, recognising the psychological and symbolic importance of violence.

He has been criticised for deficiencies in his portrayal of utopian social change, the complexities of colonial relationships, his views on women and his theory of violence but his contribution has been hugely influential in theorising race and in the development of postcolonial studies.

Fanon's challenge to naïve, backward-looking and damaging mobilisation of the race idea as blackness is paralleled in more contemporary accounts. Paul Gilroy in *The Black Atlantic* (1993) and in other writings emphasises the syncretic shared culture of blackness which is not rooted in any natural, homogenous essence of being black but in the intertwining of historical experience, geographical movement and cultural hybridity arising from the period of Atlantic slavery. Here, nation and race are treated as thoroughly inadequate concepts in which to ground sociological analysis, failing to capture and facilitate the narration of black subjectivities. Also, interactions between the African diaspora and the West over millennia deny any attempt to construct 'pure', separated accounts of either African and European identity, or whiteness and blackness. The economic foundation of Western European modernity depended in part on the institution of plantation slavery and paradoxically critiques of slavery influenced modernist thought. Gilroy demonstrates that the critiques of injustice which informed European arguments for liberal democracy and universal suffrage were influenced by slave resistance and abolition movements, for example in the work of Hegel. In that sense, the mutually defining relationship between Europe and Africa helped create what we know as modernity. Gilroy is fascinated by the ways in which successive generations of black intellectuals have grappled with the double consciousness of being black and being of the West, and he counterposes the conceptions of black nationalism and Africentrism which fall back on immutable, exclusive notions of 'black' and 'white', and those which emphasise forms of mixing and discussion of 'creolisation, métissage, mestizaje and hybridity'. The problems posed for racial science and racial governance by questions of racial mixing are explored in the next chapter.

The modernist universalising agenda which characterised the black power movement during the 1960s sought to construct a common collective notion of blackness, while often invoking little critique of patriarchy. The political repression of militant protest and the search for alternative strategies of resistance accompanied the theoretical development of anti-foundationalist concern for deconstructing identities and recognising difference. The shattering of the master narrative of Black Power gave way to increasing attention to divisions of gender, sexuality, class and ethnicity, multiple experiences and cross-cutting shared sensibilities. In a reflection on the meaning of 'postmodern blackness' which severs collective ties, bell hooks (1991: 28) casts suspicion on these critiques 'when they surface at a historical moment when many subjugated people feel themselves coming to voice for the first time', and when this may close down the opportunities 'for 'those who have suffered the crippling effects of colonisation and domination to gain or regain a hearing'. But hooks also acknowledges the value of essentialist critiques in challenging a stifling, stereotypical, 'constricting notion of blackness' and opening up space for the assertion of agency. She argues for a continued struggle for radical black subjectivity which involves both a search for oppositional and liberatory notions of self and identity, and a 'yearning' for the expression of that critical voice. However, Angela Davis, a communist, radical feminist and black activist, recently highlighted internal class divisions and the problems of mobilising the black constituency in the US:

> It's complicated. We used to think there was a black community. It was always heterogenous but we were always able to imagine ourselves as part of that community ... many black middle class people have internalised the same racist attitudes to working class black people as white people have of the black criminal. The young black man with the sagging pants walking down the street is understood as a threat by the black middle class as well. So I don't think it is possible to mobilise black communities in the way it was in the past.' (Interview with Gary Younge,
>
> *Guardian* 8 Nov. 2007)

Nevertheless, Davis argues for a continuing critical engagement with race and racism and cites stark figures from the US Justice Department which indicate that on current trends one in three black boys born in 2001 will end up in jail. The 'demise of the essential black subject' (Hall 1992b), which was, in its time, seen as politically and strategically useful, is now giving way to exploration of the huge variety of syncretic ethnic identities which have emerged following the establishment of worldwide migrant communities. In the UK, for example, the fragmentation of 'black' political identity into the politics of ethnic difference has resulted in the loss of anti-racist political solidarity and the absence of a coherent anti-racist politics (Kundani 2007).

Conclusion

This chapter seeks to provide an introduction to the history of the race idea and its mobilisation in systems of racial domination and in narratives of liberation and emancipation. It argues for taking race seriously in sociological and historical thinking and vigilance in interrogating the ways in which social, cultural and political significance is given to this idea in widely differing places and times. Rather than abandoning a general theory of race and racism because of the difficulties of grasping the totality of the ways and means by which race operates, it is argued that such a theory requires a global approach, avoiding the pitfalls of generalising from regional or national standpoints. These issues, and the development of global approaches, are an increasing trend in the field of racism studies (see, for example, Bowser 1995, Bhattacharya *et al.* 2002, Spickard 2005, Macedo and Gounari 2006).

End of chapter activity

Access the UN Special Rapporteur's country reports on racism at www.ohchr. org/english/issues/racism/rapporteur/visits.htm. These provide contemporary evidence of racism in different national contexts including Japan, Brazil and Russia. Look at a report for a country you know little about.

- What are the main groups subject to racism in that country?
- How has this come about?
- What has been the state's response?
- What views are given and claims made by racialised groups?

Further reading

Spickard, P. (ed.) (2005) *Race and Nation, ethnic systems in the modern world,* **London: Routledge.** This edited text provides accounts of the development of racialised identity hierarchies in a diverse range of regions and settings across the globe.

Winant, H. (2001) *The World is a Ghetto,* **Oxford; Basic Books.** This compelling account focuses on the more dominant understanding of race and racism as the products of Western slavery, colonialism and Empire, and relations between the 'West and the Rest', providing both historical developments and contemporary patterns across selected global regions.

Dikotter, F. (ed.) (1997) *The Construction of Racial Identities in China and Japan,* **London: Hurst.** This edited collection challenges the idea that race and racism are 'Western concepts' and that, as China has argued, racism therefore does not exist in that country. It also examines racial nationalisms, oppression of racialised minorities including the Ainu and the growth of anti-semitism in China and Japan.

Jones, A. (2006) *Genocide: a comprehensive introduction,* **Abingdon: Routledge.** This student text provides valuable case study material on genocide with material on indigenous people, colonial contexts and the Jewish Holocaust.

Bancroft, A. (2005) *Roma and Gypsy-Travellers in Europe,* **Aldershot: Ashgate.** This provides a pan-European account of Roma and Gypsy-Travellers, examining exclusions, identities and contemporary experiences. This book examines explanations of the development of forms of race and racism which draw on social relations inside Europe.

Zuckerman, P. (ed.) (2004) *The Social Theory of W.E.B. Du Bois,* **London: Pine Forge.** *Lewis, D.L.* This edited collection of the work of Du Bois provides the opportunity for students to explore key writings of this leading black intellectual and his views on race, racism and resistance.

Dennis, R. (2003) **'W.E.B. Du Bois's concept of double consciousness,'** in J. Stone and R. Dennis, *Race and Ethnicity, comparative and theoretical approaches,* **Oxford: Blackwell.** This chapter examines the extent to which Du Bois used the concept of double consciousness as a central problem for oppressed groups and critically reviews some contemporary re-statements of this idea by Heinze and Gilroy.

Web resource

The *Africans in America* website, www.pbs.org/wgbh/aia/home.html is a companion to Africans in America, a six-hour public television series. The website chronicles the history of racial slavery in the United States – from the start of the Atlantic slave trade in the sixteenth century to the end of the American Civil War in 1865 – and explores the central paradox that is at the heart of the American story: a democracy that declared all men equal but enslaved and oppressed one people to provide independence and prosperity to another. *Africans in America* examines the economic and intellectual foundations of slavery in America and the global economy that prospered from it and reveals how the presence of African people and their struggle for freedom transformed America.

References

Allen, T. (1994) *The Invention of the White Race*, Vol. 1, London: Verso.

Appiah, A. (1986) 'The uncompleted argument: Du Bois and the illusion of race, in H.L. Gates Jnr (ed.) *'Race', writing and difference*, Chicago, IL: University of Chicago Press.

Bauman, Z. (1989) *Modernity and the Holocaust*, Cambridge: Polity Press.

Bernal, M. (1987) *Black Athena: the Afroasiatic Roots of Classical Civilisation*, Vol. 1, London: Vintage.

Bonnett, A. (2000) *White Identities*, Harlow: Pearson Education.

Bhattacharya, G., Gabriel, J. and Small, S. (2002) *Race and Power, global racism in the twenty-first century*, London: Routledge.

Bowser, B. (ed.) (1995) *Racism and Anti-Racism in World Perspective*, London: Sage.

Césaire, A. (1952) *Discourse on Colonialism*, London: Monthly Review Press, first published 1972.

Chow, K. (1997) 'Imagining boundaries of blood: Zhang Binglin and the invention of the 'Han' race in modern China', in F. Dikotter (ed.) *The Construction of Racial Identities in China and Japan*, London: Hurst.

Delacampagne, C. (1983) *L'Invention du Racism*, Paris: Fayard.

Delacampagne, C. (1990) 'Racism and the West: from praxis to logos, in D. T. Goldberg, *Anatomy of Racism*, Minneapolis: University of Minnesota Press.

Dikotter, F. (1992) *The Discourse of Race in Modern China*, London: Hurst.

Dikotter, F. (ed.) (1997) *The Construction of Racial Identities in China and Japan*, London: Hurst.

Drescher, S. (1990) 'The ending of the slave trade and the evolution of European scientific racism', *Social Science History*, 14, pp.415–449.

Du Bois, W. E. B. (1987) *The conservation of races*, The American Negro Academy Occasional Papers, No. 2, http://www.webdubois.org/dbConsrvOfRaces.html.

Du Bois, W. E. B. (1903) *The Souls of Black Folks*, Chicago: McClurg and Co, Penguin edition 1996.

Edwards, J. (1994) *The Jews in Western Europe, 1400–1600*, Manchester: Manchester University Press.

Elias, N. (1982) *The Civilizing Process, state formation and civilisation*, Oxford: Basil Blackwell.

Fanon, F. (1967) *Black Skin, White Masks*, New York: Grove Press.

Gibson, N. (2003) *Fanon, the Postcolonial Imagination*, Cambridge: Polity.

Gilroy, P. (1993) *The Black Atlantic, modernity and double consciousness*, London: Verso.

Goldberg, D. (1993) *Racist Culture, Philosophy and the Politics of Meaning*, Oxford: Blackwell.

Goldenberg, D. M. (2003) *The Curse of Ham, race and slavery in early Judaism. Christianity and Islam*, Princeton, NJ: Princeton University Press.

Hall, S. (1992a) 'The West and the rest: discourse and power', in S. Hall and B. Gieben (eds), *Formations of Modernity*, Cambridge: Policy Press.

Hall, S. (1992b) 'The question of cultural identity', in S. Hall, D. Held and T. McGrew (eds) *Modernity and its Futures*, Cambridge: Policy Press.

Hancock, I. (1997) 'The roots of antigypsyism: to the Holocaust and after', in G. J. Colin and M. S. Littell (eds) *Confronting the Holocaust: a mandate for the 21st Century*, Lanham, MD: University Press of America.

Hannaford, I. (1996) *Race, the history of an idea in the West*, London: Johns Hopkins University Press.

Hesse, B., (1999) 'Reviewing the Western Spectacle: reflexive globalisation through the Black Diaspora', in A. Brah, M. Hickman and M. Mac an Ghaill (eds.) *Global Futures, Migration, Environment and Globalisation*, Basingstoke: Macmillan.

hooks, b. (1991) *Yearning, Race, Gender and Cultural Politics*, London: Turnaround.

Hulme, P. (1986) *Colonial Encounters, Europe and the Native Caribbean, 1492–1797*, London: Methuen.

Isaac, B. (2004) *The Invention of Racism in Classical Antiquity*, Woodstock: Princeton University Press.

Jahoda, G. (1999) *Images of Savages, the ancient roots of modern prejudice in Western culture*, London: Routledge.

Jones, A. (2006) *Genocide: a comprehensive introduction*, Abingdon: Routledge.

Karras, A. L. and McNeill, J. R. (eds) (1992) *Atlantic American Societies*, London: Routledge.

Kundani, A. (2007) *The End of Tolerance*, London: Pluto Press.

Laquer, W. (2006) *The Changing Face of anti-semitism*, Oxford: Oxford University Press.

Law, I. (1985) *White Racism and Black Settlement in Liverpool*, Liverpool: Department of Sociology, unpublished PhD thesis.

Lewis, B. (1971) *Race and Colour in Islam*, New York: Harper and Row.

Lewis, D. L. (2000) *W.E.B. Du Bois, The Fight for Equality and the American Century, 1919–1963*, New York: Henry Holt and Co.

Loomba, A. (2005) *Colonialism/Postcolonialism*, London: Routledge, 2nd edn.

Louis, B. St. (2002) 'Post-race/post-politics? Activist-intellectualism and the reification of race', *Ethnic and Racial Studies*, 25, 4, July, pp. 652–675.

Lynch, H. R. (ed.) (1971) *Black Spokesman, selected published writings of Edward Wilmot Blyden*, London: Frank Cass.

Macedo, D. and Gounari, P. (eds.) (2006) *The Globalisation of Racism*, Boulder, Colorado: Paradigm

Madley, B. (2005) 'From Africa to Auschwitz: how German South West Africa incubated ideas and methods developed by the Nazis in Eastern Europe', *European History Quarterly*, 35, 3, p. 181.

Mann, M. (2005) *The Dark Side of Democracy, explaining ethnic cleansing*, Cambridge: Cambridge University Press.

Memmi, A. (1967) *The Colonisers and the Colonised*, Boston, MA: Beacon Press.

Miles, R. (1993) *Racism After 'Race Relations'*, London: Routledge.

Piertese, J. (1994) 'Unpacking the West: how European is Europe' in A. Rattansi and S. Westwood (eds.) *Racism, Modernity and Identity, on the Western front*, Cambridge: Polity.

Poliakov, L. (1975) *The History of Anti-semitism*, Vol. 1, Philadelphia: University of Pennsylvania Press.

Reed, K. (2006) *New Directions in Social Theory, race, gender and the canon*, London: Sage.

Said, E. W. (1985) *Culture and Imperialism*, London: Chatto & Windus.

Sato, K. (1997) 'Same language, same race: the dilemma of *Kanbun* in modern Japan', in F. Dikotter (ed.) *The Construction of Racial Identities in China and Japan*, London: Hurst.

Smaje, C. (2000) *Natural Hierarchies, the historical sociology of race and caste*, Oxford: Blackwell.

Snowdon, F. (1970) *Before Colour Prejudice: the ancient view of Blacks*, Cambridge, MA: Harvard University Press.

Spickard, P. (ed.) (2005) *Race and Nation, ethnic systems in the modern world*, London: Routledge.

Takezawa, Y. (2006) 'Race should be discussed and understood across the globe', *Anthropology News*, American Anthropological Association, Feb./March 2006.

Thomas, N. (1994) *Colonialism's Culture*, Cambridge: Polity Press.

UNHCR (2006) *Report of the Special Rapporteur on contemporary forms of racism, racial discrimination, xenophobia and related intolerance, Mission to Japan*, Doudou Diène, UNHCR, www.ohchr.org/english/issues/racism/rapporteur/visits.htm.

Walvin, J. (1992) *Slaves and Slavery: the British colonial experience*, Manchester: Manchester University Press.

Weiner, M. (1997) 'The invention of identity: race and nation in pre-war Japan', in F. Dikotter (ed.) *The Construction of Racial Identities in China and Japan*, London: Hurst.

Weiner, M. (ed.) (2004) *Race, Ethnicity and Migration in Modern Japan*, London: Routledge.

Winant, H. (2001) *The World is a Ghetto*, Oxford; Basic Books.

World Conference Against Racism (WCAR) (2001) *World Conference Against Racism, Racial Discrimination, Xenophobia and Related Intolerance Declaration*, United Nations, WCAR: Durban, South Africa.

Xun, Z. (1997) 'Youtal: the myth of the "Jew" in modern China', in F. Dikotter (ed.) *The Construction of Racial Identities in China and Japan*, London: Hurst.

Young, R. (1994) 'Egypt in America: black Athena, racism and colonial discourse', in A. Rattansi and S. Westwood (eds.) *Racism, Modernity and Identity, on the Western front*, Cambridge: Polity.

Young, L. (1997) 'Rethinking race for Manchuko: Self and Other in colonial contexts', in F. Dikotter (ed.) *The Construction of Racial Identities in China and Japan*, London: Hurst.

Younge, G. (2007) 'We used to think there was a black community', Interview with Angela Davis, *Guardian*, 8 November.

Zuckerman, P. (ed.) (2004) *The Social Theory of W.E.B. Du Bois*, London: Pine Forge.

2 Categorising peoples: race science, genomics and naming

Key issues in this chapter:

- The development of scientific racism
- The growing opposition to Nazi racial science
- Race and IQ debates and the role of the Pioneer Fund
- The use of race in contemporary genomics
- Genetic anthropology and tracing ancestry
- The construction of racial, ethnic and national identities

At the end of this chapter you should be able to:

- Understand the development of racial science and eugenics
- Assess the challenge to racial science
- Discuss the persistence of debates over race and intelligence
- Understand contemporary debates over racial classification in genetics and genomics
- Evaluate the operation of and response to bio-colonialism
- Understand the construction and inter-relation of racial and ethnic categorisation and identities
- Understand the conceptualisation of Roma and indigenous peoples identities

Introduction

The double use of the race idea, being mobilised to carry through colonialism and imperial domination and also being used to mobilise and champion resistance, was introduced in Chapter 1. This chapter builds on this argument by a close inspection of the field of science. Science has provided the terrain for both the most theoretically elaborated notions of race and racism, and for the most fundamental anti-racist challenge to these ideas. This terrain, more than any other, shows the centrality of race in European/non-European modernity and the contradictions within it (Hesse 2007). Over 200 years after the inauguration of scientific racism exemplified in the writings of French scientist Georges Cuvier in 1800, the pioneering gene scientist and co-discoverer of DNA, James Watson restated similar arguments. Cuvier linked race with hierarchies of inferiority and superiority with whites at the top, Watson does the same. In 2000 he suggested that there was a link between skin colour and sex drive, hypothesising that dark-skinned people have stronger libidos, and drawing on the old discursive strategy of sexual fantasy long associated with the language of exploitation, conquest and domination (Hall 1992). In 2007 he said that he was 'inherently gloomy about the prospect of Africa' because 'all our social policies are based on the fact that their intelligence is the same as ours – whereas all the testing says not really', arguing that 'there is no firm reason to anticipate that the intellectual capacities of peoples geographically separated in their evolution should prove to have evolved identically' (Watson as quoted in Hunt-Grubbe 2007). These statements led to an international storm of protest and a denial from Watson, who apologised and went on to state that Africans were not 'genetically inferior'. This episode illustrates both the durability of racial science and the strength of anti-racism in this field.

The first part of this chapter examines the rise of racial science. The mobilisation of race in scientific disourse is a key theme for this chapter, which will examine the rise of race and hierarchical, inegalitarian forms of racial categorisation as elaborated in the natural sciences and in the construction of academic knowledge in a variety of fields. The development of scientific classification of races originated in the field of natural history. The construction of races as vague physical types developed from the early 1800s onwards based on ideas of fixed racial hierarchies with fixed and often limited capacities for civilisation and cultural development. Charles Darwin saw races as distinct sub-species, but broke with earlier scientific racism by replacing the idea of static, fixed, racial and cultural hierarchies with the idea of an evolving world. He also established the principle of common descent, in that races were all seen as sub-species of homo sapiens, and laid the basis for a change from typological to population thinking (Banton 1997).

The fall of racial science is also examined here and this was part of a wider anti-racist challenge to hierarchical and biological constructions of race driven by the imperative to challenge Nazi ideologies from the 1930s onwards. The use of blood grouping and other variable protein markers has recently been used to trace and chart the heterogeneous and highly mixed origins of the British population. Social Darwinism, physical anthropology, eugenics, social ecology and socio-biology have, however, retained the use of racial categories and attempted to elaborate a physical or biological basis for social and cultural difference. Race science has not disappeared, as more recently debates over the Human Genome Project and the work of scientists developing genetic databases has highlighted the continuing use of race categories. This chapter will examine the prospects for the return of race science in the context of genetics and genomics, and related debates over intelligence and tracing ancestry, or recreational genomics. Lastly, attention will be given to contemporary debates over differing forms of racial and ethnic classification, bureaucratic categorisation and the dilemmas of naming groups of people.

The rise and fall of racial science

Proto-racial science has been identified in different pre-capitalist contexts, but the major rise of racial science across Europe and North America occurred at the end of the eighteenth century and formed a key part of the wider move from religious to scientific explanation, paralleling the rise of European colonialism. Racial science did not abate with the abolition of plantation slavery, instead it developed increasing social momentum culminating in Nazi eugenics. The decline of Christian monogenism (the theory that we are all descended from the same ancestors such as the biblical story of descent from Adam and Eve), was due to its inability to account for differences between people which arose from the stories, myths and reports of contact and discovery and the archives of 'the West and the Rest' (Hall 1992). In coping with a multiplicity of data about human diversity, natural historians and other scientists were freed from the need to conform with religious accounts and could develop a multitude of racist speculations and rhetorics of descent and 'racial theory quickly grew into the leading explanatory device for human history' (Augstein 1996: xxxii). Racism passed the test of practical adequacy, effectively making sense of the world for those in the West. For example, failure to improve the 'savage' Aboriginal in Australia could be explained by innate human difference, and the conviction that they were a 'doomed race', unable to sustain themselves as human, became a dominant view (Anderson 2006).

Race and natural history

Racial taxonomies were developed in natural history, anthropology and ethnology. Carl Linnaeus in his *Systema Naturae* (1758) attempted to classify all living things into genus, species and variety, or subspecies, and identified six varieties of *Homo sapiens*; including *europaeus* (white, ruddy and muscular), *asiaticus* (yellow, melancholic and inflexible), *afer* (black, indulgent, phlegmatic and monstrous; other deviant – disabled – forms). Johann Friedrich Blumenbach, a German anatomist with a great collection of human skulls, revised Linnaeus' classification and identified five different human varieties: Caucasian, Mongoloid, Ethiopian, American and Malay. 'A blind person' he argued could 'distinguish at first grasp the scull of a Calmuck from a negroe' (1796, quoted in Augstein 1996: 65). Georges Cuvier's account of race involved dividing *Homo sapiens* into three subspecies, Caucasian, Mongoloid and Ethiopian; whites, yellows and blacks. Presenting us with a description of a world where three major races developed in isolation from each other, resulting in a hierarchy of differences in culture and mental ability produced by natural physical characteristics. For Cuvier, therefore, it was clear why 'the Caucasian race has gained dominion over the world', why the Chinese were less advanced and why the Negroes were 'sunken in slavery and the pleasures of the senses' (quoted in Banton 1997: 30). In the USA, Andrew Morton in his *Crania Americana* (1839) used measurements of the internal capacity of skulls to construct a hierarchy of those with the biggest brains, Caucasians at the top and Ethiopians ('unmixed Negroes' and 'Africans') at the bottom. The misleading and false use of this evidence was demonstrated by Stephen Jay Gould (1981), who re-examined the skulls used by Morton. The American School, typified by Morton, developed some of the most systematically elaborated accounts, due particularly to their significance for slavery. These accounts laid the basis for the production of knowledge in other spheres such as epidemiology and psychiatry, for example epidemiological studies based on the Sixth US Census of 1840 were used to justify a claim that the black person was relatively free of madness in a state of slavery, 'but becomes prey to mental disturbance when he is set free' (Thomas and Sillen 1972, quoted in Fernando 1991). Infamously, Samuel Cartwright (1851) identified 'drapetomania' as the treatable mental illness that caused slaves to run away and seek freedom.

Racial types

The development of an international school of thought emerged from the work of scientists in France, the US, Britain and Germany which included Samuel Stanhope Smith, James Pritchard, George Gliddon, Josiah Nott and in the work of two of the most well-known exponents, Arthur de Gobineau and Robert Knox. Differences between people were classified into racial types and treated as historically permanent. Here, race differences were seen as existing since creation, hence these theories had great difficulty in accounting for evolution. Furthermore, racial types were seen to display innate antagonism to each other, where 'the deep rooted hatred of the Caucasian races towards the typical Negro' became inevitable and naturalised (Smith 1848 quoted in Banton 1997: 54). Gobineau addressed the global rise and fall of civilisations in his *Essai sur l'inégalité des Race humanies* (1853), and for him 'all civilisations derive from the white race', being the Aryans, including Egyptian, Greek, Roman, Chinese and Mexican. The 'preservation of the blood' of the 'white family' was central for him in explaining the success or otherwise of these civilisations. So, the history of the world is explained by the nature and development of unequal races. His emphasis here on 'noble blood' indicates an intertwining of a belief in natural aristocracy and the reality of a hierarchy of race. Robert Knox made a significant contribution to the popularisation of the race idea and in particular to its usage in medical schools where he lectured. In his book of these lectures, *The Races of Men* (1850), he sets out his key arguments, which include the claim that both external and internal (anatomical) racial differences have existed unchanged for over 6000 years, that intermingling of races leads to infertility in the 'hybrid product', and that an understanding of racial differences in intelligence, culture and morals provided an explanation of European political conflict. This account led him, for example, to the claim that for England's safety, the 'source of all evil' lay within the 'Celtic race of Ireland' that must be 'forced from the soil', and also that a physical and psychological inferiority existed in the 'darker races'. So, the scientific construction of natural races was flourishing by the mid-nineteenth century.

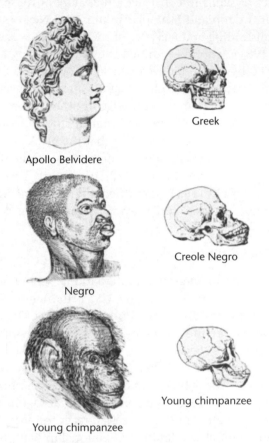

Apollo Belvidere

Greek

Negro

Creole Negro

Young chimpanzee

Young chimpanzee

Figure 2.1 Classifying race and skulls
(Source: Josiah Clark Nott and George Robert Gliddon, *Indigenous Races of the Earth*, first published 1857)

Darwin and racial evolution

The challenge to both polygenism and the notion of fixed static racial types was made by Charles Darwin in his works *On the Origin of Natural Selection or the Preservation of Favoured Races in the Struggle for Life* (1859) and *Descent of Man* (1871). He argued for the common origin of all humans through evolution, a monogenetic account which emphasised change. The struggle for survival led to natural selection and the modification of the species. *The Descent of Man* developed the argument on sexual selection which for him explained human evolution and the differentiation of races. For Darwin, races were sub-species developing with partial reproductive isolation from each other. Some, the 'savage races' with smaller brains, faced the prospect of declining fertility and extinction, whereas civilised races more cleverly adapted and survived.

Racial eugenics

Darwin's cousin, Frances Galton, both developed and influenced his thinking, applying his ideas to society (Social Darwinism) and favouring strategies which went with the grain of this set of ideas. This meant advocating forms of improving human hereditary traits through intervention: eugenics, the self-direction of human evolution. These techniques could involve either encouraging reproduction amongst the genetically advantaged or reducing populations of the inferior. Eugenics policies have included genocide, forced abortions, compulsory sterilisation and racial segregation. Japan, Korea, North America, Sweden, Australia and Nazi Germany are all examples where racial eugenics has been actively pursued by the state.

In Japan the impact of Social Darwinism 'cannot be underestimated' according to Michael Weiner (2004: 225). Elite Japanese groups combined older feudal ideas of a homogenous, native Japanese racial group with the scientific racism of the West to construct the Japanese nation as a collective race with superior civilised inherited qualities and capacities. The construction of the Yamato *minzoku* paralleled the racially pure construction of the German *volk* nation. Racism inside Japan had traditionally focussed on exclusion of groups like the Ainu and the Burakumin, the latter being described as a 'race apart ... lacking any sense of morality' (Irokawa quoted in Weiner 2004: 232) and such views were also applied to the poor and disabled. Japanese imperial expansion was seen as both necessary for the natural survival of the race and expressive of the distinctive inherited martial qualities of the Japanese people. Assimilationist policies imposed the forms of behaviour of the master race and concern over maintaining racial purity both at home and abroad led to the development of eugenic policies in the shape of Race Eugenic Protection Laws in the 1930s. In Korea, the legacy of Japanese colonialism, with its eugenic imperatives, is evident in the pursuit of forced sterilisation and aborticide for certain groups in South Korea up to the 1980s. Sweden also pursued forced sterilisation programmes aimed at ethnic and racial minorities from the late 1930s up to the 1970s. Children of mixed Aboriginal and Northern European descent were seen as a threat to racial purity in Australia, and they were forcibly taken from their parents. This practice continued for a century (1869–1969) and created the Stolen Generation, portrayed in the film *Rabbit-Proof Fence*. In Canada in the 1920s and 1930s eugenic policies included sterilisation of immigrants who failed IQ tests. Most recently, in the Czech Republic (2007) a regional court in Ostrava awarded compensation to a Romani woman for forced sterilisation by a doctor without consent.

Nazi eugenics

Nazi eugenics followed mainstream scientific research in the USA and Europe (Proctor 1988). Madison Grant's American text *The Passing of the Great Race or the Racial Basis of Human History* (1916) developed an account of the Nordic race who were primarily responsible for human achievement but who were threatened by race mixing, which was 'race suicide', thus justifying racialised immigration controls in the USA and eugenic policies which included laws banning interracial marriages, the anti-miscegenation laws. Grant's work built on William Ripley's (1899) account of Nordic, Alpine and Mediterranean races, with Nordics being seen as superior innovators and conquerors, which itself drew on Gobineau's earlier Aryan theory. Grant's account of Aryan racial supremacy was highly influential. This theory was elaborated by German eugenicist Eugen Fisher and his colleagues Erwin Barr and Fritz Lenz whose work *Human Heredity* (1921), was read by Adolf Hitler before he wrote *Mein Kampf* in 1923 (Centre for Holocaust and Genocide Studies 2007). The link between earlier colonial genocide in Namibia and the Nazi Holocaust, noted in the last chapter can be found in the work of Eugen Fisher. Fisher had established his reputation with his findings on racial supremacy and the detrimental effects of racial cross-breeding in German South West Africa which had been influential in racial hygiene policies there. He advocated enforced sterilisation of 'half-breeds', amongst other strategies. Nazi eugenics advocated 'racial hygiene', the reproduction and improvement through breeding of the master race, the elimination of racial mixing, the extermination of human beings of 'non-Aryan' or 'related' blood and the killing as 'ballast' those of no use for 'national unity' such as the chronically sick and disabled (see Jones 2006: Ch. 6 for further discussion of anti-semitism, and see extensive Holocaust resources on Wikipedia).

The refutation of race science

'The Nazi regime has compelled us all to recognize the lethal potential of the concept of race and the horrendous consequences of its misuse', as Elazar Barkan (1992: 1) has argued. Scientific racism, with all its ambiguities, inconsistencies and contradictions, operated as a regime of truth in Germany, Britain and the USA at the beginning of the twentieth century. The collapse of this dominant form of knowledge, which was active in many scientific, academic, political and military discourses, can be traced through this century. By 1950 a global declaration by a world panel of experts had come together through UNESCO to announce that there was no scientific basis for race, arguing that all races had similar mental capacities, that there was no biological deterioration due to race mixing and that race was a socially constructed myth. Although the scientific refutation of racism (as race plus hierarchy) began in the 1920s, preceding the rise of Nazism, this was relatively weak and un-influential (Barkan 1992). International efforts to produce a collective attack on scientific racism had been abandoned so as not to antagonise Hitler, but the gradual shift from politically driven anthropological and biological accounts of race to social and cultural analysis of race was underway.

Many scientists in the 1930s were dismissive or hesitant of the need to mobilise to tackle Nazi race science. Emerging signs of opposition in 1938/39 included the campaign work led by Frantz Boas and the American Anthropological Association in the USA, the 'Geneticists Manifesto' agreed at an International Conference in Edinburgh and the work of Julian Huxley and Alfred Haddon which collectively opposed racial typologies and scientific racism. Jacques Barzun's work on race had also been highly influential. His PhD thesis, published as *The French Race: Theories of Its Origins and their Social and Political Implications Prior to the Revolution* (1932), challenged the idea that the French race had arisen through conquering Gauls and Romans and argued that they had no claim to racial purity, they were 'a hopeless mixture of not only Romans, but Iberians, Syrians [and] Phoenicians' (quoted in Vinciguerra 2006). In his more famous work *Race: A Study in Modern Superstition* (1937), he argued that,

> the race question appears a much bigger affair than a trumped-up excuse for local persecution. It becomes rather a mode of thought endemic in Western civilization. It defaces every type of mental activity – history, art, politics, science and social reform.

He ridiculed the 'transmogrified phrenology' of race theories and argued strongly for the abandonment of race myths which for him denied individuality. These arguments were also elaborated in a highly influential anti-racist text written by one of Boas' PhD students, Ashley Montagu, *Man's Most Dangerous Myth, the fallacy of race* published in 1942. As the horror and evidence of Nazi racial science, experimentation and extinction policies emerged the tide turned and the refutation of scientific racism became a legitimate and widespread intellectual stance (Barkan 1992: 345).

Keeping race science alive: the Pioneer Fund and IQ debates

Running against this tide, the persistent linking of race and intelligence has maintained scientific and public attention throughout the twentieth century, and is reflected in James Watson's comments (quoted in Hunt-Grubbe 2007). William Tucker (2002) has traced the role played by the American-based Pioneer Fund in promoting these debates from the 1930s onwards in his investigation of the funding of scientific racism. The Pioneer Fund was established in 1937 for study into the problems of 'heredity and eugenics' and 'race betterment', providing grants and information as a eugenic lobby organisation. It is still highly active and its present mission statement claims it has restored the 'Darwinian-Galtonian perspective to the mainstream in traditional fields such as anthropology, psychology, and sociology, as well as fostering the newer disciplines of behavioral genetics, neuroscience, evolutionary psychology, and sociobiology' (www.pioneerfund.org). Pioneer's first president Harry Laughlin was central to the successful campaigning work to enact both immigration restriction legislation in 1924 and involuntary sterilisation in over 30 states. He was also a strong believer in Nordic supremacy, opposed Jewish migration from German persecution and as editor of the *Eugenical News* gave high praise to race hygiene policies enacted by the Nazi regime which followed the USA model he had advocated. Pioneer's first project was the distribution of a film produced by the Nazi Office of Racial Politics, *The Hereditary Defective*, to biology teachers in schools and welfare workers (Tucker 2002: 45–53). Tucker also links key individuals involved in this fund with the Ku Klux Klan crusade to repatriate blacks in the 1930s and opposition to civil rights interventions.

It has funded, and continues to fund key advocates of racial differences in intelligence and IQ including Arthur Jensen and Hans Eysenck. It also funded, together with the Bradley Foundation, much of the research that was used in *The Bell Curve* (1994) by Richard Herrnstein and Charles Murray. Currently the Fund's website asserts that firstly race is a real biological fact:

> According to Jensen, Lynn, and Rushton (among others), the scientific evidence, including the most recent genetic studies, shows that race is not a mere social construct. But you needn't take their word for it. Coroners in crime labs can identify race from a skeleton or even just the skull. They can identify race from blood, hair, or semen as well. To deny the existence of race is unscientific and unrealistic. Race is much more than 'just skin deep'.

And secondly that black people, particularly black Africans, have lower intelligence:

> Hundreds of studies on millions of people now show that around the world, the average IQ for East Asians centres around 106; for Whites, about 100; and for Blacks, about 85 in the U.S. and 70 in sub-Saharan Africa. (www.pioneerfund.org, accessed 26 Oct. 2007).

These claims, that race is real and that races are hierarchically ordered in terms of inherited genetic abilities and intelligence, illustrate the persistence and durability of scientific racism. James Watson, in publicly making this claim, as referred to at the beginning of this chapter, was therefore merely repeating a commonly held view amongst a group of scientists; he was not in this sense exceptional. The *Bell Curve Wars* (1995) brought together a range of leading intellectuals to dismantle the scientific foundations of Herrnstein and Murray's book of that name. In this collection, Stephen Jay Gould, a leading critic, argues against key central claims and finds that intelligence cannot be described by a single number, that it is incapable of ranking people in a linear order, that it is not genetically based and that it is not unchanging. Richard Nisbett, a psychometrician, challenges the evidence here and finds a zero genetic contribution to black–white differentials. For a more current perspective on the reality of race and its implications we need to turn to debates in genetics and genomics.

Contemporary race science and bio-colonialism

Examinations of the durability and persistence of race ideas in contemporary scientific contexts has been made by Bob Carter (2007) and Richard Tutton (2007). The Human Genome Project, DNA fingerprinting, forensic science, genealogy, genomics and biomedical research provide examples in their work to establish how concepts of race and, particularly for Tutton whiteness, are articulated, invoked and legitimated. Despite repeated declarations from differing scientific communities in recent years that the concept of race is not supported by current research, Tutton's work shows clearly that this is not the case, drawing on empirical work with researchers involved in the construction of population genetic databases.

Race and science in the UK: current debates

Claims for the beneficial use of race in medicine and in tracing ancestry have recently led to a resurgence of interest in race science. A 'breakthrough in racial medicine' was announced when the US Federal Drug Administration approved BiDil for the treatment of heart failure in black Americans. In 2006 an expert forum was held in the UK, organised by the Economic and Social Research Council to discuss the relevance of using categories of race and ethnicity in medicine (www.genomicsforum.ac.uk). At this meeting Joseph Graves elaborated on his work and argued that we cannot construct races using genetics, that within geographical and cultural regions variations in physical feature are enormous e.g. 85 per cent of variation in skull shape is found within regions, and that the way we look depends as much on genes as environmental factors such as solar intensity, diet, and the pattern of disease. Most of the human species evolutionary time has been spent in North-Eastern Africa and subsequently migration and gene-flow have ensured that there is substantial genetic variation across human populations living in different regions.

Also, Graves argues that 'how we *chose* to identify ourselves is not necessarily related to these genetic ancestry lines'. Referring to Sinha *et al.* (2006) and other sources he notes that 94 per cent of those who self-identified as African American did not have a majority of their genetic markers indicating African origin, with a similar finding for self-identified Native Americans, that 7 per cent of those who self-identified as 'white' did not have a predominantly European genetic background, and that 96 per cent of those who self-identified as 'black' did not have a predominantly African genetic background.

Non-coding DNA (the parts that do not carry the information necessary to make a protein) is used to establish ancestry lines and cluster groups of people as populations. This may tell us something about geographical lineage but nothing about race. Irrespective of these concerns the forum concluded that:

> despite the problems of using racial categorisations in medical research and practice we seem stuck with them for the foreseeable future.

> (www.genomicsforum.ac.uk 2006: 8)

This pessimistic conclusion arose from recognition that race was seen as a useful proxy, as the limited (6–7 per cent) of genetic differences between human populations commonly called races could be medically significant, and also that social constructions of race will continue to drive medical and scientific research.

Race and science in the US: current debates

In the US the Social Science Research Council recently hosted a web forum with the title 'Is Race Real?' (http://raceandgenomics.ssrc.org/) following a claim from Armand Leroi, an evolutionary biologist based at Imperial College in London, that racial differences are genetically identifiable. Leroi argues that recognising race will improve medical care and also that it will help us to recognise, value and protect people of obscure ancient racial stock such as the Andaman Islanders. He refers to the possibilities of geneticists admixture mapping techniques being able to:

> write the genetic recipe of the fair hair of a Norwegian, the black-verging-on-purple-skin of a Solomon islander, the flat face of an Inuit, and the curved eyelid of a Han Chinese.

> (Leroi 2006)

Also he claims that analysis of the similarity of a few hundred genes can enable people to be sorted by computer into five groups which are 'the major races of traditional anthropology', groups which are native to Europe, Africa, East Asia, America and Australasia. A further paper in this web forum by Troy Duster (2005) suggests that we face the prospect of a cascading effect from present research practice which will 're-inscribe taxonomies of race across a broad range of scientific practices and fields'. The racial designations of stored samples and data sets, also identified by Tutton, are leading to a reification of race as having genetically distinctive features. Duster warns that in the US, the collection of data using racial categories, for example in national criminal justice databases, may lead to specification of racial causes in the search for biological bases of criminal behaviour.

Looking more closely at the implications of specific programmes in the US raises a wider set of global concerns. The US Human Genome Program, which ran from 1990–2003 confirms that:

> DNA studies do not indicate that separate classifiable subspecies (races) exist within modern humans. While different genes for physical traits such as skin and hair color can be identified between individuals, no consistent patterns of genes across the human genome exist to distinguish one race from another. There also is no genetic basis for divisions of human ethnicity. People who have lived in the same geographic region for many generations may have some alleles in common, but no allele will be found in all members of one population and in no members of any other.

> (US Human Genome Project 2003)

(NB. Alleles are DNA coding sequences for a type of gene)

Bio-colonialism and indigenous peoples

The controversy over bio-colonialism, where the dominant states in the world exercise control over the biological resources of others, is addressed by the Indigenous People's Council on Biocolonialism (see www.ipcb.org/). Here they highlight how the Human Genome Diversity Project has been widely criticised for its treatment of indigenous people as research subjects with little consultation and little regard for their livelihood, and for failing to adequately address a wide range of ethical issues. Studying genetic variation to determine patterns of human migration has been used in a variety of ways to challenge aboriginal rights to territory, resources and self-determination. Across the globe, states have employed 'genomic archytypes' to resolve ancestral claims and land conflicts, for example between Tibetans and Chinese, Azeris and Armenians and Serbs and Croats. A range of other concerns are identified including genetic discrimination and genetic bio-warfare. Genetic exploitation of the economic value of indigenous peoples' blood has been indicated by a series of patent applications arising from this work.

Other studies underway include the Genographic project which aims to construct a DNA database for genetic anthropology, structuring its sampling across East Asia, India, Middle East, North America, North Eurasia and Sub-Saharan Africa. This project claims its work also helps to revitalise indigenous and traditional cultural projects such as sustaining threatened languages while gathering DNA data with those groups. Here, the benefits of genetic anthropology may include highlighting common ancestry, increased understanding of migration, the impact of culture on human genetic variation and patterns of genetic diversity and potential use for medical research to produce cures for genetic diseases. Ethical and controversial issues raised include reifying racial categories through database classifications, participants' rights in terms of consent and ownership of genetic material, addressing how bio-piracy, foreign exploitation of biological samples from traditional or indigenous peoples, will be prevented. In terms of impact on groups, this may arise as DNA evidence contradicts traditional origin stories amongst traditional cultures and, as knowledge of which peoples' ancestors arrived first, it may affect governmental decisions for land rights. More widely this raises the wider question, how will these studies affect views on race, ethnicity and minorities in wider society?

Recently the United Nations Permanent Forum on Indigenous Issues (UNPFII) announced its recommendation 'that the Genographic Project be immediately suspended and report to the Indigenous peoples on the free, prior and informed consent of all the communities where activities are conducted or planned'. Effectively stopping the collection of 100,000 DNA samples from Indigenous peoples around the world as a result of campaign work by the IPCB, and controversy and conflict in this area are highly likely to continue (see Tall Bear 2007 for a further critique of this project).

Mapping race?

Another project, the HapMap, is cataloguing common genetic variants that occur in human beings. It describes what these variants are, where they occur in our DNA, and how they are distributed among people within populations and among populations in different parts of the world (www.hapmap.org/; see 'Y Haplogroups of the World' Map from www.scs.uiuc.edu/~mcdonald/WorldHaplogroupsMaps.pdf#pref). An example of a classification of the different peoples of the world used in haplotype mapping is given below.

Haplotype Classification of Populations

Alaskan: Inuit peoples of Alaska.

Athabaskan: Athabaskan speaking peoples of Western North America.

Northeast Amerindian: Native peoples of Northeastern North America.

Salishan: Salish speaking peoples of the American Pacific Northwest.

South Amerindian: Native peoples of South America.

Mestizo ('mixed'): Native Americans blended with Europeans and Africans.

Arabian: The Arabian Peninsula.

Asia Minor: The East Mediterranean and Anatolia to the Tarim Basin.

North African: North Africa.

North Indian: Northern India.

South Indian: Southern India.

Sub-Saharan African: Africa south of the Sahara Desert.

Eastern European: The Slavic speaking region of Eastern Europe.

Basque: The Basque speaking peoples of Western Europe.

Finno-Ugrian: The Uralic speaking region of Northeastern Europe.

Mediterranean: The Romance speaking region of Southern Europe.

Northwest European: The Celtic and Germanic speaking region of Northwestern Europe.

Australian: Aboriginal peoples of Australia.

Chinese: The Chinese region of East Asia.

Japanese: The Japanese Archipelago.

Polynesian: The Polynesian Islands.

Southeast Asian: Southeast Asia and the Malay Archipelago.

Tibetan: The Himalayas and Tibetan Plateau.

Source: www.hapmap.org.

Recently data from the international haplotype has been used to suggest that human races in different parts of the world are becoming more genetically distinct, with a rider that this is likely to reverse in the future as populations become more mixed (*Guardian* 11 Dec. 2007, *Times* 11 Dec. 2007, *New York Times* 11 Dec. 2007). This study led by an anthropologist, John Hawks from the University of Wisconsin, and reported in the *Proceedings of the National Academy of Sciences*, used genetic markers from four groups: Han Chinese, Japanese, Africa's Yoruba and Northern Europeans. Evolutionary differentiation is argued to be speeding up and this was identified in, for example, lighter skin and blue eyes in Northern Europe and partial resistance to malaria in Africa. The growing debate in the news media, in blogs and in other forums on the genetic basis of racial differences and the proposition that this is accelerating indicates both the increasing legitimacy accorded to racialised biology and anthropology as well as increasing social concern and opposition to such accounts. The completely uncritical statements made by journalists, for example 'races have evolved away from each other over the last 10,000 years' by the Science editor of *The Times*, in reporting this story is a deeply worrying trend that has been evident for some time. The symbolic representation of the peoples of the world as four different coloured races was embodied in their presentation as 38-ton plastic giants in the opening parade of the 1998 football World Cup in Paris. This provided a solid reminder to global viewers of the normality of such perceptions as they were shown to a huge television audience slowly clanking down the streets of the French capital. *The Times* captured this scene on its front page with a photograph of the yellow 'plastic oriental giant shuffling towards three counterparts' (10 June 1998). This use of the idea of race was reported unquestioningly by the world's media.

Racial ancestry and identity

The use of haplotypes, which are a combination of alleles, is being marketed as a way to discover your racial ancestry and illustrates the continuing reification of race in the application of genomics, see the DNA Ancestry advert below. The African Ancestry project illustrates the emotional appeal of such applications.

Discovering race: Web advert for the DNA Ancestry project

Find the race of your ancestors by discovering your haplogroup. Were they European, and if so, which haplogroup did they belong to? Do you have a Native American Ancestry? What about African ancestry? Do you belong to the famous Jewish Cohanim line? Were you related to Niall of the Nine Hostages? Find out these interesting facts and many more.

(www.dnaancestryproject.com/)

Discovering African ancestry

African Ancestry uses DNA to trace ancestry of maternal and paternal lineages. We specialize in reconnecting people to their lost ancestral histories. We are the only company that can tell a person the present-day country(ies) in Africa with which he or she shares ancestry.

(www.africanancestry.com/)

African Ancestry Traces DNA Roots

Dr. Rick Kittles, an African-American realized that conventional genealogical methods for exploring one's family tree couldn't find him answers more specific than a continent. As a molecular geneticist, though, Kittles was in a position to use the latest DNA technology to ask questions that hadn't been feasible before. Kittles' day job is co-directing the National Human Genome Center at Howard University in Washington. To find out more about his mother's ancestors, Kittles examined his own mitochondrial DNA, which is a special kind of genetic material that is inherited exclusively down the maternal line of his family tree. In other words, his came down virtually unchanged from his mother's mother's mothers, back for hundreds of generations. Every so often, tiny mutations in the DNA occur. People who have the same mutation have the same 'foremother' somewhere back in their ancestry. For comparison, Kittles began assembling genetic data from published studies and collecting DNA samples in Africa. He said, 'My female line goes back to Northern Nigeria, the land of the Hausa tribe. I then went to Nigeria and talked to people and learned a lot about the Hausa's culture and tradition. That gave me sense about who I am. In a way, it grounded me.' 'Two people there looked like cousins I have – they even behaved like them!' Kittles laughed. Like a number of other geneticists, Kittles eventually decided to launch a for-profit side business helping people learn more about their ancestry. His is the first to specialize in serving the African diaspora. For $349, African Ancestry Inc. will test either your female or male lines. The male line is the one down which your last name is passed. The test to find where your father's father's fathers came from relies on the male Y-chromosome and thus it only works in men. Women who want to track their male line heritage can have a male relative on their father's side take the Y-chromosome test. African Ancestry sends you a kit containing two swabs. You rub them along the inside of your cheeks, then use an overnight delivery service to get the samples to the company's laboratory. There, they will be compared to African Ancestry's competitive advantage: it's exclusive African Lineage Database. This contains the DNA maps of about 9,000 African individuals from 82 population groups drawn from across all the regions exploited by the trans-Atlantic slave trade, from Senegal in the northwest of Africa to Mozambique in the southeast.

Many customers like the direct emotional connection they feel to individual ancestors found through this process. The original ancestors of all humans probably lived in Africa, but from the end of the Ice Ages 12,000 years ago up until the Age of Discovery beginning in the 15th century, Europeans and sub-Saharan Africans were relatively isolated from each other. During these millennia, some separate genetic markers emerged on each continent. So, geneticists don't have much trouble distinguishing African and European ancestors. Kittles' Y-chromosome test can raise an issue that might be sensitive to some customers wanting to get more in touch with their African paternal ancestors. The test may uncover white forefathers instead. This can be disconcerting because one of them may have owned a black female ancestor. How common is it? According to Shriver, of the several thousand people he studied who identify as African-Americans, about 90 percent are at least half black genealogically (and thus genetically). On average, about 82–83 percent of the genes found in African-Americans are indeed from Africa. Still, the odds that a Y-chromosome test will find a forefather from Europe are significant. Kittles noted that about 30 percent of African-Americans' Y-chromosomes originated in Europe. Kittles, for example, has a Y-chromosome common in Germany, not Africa. 'My father had told me for a long time that I had a white ancestor on our paternal line. So, the test confirmed it goes back to Germany.' In contrast, only about 5 percent of African-Americans' mitochondrial DNA comes from Europe, making the maternal line test a surer bet for those primarily interested in their black ancestors.

Source: The Washington Post 05/28/2003, Steve Sailer (edited article from www.racesci.org).

The exciting potential for challenging notions of race and racial descent and provision of a better understanding of ancestry has been promised by contemporary genetics research as indicated in the Africa Ancestry project, and its use by talk show host Oprah Winfrey to match her to the Kpelles tribe in Liberia. A similar approach has been taken to tracing Native American ancestry with geneticists marketing a test to determine tribal membership and Native American identity and this has been highly controversial. Demonstrating tribal membership has had increased significance where large profits from tribal-owned casinos have been distributed amongst tribal members in the US. Deciding on such claims has been described as a 'false and impossible goal' given that tribal membership is a political status and is the product of mixture between populations (Shelton and Marks quoted in Marks 2006). To date no recognised North American tribe regards DNA testing as proof of membership and greater validity is based on ancestral names used in Native American censuses. Genetic testing also has a high margin of error (+/– 15 per cent) and can confuse many groups, e.g. Mongolian and Native American ancestry. More generally, the results of genetic testing can be confusing and ambiguous, requiring a high level of understanding to interpret, with the danger of simplistic and inaccurate meaning being drawn by non-professional people. The reliance by professionals on racially constructed categories of populations remains a fundamental problem, which leads to the reproduction of more 'common-sense' racial thinking. These issues indicate the dilemmas of the contemporary commodification of identity in the use of genetic anthropology. Genomics is all about human identity, as Christine Hauskeller (2004) has argued.

Racial science and crime

One of the most important developments in crime science has been the establishment of a national database for DNA samples. The England and Wales National DNA Database now holds 2.3 million DNA profiles from individuals, and 230,000 profiles from crime-scene stains (Institute of Physics 2004). It is the biggest and most successful in the world. The established method of DNA fingerprinting depends on analysing frequency patterns of repeating sections of DNA of different lengths, which vary from individual to individual. Today, even more complex methods of gene analysis are being developed using other patterns of DNA repeats. These patterns may be related to the sex of an individual (Y chromosomes in rape cases), or their ancestry – racial mix, or more contentiously, physical characteristics (the phenotype). Mitochondrial DNA which is inherited maternally can be used on very degraded samples of DNA. Another technology, rapidly gaining interest, is based on single nucleotide polymorphisms (SNP, pronounced 'snip') whereby single base changes in a DNA sequence can be mapped and variations compared in individuals. Again it is suitable for badly degraded samples. Since SNPs remain stable when inherited they have already been used to establish geographical origins and racial mix of a suspect (Institute of Physics 2004). So, the active construction of racial categories are an intrinsic part of crime science and this has worrying implications. SNP mapping of police DNA databases, which themselves reflect the class, gender and racist biases of policing, generates correlations between the genetic profiles of different types of criminals (Carter 2007). This in turn informs debates about public safety, about the possibility of reducing crime and the notions of 'legitimate suspects' that pervade the routine practices of policing. The search for genetic markers of criminality reinforces the notion that there are genetic explanations for crime (Carter 2007). This search for markers resembles the similar searches undertaken by the 'scientific racism' of the nineteenth century. Here the markers of criminality (and many other things) were sought in skull shape and other physiognomic features but, as with modern genomics, these were merely markers, not explanations, and the categorisations of difference that they both rested upon and sought to establish were themselves the product of broader social forces connected in large part with slavery, colonialism and imperialism. Ironically, these historical sequences were expressive of a more general shift in global order and global governance, one of whose significant effects was to challenge directly nineteenth century notions of belonging and identity and the unstable systems of classification upon which they depended (Carter 2007). Concern with identity, about what it is to be human and how we are related to other human beings is a key part of current debates on genetics, genomics and classification of peoples.

Categorisation, identity and naming

The construction of identity and identification is a central feature of human life and the development of sophisticated strategies to know who we are is clearly indicated in contemporary genetics. The assertion of who we are, reflexive self-identification, can be seen to be a 'universal aspect of being human' (Jenkins 2004). External categorisation of race and ethnicity by states, bureaucracies and scientists has sought to impose order on the inter-subjective process of human identification. Affirmation of 'identity politics' has frequently been of intense concern in racial and ethnic conflict and here the precise ways in which racial, ethnic and national identities have been constructed and mobilised is often of central importance. Also in the making of race in the modern world challenging categorisation and resisting external imposition of names, hierarchies and classifications has often been a strong driving impulse in strategies of opposition and resistance. The affirmation of common humanity has been central to both anti-slavery struggles and the opposition to racial hierarchies in science.

The persistence of racial categorisation

Genetic anthropology is now being used to answer the questions 'where did we come from and how did we get here?' DNA evidence indicates that all humans share a common female ancestor who lived in Africa 140,000 years ago and all men share a common male ancestor who lived in Africa 60,000 years ago, and also that separate classifiable sub-species (races) do not exist within modern humans (Human Genome Project 2007). The genetic fluidity of human populations and commonalities across the human species make racial categorisation and measurement highly dubious. However, current UK ESRC guidelines for using race and ethnic categories suggest that we should develop procedures for scientists to apply and consider in deciding whether to use such categories (see Taylor 2006: Appendix 1). Here it is suggested that race and ethnicity categories can be used under specific circumstances. Firstly, where it is possible to reliably measure race/ethnicity categories, and where it is possible to refine the categories or the population sampled. Secondly, where race/ethnicity is either being used to assess the risk or impact of discrimination, or where race/ethnicity is a reliable proxy for other variable(s) of interest and where there is no more reliable, or less contentious, proxy than race/ethnicity which can be measured. Lastly, where the benefits of using race/ethnicity outweigh any disadvantages. These allow significant room for interpretation and discretion and clearly do not attempt to provide a definitive rejection of their usage. Such an approach has been characterised as 'capitulation to a reductive scientific formalism' where ethical and moral issues are resolved through a system of institutional procedures (St Louis 2005). In resolving the disputes over the use of race St Louis (2005: 30) argues that 'one either is or is not well disposed towards the biological notion of race in part because of a moral appreciation of its social connotation and implications'. The American Sociological Association in responding to the California referendum on prohibition of the collection of racial data by government agencies in 2004 argued strongly against this position, proposing that collecting socially significant racial data was necessary to research and identify patterns of racial discrimination and racial inequality. Here, the ASA defines race as socially constructed and as a primary area for sociological investigation identifying the important consequences of racial classification in three areas: as a sorting mechanism for mating, marriage and adoption, as a stratifying practice for providing or denying access to resources and as an organising device for mobilisation to maintain or challenge systems of racial stratification. So, categorisation of racial groups persist both in natural science, in government censuses and surveys across many societies and in social science. Examining and interrogating the moral, social and political motivations and effects of using racial categories continues to be an urgent task in the modern world.

Categorising the Roma

Racial and ethnic categories and identities are not fixed, they are the product of particular histories, conflicts, mis/recognitions, belongings, boundary drawing, imagining and forms of regulation. The question 'who is African?' appears to be conclusively answered by genetics: we all are. However who is African-American or black British may be qualified by a much more historically recent set of conditions and qualifications. In many senses race, ethnicity and nation have a common component: they seek to construct an understanding of descent

(Fenton 2003). Anti-gypsyism was briefly examined in Chapter 1, but who are Gypsies and why is the term Roma now used more widely for Europe's largest and most persecuted minority?

Who are the Roma?

Three competing forms of understanding and conceptualising Romani identity have been set out in recent debate (Vermeersch 2006). Firstly, as a historical diaspora, emphasising common origin and descent of a group of people from a military caste in India with a common Romani language now scattered across Europe. This 'deliberate fabrication' of classic 'gypsyologists', Nazi scientists and contemporary academics has been challenged for its homogenising exoticism (Oakley 1983; Vermeersch 2006: 14). Secondly, others have argued the Roma can be recognised by their affection for travelling/itinerant lifestyles, being marginal in national contexts and having a specific set of cultural practices and musical traditions. Yet movement and migration characterises humanity and also most Roma in Central Europe do live in settled communities. Thirdly, others have argued that the Roma are genetically related and have biological kinship. A recent case in Norwich, UK involved a claim to be able to identify a Romani gene which continuing recourse to science in arbitrating patterns of human descent.

Experts find rare Romani DNA in Norwich Anglo Saxon skeleton

The recent discovery of Romani DNA in an Anglo Saxon skeleton has made experts re-think the nature of the city's early population. Experts from Norfolk Archaeology Unit based at Norwich Castle have discovered a rare form of mitochondrial DNA identified as Romani in a skeleton discovered during excavations in a large area of Norwich for the expansion of the castle mall. The DNA was found in an eleventh century young adult male skeleton, and with the first recorded arrival of the Romani gene in this country put at 500 years later historians may need to re-think the ethnic mix of the city's early population. Extracting DNA from ancient bones is a complicated procedure involving removing the DNA from the tooth pulp as the hard tooth enamel preserves the gene. This form of mitochondrial DNA is passed down the female line and the identified gene is only found in the descendants of Romani. According to DNA records, the first recorded Romani gene found in England was in the sixteenth century. (Norwich City Council, Sarah Morley 12 May 2006)

http://journeyfolki.org.uk/Community/Forums/tabid/690/forumid/36/tpage/1/view/topic/postid/12098/Default.aspx#12098

In terms of estimates of the size of the Roma population by official categorisation and measurement there are huge differences between estimates and census figures, and between self-declarations of ethnic origin and external categorical estimation. So, despite deep controversy over Roma identity and Roma categorisation, there is commonality in constructing Roma group identity from a wide range of groups identified differently across Europe. There are a multitude of group labels such as Gypsy and Tsigane and sub-group names such as Vlach, Sinto, Kalderash and Beash (Vermeesch 2006). In Slovakia, some schools segregate their children into 'blacks', Roma, and 'whites', non-Roma (*Guardian* 16 Nov. 2007). The political mobilisation of these groups across Europe into the category of Roma has faced tremendous obstacles in unifying disparate groups in response to common patterns of exclusion, violence and discrimination. This has been increasingly successful in winning recognition and intervention, particularly at the EU level (see the European Commission's website on the Roma at http://ec.europa.eu/employment_social/fundamental_rights/roma/index_en.htm). EU and national governments are beginning to develop Romani programmes of action in response to these claims which may offer some prospect of material improvement for this group, but will certainly lead to greater institutionalisation and categorisation of Romani identity (see further discussion in Chapter 7). Identity, category and names matter here and they are vitally important in the struggle for fundamental rights.

Categorising Indigenous People

Paralleling the rise of the Roma as a pan-European political identity is the rise of 'Indigenous Peoples' as a collective global identity and legally recognised category by the International Labour Organisation and the UN (Niezen 2003). The claims of these peoples for global recognition as victims of racism, colonialism and globalisation were officially confirmed in the declarations of the World Conference Against Racism in 2001. But who are this group and how has their identity been constructed, conceptualised and categorised? Indigenism is the term, used by Niezen (2003), to describe the international movement that aspires to promote the rights of the world's 'first peoples'. That is the estimated 3 million people from many different societies who live in 'wild places', often formerly referred to as 'primitive'. As noted above, given the pattern of human migration and shifting settlement, and the commonality of genetic make-up claims to distinctiveness as the 'first people' in a particular territory may be highly dubious and contestable. The notion of what constitutes wilderness is also highly variable across different geographical and social contexts. Nevertheless, for this group, notions of 'unbroken ancestry' and affective attachment to lands coincide with historical identities derived from experiences of 'state genocide, forced settlement, relocation, political marginalisation, and various formal attempts at cultural destruction' (Niezen 2003: 5). Identifying this group by reference to 'traditional' lifestyles and types of economic activity is also deeply unsatisfactory when indigenous people move away from such 'traditional' spheres and still claim indigenous identity. José Martinez Cobo, Special Rapporteur for the UN Commission on Human Rights, formulated an often quoted definition of what constitutes an indigenous people:

> Indigenous communities, peoples and nations are those which, having a historical continuity with pre-invasion and pre-colonial societies that developed on their territories, consider themselves distinct from other sectors of the society now prevailing in those territories or parts of them. They form at present non-dominant sectors of society and are determined to preserve, develop and transmit to future generations their ancestral territories and their ethnic identity, as the basis of their continued existence as peoples in accordance with their own cultural pattern, social institutions and legal systems.
>
> (Martinéz Cobo, quoted in Caumartin 2005: 6)

Ethnic identity is primarily seen as having a concern with particularity, ideas of a common homeland, culture and historical memory and so on for that group. Indigeneity is not an ethnic identity, then, but a collective category for different peoples who share similar histories of oppression and exploitation but not homeland and culture, and who may have highly distinctive characteristics, for example of dress, mythologies and language. For example, such differences exist between the Touregs of North Africa, the Crees of North Canada, the Sami of Finland and the Herero of Namibia, all of whom lay claim to a common indigenous identity. Global political recognition acknowledges indigenous people's long struggle against racism and colonialism and recognises a range of rights including:

> to call themselves by their own names; to participate freely and on an equal footing in their country's political, economic, social and cultural development; to maintain their own forms of organization, lifestyles, cultures and traditions; to maintain and use their own languages; to maintain their own economic structures in the areas where they live; to take part in the development of their educational systems and programmes; to manage their lands and natural resources, including hunting and fishing rights; and to have access to justice on a basis of equality.
>
> (WCAR 2001: para 42)

Most indigenous people around the world remain victims of internal colonialism (Weaver 2005) where native populations are marginalised by a mass of colonial settlers. For example the Maya in Guatemala have been fighting centuries of oppression and a 36-year civil war to secure recognition of their rights. The intersections of descent, racism, ethnicity, identity and categorisation are usefully elaborated for both indigenous and mixed/mestizo groups in the Guatemala case.

Identity and categorisation and naming in Guatemala

The indigenous peoples of Guatemala are descended from aboriginal populations at the time of the Spanish conquest, specifically those groups descended from the Mayan civilisation and Xinca peoples. The black Garifuna communities of Guatemala are often considered as belonging to 'indigenous' groups where the non-white and non-dominant status of Garifunas plays a key role in the ascription of identity. The task of finding 'objective' criteria that permit one to identify indigenous people has long preoccupied researchers and census authorities alike. It is important to give consideration to two key traditional cultural markers of identity in Guatemala, wearing indigenous clothing and speaking indigenous languages. These two markers have long been used for the ascription of ethnic identity, including by population census officials. To a degree these two attributes are still strong markers of identity, in the sense that individuals wearing traditional indigenous clothing and those whose first language is an indigenous language will frequently self-identify as indigenous. However, the reverse is not true and individuals who have ceased to speak indigenous languages, or who no longer wear traditional clothing may still self-identify as indigenous. Fewer and fewer indigenous people (especially men) wear traditional indigenous clothing on a daily basis, not least because of the expense incurred in purchasing such items of clothing. Similarly, languages are important for indigenous cultural identity but the loss of indigenous language does not necessarily lead to a loss of indigenous identity. The 'indigenous' or Mayan categories encompass a diversity of groups that are differentiated on the basis of language and whose populations tend to be concentrated in specific geographical areas. The main ethno-linguistic

➔

indigenous groups in Guatemala (that is, spoken by more than 100,000 people) are K'ichee' (over a million speakers), Mam (almost three-quarters of a million speakers), Kakqchikel (over 400,000 speakers) and Q'eqchi' (just under 400,000 speakers). Thus, it is important to acknowledge the coherence in 'indigenous' or 'Mayan' identity which is rooted in shared history and a degree of cultural affinities, as well as the diversity within the indigenous category which mitigates against the emergence of a united indigenous-based movement and leadership.

The ladino category is also a composite group. The meaning of ladino changed drastically during the course of the nineteenth century. Up until then, the ladino category related to 'meztizos' (individuals of mixed Indian–Spanish parentage). Thus, the definition had clear racial undertones. Towards the end of the nineteenth century, ladinos gradually came to include 'assimilated' indigenous peoples who adopted Western clothing and spoke Spanish. The latter reflected the fact that integrating into the ladino ranks was not accessible to all, but presumed access to (Spanish) language or education and a degree of interaction with the ladino world. Over the years, the meaning of 'ladino' gradually evolved from a racial concept to one rooted both in class and in anti-indigenous sentiment. To be ladino now denoted until recently an essentially 'non-indigenous' identity of individuals. Groups that were once clearly distinct from meztizos and indigenous peoples such as the white Criollo elite (of white European descent) now barely seem to register on the ethnic scales of the country. This group, which is unlikely to self-define as ladino, tends to be ascribed by default a 'ladino' identity by virtue of their non-indigenous status. It must be noted however that in the past decade important cracks are appearing in the bi-polar Guatemalan model. Many indigenous movements and organisations distance themselves from the 'indigenous' category with its pejorative and colonial connotations, opting instead for a more positive 'Mayan' category. On the other hand many individuals no longer feel comfortable with a ladino label that some associate with negative connotations of racism, violence and exploitation, opting instead for a more positive 'mestizo' category. Physical appearance and skin colour, region of origins, culture, class and lifestyle all play a part in the processes of ascription and self-definition of identity.

Source: edited extracts from Caumartin 2005.

Conclusion

This chapter has shown how racial systems of classification have been elaborated in scientific contexts and how political imperatives to challenge such racial science developed. It has examined current debates in both the US and the UK over the validity and status of the race idea and in particular has established ongoing ambivalence and conflict over whether or not it should be systematically and consistently rejected. The use of genetics to construct human identities has been explored and ethical debates in the use of race have been examined, with particular attention to indigenous people and issues of bio-colonialism. Tracing ancestry and establishing genealogies raises interesting questions for the understanding and challenge of simplistic, pure notions of kinship, tribal membership and racial and ethnic identity. Anchoring identities in the past has been shown to be highly illusory and the changing fluid character of racial and ethnic identities has been confirmed. The social and political significance of developing categories and identities has been illustrated by review of the social and political construction of both the Roma in Europe and indigenous people across the world.

End of chapter activity

Read submissions to the ESRC Genomics Forum website (www.genomicsforum. ac.uk) and identify the different positions taken by scientists in using race in contemporary research. Compare this with the American Sociological Association race guidelines, (www.asa.org). How do they differ and what implications would you draw from these debates for best social scientific practice in using concepts of race? (American Sociological Association (2002) *The Importance of Collecting Data and Doing Social Science research on Race*, www2.asanet.org/media/asa_race_statement.pdf)

Further reading

Augstein, H. F. (ed.) (1996) *Race, the Origins of an Idea, 1760–1850,* **Bristol: Thoemmes Press.** This edited collection of original sources presents extracts from the work of leading philosophers and natural historians on racial science. These texts document the rise of racial theory in Germany, France and England which was used to justify imperialism and colonial rule.

Clarke, A. and Ticehurst, F. (eds.) (2006) *Living with the Genome, ethical and social aspects of human genetics,* **Basingstoke: Palgrave.** This edited collection examines a variety of key issues from a variety of standpoints and includes contributions on Nazi eugenics, contemporary eugenics, the impact of the Human Genome Diversity Project on indigenous communities, race and IQ, and contemporary debates on racism, ethnicity and biology.

Vermeesch, P. (2006) *The Romani Movement, minority politics and ethnic mobilisation in contemporary Central Europe,* **Oxford: Berghahn Books.** This text examines the development of Romani political identities drawing on empirical research with activists and politicians in Czech Republic, Hungary and Slovakia.

References

American Sociological Association (2002) *The Importance of Collecting Data and Doing Social Science Research on Race*, www2.asanet.org/media/asa_race_statement.pdf.

Anderson, K. (2006) *Race and the Crisis of Humanism*, London: Routledge.

Augstein, H. F. (1996) *Race, the origins of an idea, 1760–1850*, Bristol: Thoemmes Press.

Banton, M. (1997) *Racial Theories*, Cambridge: Cambridge University Press.

Barkan, E. (1992) *The Retreat of Scientific Racism, changing concepts in race in Britain and the US between the world wars*, Cambridge: Cambridge University Press.

Barzun, J. (1937) *Race: a study in modern superstition*, New York: Harcourt.

Carter, R. (2007) 'Genes, genomes and genealogies: the return of scientific racism', *Ethnic and Racial Studies*, 30, 4, pp. 546–556.

Cartwright, S. A. (1851) 'Report on the Diseases and the Physical Perculiarities of the Negro Race', *New Orleans Surgical and Medical Journal*, pp. 691–715, http://www.google.com/books?id=mjkCAAAAYAAJ&pg=RA2-PA707&.

Caumartin, C. (2005) *Racism, Violence, and Inequality: an overview of the Guatemalan case*, Oxford: CRISE.

Centre for Holocaust and Genocide Studies (2007) *Racism: elimination of human beings of minor value*, Minneapolis: University of Minnesota.

Duster, T. (2006) *Race and Reification in Science*, http://raceandgenomics.ssrc. org/Duster/.

Fenton, S. (2003) *Ethnicity*, Oxford: Polity.

Fernando, S. (1991) *Mental Health, Race and Culture*, London: Macmillan.

Gould, S. J. (1981) *The Mismeasure of Man*, Harmondsworth: Penguin.

Hall, S. (1992) 'The West and the Rest: discourse and power', in S. Hall and B. Gieben (eds), *Formations of Modernity*, Cambridge: Policy Press.

Hauskeller, C. (2004) 'Genes, genomes and identity. Projections on matter', *New Genetics and Society*, 23, 3, pp. 285–299.

Hesse, B. (2007) 'Racialised modernity: an analytics of white mythologies', *Ethnic and Racial Studies*, 30, 4, pp. 643–663.

Hunt-Grubbe, C. (2007) 'The elementary DNA of Dr. Watson', *Times Online*, Oct 14.

Institute of Physics (2004) 'Science and Crime, report of a seminar', www.iop.org/activity/policy/Events/Seminars/file_3516.pdf.

Jenkins, R. (2004) *Social Identity*, London: Routledge.

Knox, R. (1850) *The Races of Men*, Philadelphia: Lea & Blanchard.

Leroi, A. (2006) *A Family Tree in Every Gene*, http://raceandgenomics.ssrc.org/Leroi/.

Marks, J. (2006) 'HGDP: impact on indigenous communities' in A. Clarke and F. Ticehurst (eds.) *Living with the Genome, ethical and social aspects of human genetics*, Basingstoke: Palgrave Macmillan.

Niezen, R. (2003) *The Origins of Indigenism, human rights and the politics of identity*, London: University of California Press.

Oakely, Judith (1983) The Traveller Gypsies, Cambridge: Cambridge University Press.

Proctor, R. (1988) *Racial Hygiene: medicine under the Nazis*, Cambridge, MA: Harvard University Press.

Ripley, W. Z. (1899) *The Races of Europe: a sociological study*, New York: D. Appleton & Co.

Sinha, M., Larkin, E., Elston, R., and Redline, S. (2006) 'Self-reported race and genetic admixture', *New England Journal of Medicine*, 354, 4,pp. 421–422.

St Louis, B. (2005) 'Racialization in the "Zone of Ambiguity"', in K. Murji and J. Solomos (eds), *Racialization, studies in theory and practice*, Oxford: Oxford University Press.

Tall Bear, K. (2007) 'Narratives of race and indigeneity in the Genographic Project', *Journal of Law, Medicine and Ethics*, 35, 3, pp. 412–424.

Taylor, R. (2006) Policy and practice implications arising from the workshop 'Classifying Genomics: how social categories shape scientific and medical practice', www.genomicsforum.ac.uk.

F. Ticehurst, (eds.) *Living with the Genome, ethical and social aspects of human genetics*, Basingstoke: Palgrave Macmillan.

Tucker, W. (2002) *The Funding of Scientific Racism, Wickliffe Draper and the Pioneer Fund*, Champaign, IL: University of Illinois Press.

Tutton, R. (2007) 'Opening the white box: exploring the study of whiteness in contemporary genetics research', *Ethnic and Racial Studies*, 30, 4, pp. 557–569.

US Human Genome Project (2007) *Genetic Anthropology, Ancestry and Human Migration*, www.ornl.gov/sci/techresources/Human_Genome/elsi/humanmigration.sthml.

US Human Genome Project (2003) *Minorities, Race and Genomics*, www.ornl.gov/sci/techresources/Human_Genome/elsi/minorities.shtml.

Vermeesch, P. (2006) *The Romani Movement, minority politics and ethnic mobilisation in contemporary Central Europe*, Oxford: Berghahn Books.

Vinciguerra, T. (2006) 'Jacques Barzun: cultural historian, cheerful pessimist, Columbia avatar', in W. T. De Bary (ed.) *Living Legacies at Columbia*, New York: Columbia University Press.

Weaver, J. (2005) 'Indigenousness and Indigeneity', in H. Schwarz and S. Ray (eds) *A Companion to Postcolonial Studies*, Oxford: Blackwell.

Weiner, M. (2004) 'Discourses of race, nation and empire in pre-1945 Japan', in M. Weiner (ed.) *Race, Ethnicity and Migration in Modern Japan*, Abingdon: Routledge.

3 Theorising racism and ethnicity: foundations

Key issues in this chapter:

- The founding figures of the sociology of racism and ethnicity
- Anna Cooper and the contribution of black feminism
- Concepts of intersectionality and racialisation
- Max Weber's theorisation of race, ethnicity and nation
- Robert Park's theorisation of race relations and the case of Hawai'i
- The emergence of the British sociology of race relations

At the end of this chapter you should be able to:

- Evaluate the relative contribution of the founding figures of this field of study
- Understand the concepts of racialisation and race relations
- Discuss the linkages between race, ethnicity and nation
- Explain how the sociology of race relations developed in the UK
- Critique both the idea of assimilation and the race relations problematic

Introduction

The field of scholarly work on racism is massive and growing. It now encompasses scholarship across a wide range of disciplines including psychology, geography, history, modern languages, area studies, economics, health, religious studies, politics, archaeology, philosophy, communication studies as well as sociology and social policy (Bulmer and Solomos 1999). What binds much of this work together is the utilisation of a set of core concepts; race, racism, ethnicity and migration. Highly contested though they may be, they are applied, explored and elaborated in the context of a multitude of theories and research settings. In compiling a recent collection Goldberg and Solomos (2002) confirm these trends and emphasise the interdisciplinary and multidisciplinary character of studies in this field combined with a quest for adequate theory. How are we to begin to examine the range of leading scholars, schools of thought, periods of thinking and fields of inquiry? A canon of key figures in sociology is increasingly opening up to scholars who have sought to examine the issue of racism (Reed 2006). It was argued in Chapter 1 that William Du Bois was the first leading sociologist in this field, as his work argues that race is the most socially significant construct of modernity, as class was for Karl Marx. His work was not purely theoretical speculation, rather it epitomised empirically informed sociological theory which marks out the best work in this discipline. Since Du Bois' classic work we have had over a century of research and scholarship seeking to make sense of racism, looking backwards to examine historical contexts and questions and, as now, seeking to make sense of urgent topical conflicts and questions that confront us all and to inform social and political action.

This chapter provides an intellectual map of key theorists and important texts which have shaped academic scholarship. W.E.B. Du Bois, Max Weber and Robert E. Park have been referred to as the 'founding fathers of the sociology of race and ethnicity' (Stone and Dennis 2003: 6) and key ideas and linkages are explored in this body of knowledge. The impact of this group of academics in stimulating and influencing the work of a second generation of scholars in the UK including John Rex and Michael Banton writing in the post-war years is also explored, together with the new contributions to knowledge that their texts provide. Neither Karl Marx nor Émile Durkheim directly made a major contribution to this field of sociology. Drawing on Marx's work on Irish migrants in the UK, on the Jewish question and on specific ethnic groups, it is possible to identify some key themes in his treatment of ethnicity. These include, firstly, the emphasis in his work on the economic determination of cultural and ethnic relations, and, secondly, seeing ethnicity as an obstacle to the universal progress of humanity (for example, claims for recognition by ethnic groups incapable of building capitalist nation states and who need to be assimilated, such as Serbs). Lastly, Marx saw ethnic and racial identities falling away as class relations became more significant, as for example anti-Irish racism being seen as leading to division and 'impotence' of the English working class (Malešević 2004). Despite the relegation of ethnicity and race to secondary significance, examining race through the lens of class has, however, inspired a significant group of scholars, as exemplified in Cedric Robinson's *Black Marxism, the making of the Black Radical Tradition* (1983), and including C.L.R. James and Richard Wright who have sought to challenge incomplete and inaccurate European models of history and social change that underplay the role of black social agents. Durkheim's work also illustrates some key themes, including the decline of ethnicity and older traditional forms of identity with the arrival of modernity and global capitalism, and his focus on the need for social integration. Despite his failure to understand the relationship of ethnicity with modernity, Durkheimian concerns over integration as being crucial for social progress dominate much contemporary political and policy debate in the UK and Europe over race and ethnicity.

Pioneer of race theory: Anna Julia Cooper's account of racism and intersectionality

The work of Anna Julia Cooper is increasingly acknowledged as constituting a core part of this classical sociological canon, as she is arguably one of the first leading pioneers of race theory. Cooper places a central focus not only on race in her work, but also on its relations with gender and class (Lemert 1995, Reed 2006). From its outset race has been theorised as being inextricably connected to overlapping structures of inequality and this focus on intersectionality is a foundational aspect of this field of study. Cooper's work inaugurated and articulated a set of key conceptual and substantive interconnections which have energised academics across the twentieth century, for example in Angela Davis' *Women, Race and Class* (1980), Fiona Williams in her work on social policy and issues of race, gender and class (1989, 2005), and most recently in the theorisation of intersectionality and multiple discrimination in current debate in Europe (Quing 2007, Walby 2007). Intersectionality is an attempt to theorise the interactions and outcomes across different structures of inequality such as race, gender and class. These core contributions collectively provided an intellectual agenda which huge numbers of writers and researchers have subsequently built upon in constructing this area of study as one of the most lively, exciting and challenging fields of inquiry in social science.

Anna Julia Cooper published *A Voice from the South* in 1892. This has been acknowledged as one of the earliest and most significant statements of black feminist thought (the full text can be read at http://docsouth.unc.edu/church/cooper/cooper.html). Although fully elaborated theory is not provided here, Cooper does combine a concern for identifying racial inequalities, racism and class in America together with analysis of the role of femininity and masculinity and related strategies for activism and progress. She considers different dimensions of the 'race problem', the representation of 'the Negro' in American literature and the interrelated status of women. She presents women as central in social, political and economic conflict:

> The woman of to-day finds herself in the presence of responsibilities which ramify through the profoundest and most varied interests of her country and race. Not one of the issues of this plodding, toiling, sinning, repenting, falling, aspiring humanity can afford to shut her out, or can deny the reality of her influence. No plan for renovating society, no scheme for purifying politics, no reform in church or in state, no moral, social, or economic question, no movement upward or downward in the human plane is lost on her.

(Cooper 1892: 142–3)

And more specifically, black women are presented as central to confronting the racial crisis apparent in that period, despite criticism of her failure to do this by some feminists:

> to be a woman of the Negro race in America, and to be able to grasp the deep significance of the possibilities of the crisis, is to have a heritage, it seems to me, unique in the ages. In the first place, the race is young and full of the elasticity and hopefulness of youth. All its achievements are before it. It does not look on the masterly triumphs of nineteenth century civilization with that blasé, world-weary look which characterizes the old washed out and worn out races which have already, so to speak, seen their best days.

(Cooper 1892: 144)

Anna Julia Cooper, A Black Woman of the South
Source: Frontispiece image, *A Voice from the South*, 1892, Xenia, Ohio: The Aldine Printing House. Used with Permission of Documenting the American South, The University of North Carolina at Chapel Hill Libraries.

Her examination of the dimensions of racial inequality begin to set out a range of concerns that have been systematically pursued in this field of social science. Firstly, she identifies some of the ways in which negro-phobia, or anti-black racism, is expressed. For example seeing Africa and Africans as contributing nothing to the world, 'not a poem, not an invention, not a piece of art', a 'race' which would not be missed if the continent was 'sunk into the ocean tomorrow'. America it appears is a place where just making reference to black people in everyday conversation produces a 'storm of feeling' that makes men 'grow wild and unfit'. Denial of racism also appears as common practice, it is not that the 'Negro is black', but that he is 'weak – and we don't like weakness'. In contrast she highlights the growing significance of black-led colleges, institutes and schools, and their presidents, teachers, lawyers and ministers, and the significance of education in developing a black contribution to society. She is also conscious of human waste, as exemplified in shockingly high rates of black mortality in comparison to whites, and sought to provide an account of its economic and political causes:

> For 1889 the relative death-rate of the two races in the District of Columbia was: whites, 15.96 per 1000; colored, 30.48, about double. Especially noticeable is the difference in the mortality of children. This is simply alarming.
>
> (Cooper 1892: 247–8)

Poverty, destitution, homelessness and insanitary housing conditions for black people are identified, together with racial discrimination, as for example in Washington 'low priced houses on streets are almost uniformly kept for the white poor' and adverts state 'not rented to colored people'. For whites, the causes of black poverty are because the 'Negro is indolent improvident and vicious'. But Cooper eloquently presents an opposite emotive picture of hard working, caring black masculinity in the face of intense economic oppression:

> Hard-working men, toiling year in and year out, from sunrise to dusk, for fifty cents per day, out of which they must feed and shelter and clothe themselves and their families! That they often have to take their wage in tickets convertible into meat, meal and molasses at the village grocery, owned by the same ubiquitous employer! That there are tenants holding leases on farms who toil sixteen hours to the day and work every chick and child in their possession, not sparing even the drudging wife – to find at the end of the harvesting season and the squaring up of accounts that their accumulations have been like gathering water in a sieve.
>
> (Cooper 1892: 252–3)

She examines economic contexts, exploring the relations between racial divisions and capitalists, labour relations and class in urban and rural contexts. Cooper's work constitutes a fundamental challenge to white governance and culture, and its moral codes and social ethics of superiority. Her wide-ranging sociological account addresses social institutions, the family, education, as well as the complexities of stratification (Reed 2006). Cooper provides a powerful account of the inter-related struggles against economic exploitation, racism and sexism, and although she draws on some idealised conceptions of womanhood and blackness her work has been highly influential in the development of black feminism.

Du Bois also wrote about women's oppression and racism, and for this is also regarded as an early black feminist. For example in the arguments presented in the *Freedom of Womenhood* (1924), where he reflects on Sojourner Truth's famous 'ain't I a woman' speech at the second National Woman Suffrage Convention in 1852. Before she spoke white women were recorded as saying to the presiding officer, 'don't get the cause mixed up with abolition and niggers'. Du Bois presents the speech in full and pays tribute to the impact of black women's struggles in contributing to wider social emancipation. A short extract from Sojourner Truth's speech as used by Du Bois, where she firmly and definitively places herself as equal to any white man or woman, is as follows:

> I could work as much and eat as much as a man (when I could get it), and bear de lash as well – and ain't I a woman. I have borne thirteen children and seen 'em mos'all sold into slavery, and when I cried out with a mother's grief, none but Jesus heard – and ain't I a woman.
>
> (quoted in Zuckerman 2004: 158)

As Angela Davis, a leading radical feminist and black activist (see final section in Chapter 1) notes, Sojourner Truth's claim to equality exposed the middle class bias and racism of both 'male supremacists' and some in the new women's movement (Davis 1980: 63). Central themes addressed by Cooper, Du Bois and Truth of racism, gender and class and the inter-related struggles for liberation, emancipation and equality also appear as central themes in Davis' key text *Women, Race and Class* (1980). She begins by examining the experience of slavery, drawing on slave narratives which nearly always reported the use of rape and sexual victimisation to terrorise and intimidate slave women, and their continual resistance, 'never subdued'. Davis argues that 'new standards for womanhood' are provided by slave women who pass on a legacy of tenacity, hard work, self-reliance and resistance. The strong connections between the anti-slavery movement and the development of women's rights are established, together with racism in the women's suffrage movement. She also argues that the centrality of national and international economic forces placed black women in a position of exploitation and servitude which severely constrained any hope of emancipation. The 1890 census confirmed that many decades after abolition significant numbers of black women still worked in the cotton mills, sugar refineries and mines doing dirty work for unequal pay, with over 30 per cent in domestic service. By the 1960s Davis (1980: 98) states that still 'one-third of black women workers remained chained to the same old household jobs' of domestic service; a key barrier to emancipation as Du Bois also argued.

Du Bois has been criticised for his uncompleted theorisation of race (see Chapter 1), failing to break with primordial, essentialist, anthropological constructions of race to provide a fully social account (also see Chapter 2 for a critique of naturalised constructions of racial categories). Similarly, Cooper's book and Davis' early work both display a tendency to idealise and homogenise black and white experience, failing to carry through an adequate account of the complexities of exclusion and discrimination within these social categories. For example, the range of ethnic groups subsumed under both the 'black' category and the 'white' category with differing experiences and social locations is not adequately addressed. A second criticism is that the relationship between race, class and gender is explicitly addressed, connections are drawn but these linkages are under-theorised. However, these ideas have not only contributed to the strong and influential field of black feminism and intersectional theory (hooks 1982, Collins 2000) but also to the wider understanding of the racialisation of both America (Goldberg 2005) and other countries, for example the UK.

In the UK, Fiona Williams (1989) has sought to address the problem of providing an integrated theorisation of race, gender and class in specific relation to the operation of the welfare state and the discipline of social policy. But she acknowledges the difficulty of doing justice to these questions and other forms of social division including disability, sexual orientation and age. She presents a new analytical framework of 'racially structured and patriarchal capitalism', with the welfare state in the UK being:

built from the exploited labour of Black and other immigrant workers and women, [reproducing] international, racial and sexual divisions of labour, as well as racial domination and female subordination, all of which are compounded by class differences.

(Williams 1989: 207)

The failure to do full justice to ethnic differentiation in this account and the acknowledged failure to fully address intersectionality do not undermine the value of this attempt to grasp and exemplify the inter-related linkages between race, gender and class in this context and carry through the type of analysis embarked on a century before by Cooper.

Following Cooper's lead, intersectional analysis remains a leading edge debate in racism and ethnicity studies, feminist studies, disability studies and related fields of social science.

Key concepts: Intersectionality

Kimberlé Crenshaw (1990, 1991) distinguishes between structural and political intersectionality, indicating the importance of examining the interactions and outcomes of structures of inequality and also examining the ways in which political ideologies and rhetoric interact to marginalise and deny key issues, such as the marginalisation of women or disabilities. Philomena Essed (1991, Essed and Gircour 1996) has used intersectionality as a tool to identify intertwined gender, race, ethnic, economic and educational factors in shaping specific expressions of everyday injustices. Their work has helped to stimulate debates in international politics, and within the UN there is now increasing recognition that women do not only experience exclusion and discrimination solely on the grounds of gender, but also through age, disability, health status, race, ethnicity, caste, class, national origin and sexual orientation.

Most recently the work of Sylvia Walby (2007) has been concerned to address the theorisation of multiple intersecting social inequalities drawing on complexity and systems theory. Her work retains a focus on gender and intersectionality in Europe and examines the wider implications of these debates in the context of sociological theory. This work on intersectionality is indicative of a trend in these debates, which has been to move away from a central focus on analysing race and racism to seeing this as just one key feature of contemporary patterns of oppression and globalisation. Even for those scholars who seek to retain a central focus on racism this can still lead to an investigation of social complexity, as the recent collection by Murji and Solomos (2005) on racialisation indicates.

Key concepts: Racialisation

The dynamic process by which racial concepts, categories and divisions come to structure and embed themselves in arenas of social life whether in thought (Fanon 1967), British post-war politics (Miles 1989), policy and legislation (Banton 1977), national states or regional and global systems (Goldberg 2002).

Key source: Karim Murji and John Solomos (eds.) (2005) *Racialisation, studies in theory and practice,* Oxford: Oxford University Press.

The century of scholarship from Cooper and Du Bois onwards that has been primarily concerned with examining the operation of racialised social divisions in America has most recently been contributed to by Goldberg (2005) in this collection. His concern about the use of the concept of racialisation as an easy and simplistic 'label' for complex social processes makes him cautious about its usage by social scientists. Race, he argues, both in the USA and across the world, 'continues to define where one can go, what one can do, how one is seen and treated, one's social, economic, political, legal and cultural, in short, one's daily experience' (Goldberg 2005: 101). For Goldberg, historical and contemporary modes of racial Americanisation revolve around the dominance of segregation. This includes 'constitutionalised' segregation, realised through white political power and evident in ghettoisation and apartheid in American cities, and 'informalised' segregation through white flight (migration by white households out of poorer, black neighbourhoods) and the choices of private households and individuals. These processes of segregation are underlain by racialised criminal justice institutions which drive racial discrimination in policing through racial profiling (equating blackness with criminality in everyday policing), racial discrimination in sentencing and racial incarceration (putting a disproportionate number of blacks and Latinos in American prisons). The role of social class is addressed, for example through identification of racial inequalities in incomes, and this is seen as further evidence of the racialisation of the USA. Racial categories are doing much of the work in this analysis and there is relatively little attention given to other structures of inequality and how they intersect, which has always been a core concern for many black feminists. However, the chapter by Rattansi (2005: 271–290) in this collection does pick up this wider agenda. He argues that the concept of racialisation is indispensable as 'race simply describes' and 'racism suggests singularity and closure' whereas analysing racialisation involves elaboration of the dynamic and complex processes through which racial categories become inscribed in specific contexts, articulate with other categories and then change and develop. Rattansi's 'call for complexity' is easy and important to make but much harder to achieve in terms of adequate, viable sociological analysis. He seeks to exemplify this concern with careful investigation of both the 'degrees of attachment' and 'degrees of commitment' political actors and bureaucrats have to overt racism in the context of British post-war debates over immigration. Also, he refers to the 'melange of notions of race, ethnicity, nation and cultural difference', and the 'questions of class, gender and sexuality' these individuals operate with. Although rather vague, these statements indicate a concern to unravel complexity rather than lapse into simplistic accusations of racism. This facilitates an analysis of racial identities and subjectivies that do not operate with the dualist labelling of racist/non-racist positions. Rattansi's framework for examining racialisation is 'the race–nation–ethnicity complex and its articulation with sexuality, gender and class', a position moving in the same theoretical direction as Crenshaw and Essed (see intersectionality above) which offers a rich seam of connections and interlinkages to explore without suggesting a rigid theory which gives primacy to only one of these factors as some forms of Marxism (class) or feminism (gender) would.

The form and relationships between these categories can be theorised as in 'continual correspondence' or as operating with 'no necessary correspondence' to each other. In other words, either these categories are always at play in historical situations and need to be revealed, or they may or may not be dependent on prevailing circumstances. This latter position allows for autonomy in racist logics, for example in law or science which are not determined by economic or gender considerations, or for close determination where, for example, legislation directly meets the needs of capital as in the definition of 'Negroes' as 'goods and commodities' for the purposes of shipping in sixteenth century English law. To argue that examination of the racialisation of particular contexts always requires treatment of this long list of intersecting factors may lead to rather mechanistic forms of analysis. A key set of intersections between race, ethnicity and nation form the specific focus for Weber's work which complements the pioneering race theory provided by Cooper.

Pioneer of ethnicity theory: Max Weber's account of the 'race-ethnicity-nation' complex

Max Weber, one of the 'founding fathers' of this field of study, also grappled with the multidimensional nature of the 'race–ethnicity–nation' complex, despite lapsing into racist slurs in his early work where it was common to find negative treatment of some ethnic and racial groups including 'Slavic' Poles in Germany (Manasse 1947). Also,

> Weber may be criticised along with almost every other social thinker from the time of the French Revolution to the outbreak of World War 1 for failing to give sufficient weight to racial, ethnic and national conflicts.

> (Stone 2003: 29)

Nevertheless, his limited analysis of these issues has been highly influential. Weber opposed what he called 'race mysticism' and increasingly came to oppose racial theories of national characters and social change. For example, he was highly critical of the development of race eugenics in Germany and in particular the views of Alfred Ploetz, who founded the German Society for Racial Hygiene in 1904, about which he said, 'with race theories you can prove or disprove anything you want', calling them a 'scientific crime' and replying to allegations of black inferiority with the comment that the most important scholar in the Southern States of the USA was black: Du Bois. (Weber 1978: 398).

Economy and Society is Weber's massive empirical comparison of social structure and social norms in global historical depth. One chapter of this treatise, 'Ethnic Groups', addresses race membership, the multiple social origins of ethnicity and the interconnections with nationality and cultural prestige. Race identity is seen as a highly problematic source of social action where a group is seen to have common traits and despises others. The hatred, loathing and disgust of blacks and of sexual relations between blacks and whites in the USA, witnessed by Weber in the early twentieth century, is explained by the monopolisation of social power and honour by whites and related social closure, partly arising from the equation of blacks with slavery and hence their exclusion from social status. The anti-black racism of the 'poor white trash' of the Southern States, being propertyless and often destitute, is therefore explained through their being able to lay claim to the honour and dignity of being white, precisely because of the social 'declassment', or the lowering of the social status and social position of black people. He identifies the 'one drop' rule which operates against black people, which is not similar for indigenous Americans. In the USA:

> the smallest admixture of Negro blood disqualifies a person unconditionally, whereas very considerable admixtures of Indian blood do not.
>
> (Weber 1978: 386)

Whether racial differences and ethnic group affinity are real or not was irrelevant for Weber, what matters are the consequences for social action that result from such categorisation and group formation of political communities. For Weber ethnic groups are those which have a belief in common descent arising from either collective memories of colonisation and migration, collective customs, physical similarities or all three. Other markers of ethnicity may include common language, the ritual regulation of life and shared religious beliefs, the perception of being the 'chosen people'. A clear distinction is drawn between ethnic groups and kinship groups as the former may rest on artificial origins of common belief which have been artificially organised through political processes, and often continuing after disintegration of that political community, rather than being based on concrete blood ties. Weber also recognised that collective perceptions of a common ethnicity may encompass many forms of difference and diversity, including class, occupation, dialect and religion.

Ethnic group and nationality are seen as sharing the notion of common descent. But the sense of a common nationality may be shattered by racism as he observes that whites were hostile to a sense of common national identity with blacks in the USA, whereas black people had both a sense of and laid claim to American nationality. This latter point is borne out in Cooper's *A Voice from the South*, where she elaborates the many contributions made by black people to the American nation. Weber uses examples of French Canadians, the Swiss, Serbs, Croats and the French to examine differing ways in which notions of nation and ethnicity interact. A shared common language, for example, may bind a people together and serve as a pre-eminent identifier of who is in the nation, as well as being insufficient to sustain that identity. Further, it is recognised that many modern nation states comprise several language groups. The Swiss, it is argued, do not have a common language, common literature or art but do have a strong sense of community and customs and strong historical memories of being united in collective defence of their distinctiveness. Here, the link between the concept of a nation and political power emerges as a key theme. The greater the emphasis on power, the stronger the idea of a nation becomes.

The hesitancy Weber has in building this rather selective account of the nature and theorisation of linkages of race–ethnicity–nation is indicated by his concern that at this level he has only presented 'vague generalisation', a classification which 'could easily be enlarged'. More fundamentally, alongside his opposition to race thinking, he also indicates an opposition to the notion of 'ethnically' determined social action. This is because he argues that both these categories conceal underlying social processes that have to be carefully identified, distinguished and evaluated in detail. Indeed, for Weber, the whole concept of an ethnic group would dissolve if this rigorous analytical process was pursued, focusing instead on the specific effects of different underlying factors including customs, traditions, the influence of language or religion, beliefs in blood ties, patterns of sexual relations and intermarriage. Further, his concern with these ideas also involved a view that ethnicity and nationalism would decline in importance due to the greater power of modernisation, industrialisation and individualism. The opposite is true, and as noted above this underestimation of the significance and scale of ethnic and national conflicts through the twentieth century also applies to race identities and racial conflict. Weber's classic chapter in *Economy and Society* constitutes a significant contribution to this field and Stone (2003) identifies four main elements of this contribution. Firstly, his insight into fundamental definitions:

Weber's key concepts

Race identity

'Common inherited and inheritable traits that derive from common descent.'

Ethnicity

'Human groups that entertain a belief in their common descent because of similarities of physical type or of customs or both, or because of memories of colonisation and migration; this belief must be important for the propagation of group formation; conversely, it does not matter whether or not an objective blood relationship exists.'

Nation

'A powerful political community of people who share a common language, or religion, or common customs, or political memories; such a state may exist or it may be desired.'

Nationality

'A sense of common distinctiveness which is felt to derive from common descent.'

Source: Max Weber (1978) *Economy and Society*, Vol. 1, Part 2: 385–398, also see John Stone (2003) 'Max Weber on race, ethnicity and nationalism', in J. Stone and R. Dennis, *Race and Ethnicity, Comparative and Theoretical Approaches*, Oxford: Blackwell.

The sharing of a notion of common descent binds these four concepts together, with other key elements defining differences between them. Race is distinguished by the social evaluation of real physical traits, ethnicity by a wider set of markers with race being used as one of this set in some situations. A nation is distinguished by political power and the actual or intended formation of a state. These definitions are acknowledged as providing a key foundation for academic work in this field along with the increasing challenge to the reality of race, as discussed in Chapter 2. The other three core Weberian contributions to this field identified by Stone (2003) are the focus on social closure (the action of social groups, who restrict entry, for example through racial and ethnic discrimination in employment, and exclude benefit to those outside the group in order to maximise their own advantage) and boundary formation which has influenced the sociology of ethnicity and the work of Hechter (1975), Barth (1969) and Brubaker (2002). For example, Brubaker's work is partly driven by the critique of 'groupism', the tendency to see the world as consisting of bounded groups. This concern to avoid the reification of ethnicity draws on Weber's position and leads to a concern to interrogate ethnicity as 'not a thing in the world, but a perspective on the world' (Brubaker 2002: 65). The focus on the search for legitimacy in social action and its significance for explaining racist belief systems and the ways in which they facilitate racial hierarchies to develop, endure and change is seen as being highly influential, for example in the work of Rex (1980). Lastly, the focus on the theoretical primacy of power, in its military, economic and political forms, as central to understanding domination in ethnic and racial hierarchies is a key contribution from Weber which has been elaborated by the 'pluralist' school (Furnivall 1948; Kuper and Smith 1969), the 'race relations' school (Banton 1967, Rex 1970), and in global studies of ethnic cleansing and fascism (Mann 2004a, 2004b). Furthermore, his work on urbanism and institutional structures of the city (Weber 1958) provided a foundation for urban sociology which has often been centrally concerned with issues of migration, ethnic diversity and racial conflict.

Pioneer of race relations theory: Robert Park and the Chicago School

Robert Park was one of the main intellectual leaders of the so-called Chicago School of sociology, and developed a highly influential theory of race relations. The Chicago School, despite its widespread reputation in sociology, was by no means a monolithic enterprise. It was not a 'School' as such and encompassed highly varied theoretical and methodological approaches.

The Chicago School: who are they?

The founders, who included Albion Small, W.I. Thomas (Thomas and Znaniecki 1918, 1920), and the philosopher George Herbert Mead (1934), created and held to a unified scheme of sociological thought, shaped by the guiding originality of Thomas and Mead, whose ideas formed a coherent and cohesive framework within which research could be done.

A second generation at Chicago undertook a vast research programme, based on the thinking of the founders and propelled by the energy and vision of Robert E. Park and his junior colleague E.W. Burgess (Park and Burgess 1921).

As a result, a generation of researchers and thinkers, trained by these people and led by Everett C. Hughes (1943, 1984) and Herbert Blumer (1939, 1969), undertook research and theoretical development which could be, and eventually was, characterised as 'symbolic interactionism'.

(Source: H.S. Becker, *The Chicago School so-called*, http://home.earthlink.net/~hsbecker/chicago.html, accessed 18 Jan. 2008)

Robert Park was at the University of Chicago from 1914 to 1936 and oversaw a huge burst of research activity, much of which was concerned with Park's primary research fields of collective social behaviour, urban ecology and race relations. His work attributed central significance to the operation of race and ethnicity in social contexts and identified these as some of the major bases of status group formation (Lal 2003). He saw social conflict as arising from the actions of status groups to achieve or defend their position and opposed the view that racial and ethnic divisions concealed more fundamental, or functional, underlying class interests. So, here racial groups may act through forms of ideological belief or sentiment which may conflict with more rational economic imperatives and interests, for example majority hostility to ethnic minority workers may not 'fit' with skills shortages in the labour market and the demands of employers. He rejected biological and psychological accounts of race and highlighted the importance of examining the social relations between cultural groups in urban contexts (Banton 1987).

Park's definition of race relations

The relations existing between peoples distinguished by marks of racial descent, particularly when these racial differences enter into the consciousness of the individuals and groups so distinguished, and by so doing determine in each case the individual's conception of himself as well as his status in the community.

Historically the races of mankind at different times and places have lived together in a wide variety of different ways ... without interbreeding ... maintaining their integrity [like] the gypsies of Europe. On the other hand, notably those that have fused to create the peoples of Europe, have lived together in an intimacy so complete that original racial differences have been distinguished [like] the Germanic and Slavic tribes.

Source: Park 1950: 81.

Drawing on ecological explanation he sought to understand these race relations in terms of processes determining all forms of human, animal and plant life. Plants may live together in peace, they may migrate, invade, suffocate others and establish dominance, or mix, change and produce hybrids. Park and Burgess (1921) describe competition for territory and resources as a key level of social organisation and saw racial prejudice as instrumental in reducing competition and maintaining control over social territory. Park developed three models of social change (Lal 2003). The first involved the incorporation of minorities into mainstream society through the efforts of a 'democratic public', public education, social reform and negotiation and reconciliation of interests through a framework of political institutions. The second model involves collective behaviour including riots, revolts, protest and the multiplicity of actions that social movements may use to win social change. Park's third model is the much criticised, race relations cycle of integration where newly arrived racial groups are seen as passing through 'four great phases on interaction': competition, conflict, accommodation and finally assimilation into an inclusive nation state (Park 1950). Here race is used to refer to a multiplicity of groups including Italians, Polish, Slavs as well as black people. As Roediger (2006) points out, this expansive use of race as a category fits well into an early twentieth century context, 'when the relationship of Poles, Irish, Italians, and Lithuanians, for example, to American whiteness was far from clear'. The redrawing of racial divisions and the repositioning of European immigrants as 'white' in Chicago and other American cities can, however, be explained more adequately by the outcome of active and differential processes of social, economic and political conflict rather than the 'natural' processes of assimilation.

Key concepts: Assimilation

A process of interpenetration and fusion in which persons and groups acquire the memories, sentiments, and attitudes of other persons and groups, and by sharing their experience and history are incorporated with them in a common cultural life.

Source: Park and Burgess 1921: 735 quoted in Rumbaut 2003: 235.

Park (1950: 84) does provide an optimistic and idealistic account, foreseeing the integration of all cultural groups into a diverse global culture and social order paralleled by the decline of racial stratification; a civilising process. In employment for example, competition for jobs led to racial discrimination, and as migrants changed their language, institutions and other practices they became accommodated and discrimination lessened. This vision was tested by Park in Hawai'i, which seemed a 'racial paradise' in comparison to the race riots, lynching and Jim Crow segregation codes of mainland America, and where there was little public or legal opposition to interracial sexual relations and marriage (Pierce 2005).

Hawai'i: the racial laboratory for Park's theory

The Hawaian islands have become a laboratory for a study of the race problem. In these islands all the races of the Pacific have come together in numbers and conditions more favourable and successful to the working of the melting pot than anywhere else on the planet. (Park 1926)

Following the arrival of 'Haole' (white Europeans and Americans), Hawai'i experienced mass deaths as a result of epidemic disease and the spread of venereal disease which decimated 90 per cent of the population between 1778 and the end of the nineteenth century. From the 1840s to 1920s foreign ownership of land, massive expansion of sugar plantations and the movement of migrant labour from China, Japan, Korea and elsewhere dramatically transformed the society (60 per cent of Hawai'i population was foreign born by 1900). White control of the political economy led to the overthrow of the indigenous monarchy and it became an official territory of the United States in 1900. By 1930 when Park visited Hawai'i, indigenous people and whites were small minorities (12–13 per cent) with a growing Asian workforce competing for work, wages and better living conditions. The increasing dominance of Western values and the establishment of white supremacy through legal and institutional means set the scene for the testing of Park's theories of assimilation and civilisation. Investigation of interracial marriage was carried out by Park's Chicago contemporary Adams (1937) in the urban setting of Honolulu. Despite finding low rates of intermarriage amongst Haole and Japanese groups, Adams concluded that historically established interracial marriage, the growing group of people with mixed origins and egalitarian values were leading to significant decline in racial and ethnic divisions. But the strength of white racism, ethnic conflict on the plantations and institutional racial discrimination showed that the 'race relations cycle' was ill-equipped to explain the realities of Hawai'is 'racial paradise'.

Sources: Adams 1937, Pierce 2005.

Other criticisms of Park's work have included his neglect of class differentiation within racial and ethnic groups, for example the rise of the black middle class, and over-estimation of social cohesion and consciousness amongst these groups, together with a lack of attention to power and violence in structuring racial and ethnic divisions (Lal 2003). Despite these criticisms, and the complex and varied paths by which differing groups interact and produce hierarchies of exclusion and inclusion in differing national contexts, the reinvention of integration/assimilation as a policy objective for both the British government and other nation states in recent years signals the ideological power of Park's contribution to this field of study (see discussion on race relations policy in the UK in Chapter 5).

Building on the pioneers: the emergence of the British sociology of race relations

American scholarship has been highly influential on British research, from the impact of the Chicago School of sociology upon studies of black and white relations in England and Wales during and since the early 1940s, to the role of the Ford Foundation in funding research into inter-ethnic problems in Britain's cities during the 1950s and 1960s (Clapson 2006). *The Philadelphia Negro* (1899) by Du Bois, the Chicago Commission on Race Relations study *The Negro in Chicago* (1922), Gunnar Myrdal's *An American Dilemma: The Negro Problem and Modern Democracy* (1944) and St Clair Drake and H.R. Clayton's *Black Metropolis: a study of Negro life in a Northern City* (1945) provided a track record of seminal empirical studies examining racism and material conditions in American urban contexts. This inspired sociological research in Britain. Kenneth Little's *Negroes in Britain: a study of racial relations in English Society* (1948) was one of the first, examining the history of the black presence in Britain and life in Cardiff's black community and the pervasiveness of racist myths of the 'mental inferiority' of black people' and the 'biological ill-effects of racial crossing' amongst children and in English culture. Continuing this tradition, John Rex along with Robert Moore produced a classic empirical study *Racism, Community and Conflict* (1967) which examines these issues in the context of Birmingham. This unites a conflict perspective (which stresses that to understand society we need to understand the struggles between groups) with a model of residential segregation and zonal structure of the Chicago ecologists, seeing the city as a class struggle for housing where interest groups use their power in the market situation. Black migrants are forced into 'zones of transition'. Differential access to employment is linked to discrimination in the housing market, which is mediated by the social and cultural resources migrant communities bring with them and the development of accommodative institutions. This study confirms that racism is embedded in post-colonial societies and is intrinsic to social relations of power and domination (Bailey 1975). It also confirms that racism can act independently from class, for example through excluding black and Asian migrants from state welfare and public services such as council housing (Williams 1989).

Rex and Banton

The contribution to the study of race, racism and ethnicity by John Rex and Michael Banton, who have been significantly influenced by Weberian ideas and the work of Park and others in Chicago, has recently been examined in two articles in the leading journal in the field, *Ethnic and Racial Studies* (Jenkins 2005, Barot 2006). They have played a leading part in the development of the British sociology of race relations in the post-war period. John Rex's core contribution to this field over many years includes placing conflict at the heart of sociological analysis of race and ethnicity, development of an internationalist, historical account of race and colonialism, applying a Weberian understanding of class to race relations situations and markets, and linking these together in analysis of the welfare state (Jenkins 2005, Williams 1989). For Rex, ethnic groups are real, races are not. But analysis of race relations, race relations situations and racial stratification in labour, housing and education is seen as appropriate where ethnic groups construct beliefs in racial hierarchy and act on them through exclusion and discrimination. Nevertheless, his focus on ethnic minorities and ethnic mobilisation, on the one hand, and on the other the primacy of Weberian conceptions of class as deriving from market position, have led to criticism that he has given inadequate attention to the centrality of racism in post-colonial contexts. In addition to the fundamental critique that the 'race relations' problematic has implicitly legitimised the notion of race as real, Rex has been criticised for focussing on black people rather than on structures of white domination (Jenkins 2005: 203–4). Drawing on a Weberian model of social action, Rex identifies the core issue for sociology as 'the problem of conflict'. It is the norm, where class relations and markets lead to structures of group formation and conflict between them producing plural societies and inequalities of power. Jenkins identifies a similar problem to Weber in the assumption that pursuit of class interests will reduce affective ethnicities and lead to fragmentation and decline of ethnicity. The dangers of such a position given the durability and renewal of ethnic conflict across the globe are clear. The value of Rex's focus on class and conflict, despite the problem of economic reductionism and a failure to address gender, is that this suggests the 'utter implausibility of peaceful co-existent (egalitarian) multiculturalism' (Jenkins 2005: 207). Overall, Rex has made a major contribution to this field, which has recently been acknowledged in a wide-ranging collection (Abbas and Reeves 2007).

Michael Banton was similarly concerned to examine the settlement and experiences of colonial migrants in the UK, for example in his first book, an ethnographic study of *The Coloured Quarter* in London's East End (1955). Following Little and anticipating Rex, Banton provides a sociological account of British 'race relations', locating this in the international context of colonialism. Similarly, the interests and issues of black Caribbean migrants to the UK in the 1940s and 1950s were dealt with by the government's Colonial Office, which was part of the Foreign Office. It was the race riots in British cities in 1958 that brought home the significance of managing domestic 'race relations' and thereafter these issues became the concern of the Home Office and British race relations policy followed. Banton (1967: 68–76) provided a comparative account of social action and the utilisation of race to construct differing systems of race relations around the world identifying a typology of race relations situations including domination, integration and pluralism. Rex sets out a more specific typology of these situations, which included frontier competition, unfree labour, exploitative/harsh labour, inequality in caste systems, other hierarchies of inequality, cultural pluralism, urban stratification/underclass, pariah outsiders and scapegoats. In all these contexts racial belief systems are seen as politically linked to structures of exploitation and oppression. To these rather over-simplified and macro-accounts, Banton contributed a counterbalancing focus on micro-individual social action through his rational choice theory and a central focus on competition in shaping racial and ethnic relations (Banton 1983; Barot 2006). Here, individuals use physical and cultural differences to create groups and categories through inclusion (ethnic groups) and exclusion (racial groups). Group interaction produces boundaries determined by the intensity and form of competition. Here a focus on individual action, for example in the housing market, led to a sustained concern to address racial discrimination, as for 'every act of discrimination someone is responsible and should be brought to account' (Banton 1996). Banton pursued this objective in his work on the International Committee on the Elimination of Racial Discrimination from 1986 to 2001. The political value of this activism is much less open to attack than a rational choice theory approach to understanding ethnicity. Rational choice theory prioritises the study of individual action which atomises the social. It also neglects the collective sphere of human action and the structural causes of human behaviour. Lastly, the core notion of individual optimisation in rational choice theory cannot be tested or falsified (Malešević 2004: 119). But, one of the contributions of this theory is to encourage calculation of the benefits derived by social actors from such actions as race/ethnic hate or discrimination (see motives of racist violence discussed in Chapter 6). This assists in elaborating the motives for such behaviours but these accounts need to be placed in wider macro and meso structural, political and cultural contexts, as will be examined further in the analysis of racial violence.

Race relations and beyond

The 'race relations problematic', which tends to assume that races were real things which came into conflict with each other, interacted and, hence, these processes became an object of study, has been much criticised. Miles (1993), Goldberg (1990) and Guillaumin (1980) have consistently argued against the use of the race idea in social analysis as it is seen to necessarily suggest that certain social relationships are natural and inevitable. The belief or implicit suggestion that races are real is therefore treated with the utmost suspicion; race is seen to be essentially ideological and the analytical task is to explain why social relationships are interpreted in this way.

This position has been inflated into a general criticism of the resulting experience of race relations policies in the UK from the 1960s onwards by Lloyd (1994: 230) since they are seen as 'reinforcing the racialisation of social relations in contemporary Britain'. So, racial divisions are considered to have been actively created by policies concerned to challenge racism and racial discrimination. This is seen as resulting from the persistent use of the notion of race in bureaucratic, technical, academic and political discourse. Race has been given an official reality in race relations legislation, race relations policies, race relations courses and programmes of study, and party political agendas. In other words, the continued use of the race idea is seen as reinforcing dominant common-sense ideas that different races exist and have a biological reality.

The rejection of race as an analytical tool in this way raises a number of problems. Firstly, thorough critique of the mythical notions of race and race relations implies that not only are there no real relations between races but that it is meaningless to search for equality or justice between races. Are we to reject these ideas as well? How far should political calculation of the potential effects of using such terms, or indeed research to establish the previous impact of race discourse be considered before use of such terms is dismissed. The race idea can be employed to articulate strategies of liberation and emancipation, as discussed in Chapter 1, and to highlight existing racial divisions in order to facilitate political mobilisation without necessarily increasing those divisions. Indeed, it may be established that such action achieved its objective of a reduction of some aspects of racial divisions, for example in political participation. The value of such strategic essentialism, where race may be invoked in political struggle, cannot be theoretically assumed to have a racist political effect. The use of particular concepts and their discursive articulation with others, e.g. biology, sexual difference, or rights, will determine their political and policy implications. So, it cannot be assumed that the concepts of race and nation will only be used to articulate domination and exclusion or that ethnicity will only be used to articulate cultural pluralism. This points to a set of analytical concerns as the object of study. These include, firstly, the active construction of the social world by those who articulate racism, secondly, the political, economic and ideological processes which have determined the use of race to comprehend patterns of migration and settlement, and thirdly, analysis of law, policies and practices which have drawn on ideas of race and which have been concerned to respond to or regulate such real social processes.

The work of Little, Banton and Rex shares a common concern to address these issues and to map the British and international context and, together with an increasingly wide range of other scholars, they helped to inaugurate a major field of study (Banks 1983). In moving beyond the sociology of race relations, academic scholarship has moved in a number of directions and many scholars have made a 'turn to ethnicity', seeking to prioritise investigation of this more 'real' set of social phenomena. The nature and dynamics of ethnicity are the focus of the next chapter.

Conclusion

This chapter has identified the central contribution of Cooper, Weber, Park, Rex and Banton to the development of this field of study. It has shown the importance of examining both the inter-relationships between race, gender, class, ethnicity and nation and the logic of racialisation. Whether examining racism and ethnicity in inter-war Hawai'i or post-war Britain, the ways in which these factors are mobilised in specific contexts needs careful scrutiny. Over-generalisation of both the nature of these situations and the processes and prospects for social change have been shown to be problematic for all these scholars. The durability, dynamics and resurgence of both racial and ethnic conflict and segregation has often been under-estimated. However, collectively these contributions have built and shaped a coherent field of intellectual and political endeavour. The desire to interrogate, understand and challenge the highly varied forms of racial and ethnic exclusion examined in the work of this core group has driven this output, and it continues to motivate the rapidly expanding ranks of social researchers in this field.

End of chapter activity

Read Anna Cooper's *A Voice from the South* at http://docsouth.unc.edu/church/cooper/cooper.html. In what ways does the first part of the book, which provides a solo voice of the black woman, differ from the second, which seeks to represent the concerns of black people more generally? How has she contributed to the understanding of the linkages between race, gender, class and nation? To what extent does she adequately explore institutional racism in American society?

Further reading

Reed, K. (2006) *New Directions in Social Theory, race, gender and the canon,* **London: Sage.** This text examines both the contribution of theorists of race and gender to classical, modern and contemporary sociology, and the extent of their exclusion from the mainstream of social theorising.

Stone, J. and Dennis, R. (2003) *Race and Ethnicity, comparative and theoretical approaches,* **Oxford: Blackwell.** This reader examines the contribution of Du Bois, Weber and Park to this field and provides extensive international coverage of theoretical issues and contemporary problems.

Bulmer, M. (1984) *The Chicago School of Sociology: institutionalization, diversity, and the rise of sociological research.* Chicago: University of Chicago Press. This book provides a thorough review of the key actors and studies produced by the 'so-called' Chicago school.

References

Abbas, T. and Reeves, F. (eds.) (2007) *Immigration and Race Relations, sociological theory and John Rex,* London: I. B. Tauris.

Adams, R. (1937) *Interracial Marriage in Hawaii: a study of the mutually conditioned processes of acculturation and amalgamation,* London: Macmillan.

Bailey, J. (1975) *Social Theory for Planning,* London: Routledge and Kegan Paul.

Banks, M. (1983) *Ethnicity, anthropological constructions,* London: Routledge.

Banton, M. (1955) *The Coloured Quarter,* London: Cape.

Banton, M. (1967) *Race Relations,* London: Tavistock.

Banton, M. (1977) *The Idea of Race,* London: Tavistock.

Banton, M. (1983) *Racial and Ethnic Competition,* Cambridge: Cambridge University Press.

Banton, M. (1987) *Racial Theories,* Cambridge: Cambridge University Press.

Banton, M. (1996) *International Action against Racial Discrimination,* Oxford: Clarendon Press.

Barot, R. (2006) 'Reflections on Michael Banton's contribution to race and ethnic studies', *Ethnic and Racial Studies,* 29, 5, pp. 785–796.

Barth, F. (ed.) (1969) *Ethnic Groups and Boundaries: the social organisation of cultural difference,* London: Allen & Unwin.

Becker, H.S., *The Chicago School so-called,* http://home.earthlink.net/~hsbecker/chicago.html (accessed 18 Jan. 2008).

Blumer, H. (1939) *An Appraisal of Thomas and Znaniecki's The Polish Peasant in Europe and America,* New York: Social Science Research Council.

Blumer, Herbert (1969) *Symbolic Interactionism,* Englewood Cliffs, NJ: Prentice-Hall.

Brubaker, R. (2002) *Ethnicity without groups,* Cambridge: Cambridge University Press.

Bulmer, M. and Solomos, J. (eds.) (1999) *Ethnic and Racial Studies Today*, London: Routledge.

Chicago Commission on Race Relations (1922) *The Negro in Chicago: a study of race relations and a race riot*, Chicago: University of Chicago.

Clapson, M. (2006) 'The American contribution to the urban sociology of race relations in Britain from the 1940s to the early 1970s', *Urban History*, 33, pp. 253–273.

Collins, P. H. (2000) *Black Feminist Thought*, London: Routledge.

Cooper, A. J. (1892) *A Voice from the South*, Xenia, Ohio: Aldine Printing House, http://docsouth.unc.edu/church/cooper/cooper.html.

Crenshaw, K. (1990) Demarginalizing the Intersection of Race and Sex: a black feminist critique of antidiscrimination doctrine, feminist theory and antiracist politics, 1989 *University of Chicago Legal Forum* 139–67 (1989), reprinted in David Kairys (ed.) *The Politics of Law: a progressive critique,* New York: Pantheon, pp. 195–217, 2nd edition.

Crenshaw, K. (1991) Mapping the Margins: intersectionality, identity politics, and violence against women of color, *Stanford Law Review,* 43, pp. 1241–99.

Davis, A. (1980) *Women, Race and Class*, London: Women's Press.

Drake, St. C. and Clayton, H. R. (1945) *Black Metropolis: a study of Negro life in a Northern City,* Chicago: Chicago University Press.

Du Bois, W. E. (1899) *The Philadelphia Negro, a social study*, Philadelphia: University of Pennsylvania Press.

Du Bois, W. E. (1924) *The Freedom of Womanhood,* in P. Zuckerman (ed.) (2004). *The Social Theory of W.E.B. Du Bois*, London: Pine Forge.

Essed, P. (1991) *Understanding Everyday Racism*, Newbury Park, CA: Sage.

Essed, P. and Gircour, R. (1996) *Diversity, Gender, Color and Culture*, Amherst, MA: University of Massachusetts Press.

Fanon, F. (1967) *Black Skin, White Masks*, London: Grove Press.

Furnivall, J. S. (1948) *Colonial Policy and Practice, a comparative study of Burma and Netherlands India*, Cambridge: Cambridge University Press.

Goldberg, D.T. (ed.), (1990) *Anatomy of Racism*, Minneapolis: University of Minnesota Press.

Goldberg, D. T. (2002) *The Racial State*, Oxford: Blackwell.

Goldberg, D. T. (2005) 'Racial Americanisation', in K. Murji and J. Solomos (eds) *Racialisation, studies in theory and practice*, Oxford: Oxford University Press.

Goldberg, D. T. and Solomos, J. (eds) (2002) *A Companion to Racial and Ethnic Studies*, Oxford: Blackwell.

Guillaumin, C. (1980), 'The idea of race and its elevation to scientific and legal status', in UNESCO, *Sociological Theories: Race and Colonialism*, Paris: UNESCO.

Hechter, M. (1975) *Internal Colonialism, the Celtic fringe in British national development, 1536–1966*, Berkeley: University of California Press.

Hooks, B. (1982) *Ain't I a Woman*, London: Women's Press.

Hughes, E. C. (1943) *French Canada in Transition,* Chicago: University of Chicago Press.

Hughes, E. C. (1984) *The Sociological Eye,* New Brunswick, NJ: Transaction Books.

Jenkins, R. (2005) 'The place of theory: John Rex's contribution to the sociological study of ethnicity and "race"', *Ethnic and Racial Studies*, 28, 2, pp. 201–211.

Kuper, L. and Smith, M G. (eds) (1969) *Pluralism in Africa*, Berkeley: University of California Press.

Lal, B. B. (2003) 'Robert Ezra Park's approach to race and ethnic relations', in J. Stone and R. Dennis, *Race and Ethnicity, comparative and theoretical approaches*, Oxford: Blackwell.

Lemert, C. (1995) *Sociology after the Crisis*, Boulder, CO: Westview Press.

Little, K. (1948) *Negroes in Britain: a study of racial relations in English society*, London: Routledge.

Lloyd, C. (1994) 'Universalism and Difference: The crisis of anti-racism in Britain and France', in A. Rattansi, and S. Westwood (eds.) *Racism, Modernity and Identity*, Cambridge: Polity Press.

Malešević, S. (2004) *The Sociology of Ethnicity*, London: Sage.

Manasse, E. (1947) 'Max Weber on race', *Social Research*, 14, pp. 191–221.

Mann, M. (2004) *Fascists*, Cambridge: Cambridge University Press.

Mann, M. (2005) *The Dark Side of Democracy, explaining ethnic cleansing*, Cambridge: Cambridge University Press.

Mead, G. H. (1934) *Mind, Self, and Society*, Chicago: University of Chicago Press.

Miles, R. (1989) *Racism*, London: Routledge.

Miles, R. (1993) *Racism after 'Race Relations'*, London: Routledge.

Murji, K. and Solomos, J. (eds.) (2005) *Racialisation, studies in theory and practice*, Oxford: Oxford University Press.

Myrdal, G. with Sterner, R. and Rose, A. (1944) *An American Dilemma: the Negro problem and modern democracy*, New York: Harper.

Park, R. (1950) *Race and Culture*, Glencoe, IL: The Free Press.

Park, R. E. (1926) 'The urban community as a spatial pattern and a moral order', in E. W. Burgess (ed.) *The Urban Community*, Chicago: University of Chicago Press.

Park, R. E. and Burgess, E. W. (1921) *Introduction to the Science of Sociology*, Chicago: University of Chicago Press.

Pierce, L. (2005) 'Creating a racial paradise: citizenship and sociology in Hawai'i', in P. Spickard (ed.) *Race and Nation*, London: Routledge.

Quing (Quality in Gender and Equality Policies) (2007) *STRIQ Project*, www.quing.eu/index.php?option=com_content&task=view&id=20&Itemid=37.

Rattansi, A. (2005) 'The uses of racialisation: the time-spaces and subject-objects of the raced body', in K. Murji and J. Solomos (eds) *Racialisation, studies in theory and practice*, Oxford: Oxford University Press.

Reed, K. (2006) *New Directions in Social Theory, race, gender and the canon*, London: Sage.

Rex, J. (1970) *Race Relations in Sociological Theory*, London: Weidenfeld and Nicolson.

Rex, J. and Moore, R. (1967) *Racism, Community and Conflict*, London: Institute of Race Relations/Oxford University Press.

Robinson, C. (1983) *Black Marxism, the making of the black radical tradition*, London: Zed Press.

Roediger, D. R. (2006) *Working Towards Whiteness: how America's immigrants became white, the strange journey from Ellis Island to the suburbs*, New York: Perseus.

Rumbaut, R. G., (2003) 'Assimilation and its discontents', in J. Stone and R. Dennis (eds) *Race and Ethnicity, comparative and theoretical approaches*, Oxford: Blackwell.

Stone, J. (2003) 'Max Weber on race, ethnicity and nationalism', in J. Stone and R. Dennis (eds) *Race and Ethnicity, comparative and theoretical approaches*, Oxford: Blackwell.

Stone, J. and Dennis, R. (eds) (2003) *Race and Ethnicity, comparative and theoretical approaches*, Oxford: Blackwell.

Thomas, W. I. and Znaniecki, F. (1918) *The Polish Peasant in Europe and America*, vols. 1–3, Chicago: University of Chicago Press.

Thomas, W. I. and Znaniecki, F. (1920) *The Polish Peasant in Europe and America*, vols. 4–5, Boston: Badger Press.

Walby, S. (2007) 'Complexity theory, systems theory, and multiple intersecting social inequalities', *Philosophy of the Social Sciences, 7,* 37, pp. 449–470.

Weber, M. (1958) *The City*, Chicago: Free Press.

Weber, M. (1978) *Economy and Society: an outline of interpretive sociology*, Berkeley, CA: University of California Press.

Williams, F. (1989) *Social Policy, a critical introduction, Issues of race, gender and class*, Cambridge: Polity.

Williams, F. (2005) 'Intersecting issues of gender, "race", and migration in the changing care regimes of UK, Sweden and Spain', Paper presented to the ISA, Chicago.

Zuckerman, P. (ed.) (2004) *The Social Theory of W. E. B. Du Bois*, London: Pine Forge.

4

Understanding ethnicity: theorectical and conceptual debates

Key issues in this chapter:

- The conceptualisation and theorisation of ethnicity
- Patterns of ethnic relations
- Ethnic and super-diversity in the UK
- State-of-the-art research on ethnicity in the UK

At the end of this chapter you should be able to:

- Understand why ethnicity matters
- Identify the key markers of ethnic groups
- Assess alternative theoretical approaches to ethnicity
- Explain the changing dynamics of English ethnicity
- Identify leading-edge ethnicity research questions

Introduction

The foundational understanding of ethnicity provided by Max Weber examined in the previous chapter provides the basis for moving on to examine contemporary debates and evidence in this chapter. For Weber, ethnic groups are those which have a belief in common descent arising from either collective memories of colonisation and migration, collective customs, physical similarities or all three. Also ethnic groups are marked out by a range of dimensions of ethnicity including common language, the ritual regulation of life and shared religious beliefs. The scale and significance of ethnicity and related conflict across the globe is of major social significance as it is the 'leading source of violence in international affairs' (Esman 2004: 26). In this chapter we firstly examine the conceptualisation of ethnicity, a range of theoretical and sociological approaches to ethnicity and the nature of ethnic relations. Secondly, to ground these arguments we look closely at the operation of ethnicity in the UK. Here the development of ethnic diversity and 'super'-diversity are explored, together with examination of the ways in which ethnicity is surveyed and measured and how ethnic identities have developed, changed and been studied. Lastly, we consider the state of the art of ethnicity research in the UK and identify both what we know and what we have yet to understand and find out.

How and why does ethnicity matter? In fleshing out some of the ways in which ethnicity matters we need to look closely at specific social contexts (Jenkins 1997). In wars, organised politics, market relationships and in organised structures of domination ethnicity is central for many societies. Apart from these more formal contexts, ethnicity may also be of high importance in informal social contexts such as:

Primary socialisation: in the social construction of children's identities encountering and learning about oneself, who we are, and others may involve the use of ethnic labels and categories alongside other primary identities of gender, selfhood and human-ness.

Routine public interaction: informal ethnic categorisation may often help to organise and interpret social interaction. Verbal and non-verbal cues including dress, language, humour and verbal abuse may often be key to the expression and mobilisation of ethnic identities and group boundaries: who is part of my group and who is not. Everyday cultural ignorance, miscommunication and misrecognition of difference, where individuals coming from two contrasting ethnic communities may bring with them different value assumptions, expectations, verbal and non-verbal habits that influence social interaction and communication, may result in offensive behaviour, affronts to dignity and lack of respect which can all lead to ethnic conflict and violence.

Sexual relationships and marriage: inter-ethnic sexual relationships have often been a key site for violence and conflict, for example in the British race riots of 1919 and 1948, and also for aspects of patriarchal power and control which may often be concerned to enforce ethnic exclusivity or group possession of women, for example where a female English Traveller may be 'outcast' if she marries outside the group.

So, the extent to which ethnicity matters may be highly variable, dependent on society, time and context, but it is arguably 'a basic universal facet of the human cultural repertoire' (Jenkins 1997: 77).

Ethnicity: concepts, approaches and relations

Conceptualisation

Ethnicity refers to the differentiation of groups of people who have shared cultural meanings, memories and descent, produced through social interaction. In classical Greek the terms *ethnos/ethnikos* were used in a number of ways to refer to a collectivity that share similar cultural or biological characteristics, for example a tribe of people or a band of friends, and who were not Greek, outside the nation, foreign, different and also inferior, barbarian and less civilised. This distinction between ethnically marked 'others' and non-ethnically marked 'us' persists in modern popular usage with references to ethnic fashion or food. Sociological accounts of ethnicity are highly varied but tend to break the classical linkage between ethnicity and 'other' in asserting that we are all ethnically located in that our subjectivity and identity are contextualised by history, language, descent and culture.

Ethnicity usually refers to the differentiation of social groups on the basis of five distinct criteria. Firstly, a notion of a 'homeland' or place of common origin is a key element, which is linked to the idea of a diaspora where an ethnic group has migrated from that place to form communities elsewhere which identify with their place of origin. Secondly, a common language, either distinctive in itself or a distinctive dialect of a language shared with others, may be central to the construction of shared memories and emotional attachment to a group. Identification with a distinct religion, e.g. Sikhism, or a religion shared with others can be a central feature of many ethnic groups. A common culture with distinctive social institutions and behaviour, diet and dress and a common tradition or shared history of one's own 'people' or nation are other criteria used in specifying ethnic groups.

Ethnicities may be highly durable over millennia and space, and can also be formed from new conjunctions of social contexts, for example through migration where backward-looking ethnic belonging is newly shaped with the construction of national context to produce hyphenated forms, e.g. British-Asian or Hispanic-American. Ethnic solidarity can provide a deep sense of physical and psychological security allowing the individual to identify and find a sense of common purpose with a great and long-lasting tradition of people. But if shared beliefs underlie ethnic differentiation, then the boundaries of ethnic groups are inevitably unclear and caution is required in assessing the extent to which external categories reflect accurately social meanings, social roles and wider social inequalities. There may often be a poor fit between state and bureaucratic constructions of ethnic categories and dynamic forms of ethnic identity held by people and groups themselves.

Sociological approaches

Sociological approaches to conceptualising ethnicity have been distinguished as falling into two camps. Primordial approaches, first suggested by Edward Shils in 1957, see ethnic ties of blood, race, language, region and custom as primary and inescapable: you are born into membership of an ethnic group and cannot escape or change your identity. This approach has been criticised as static, failing to acknowledge those positions where identities can change, for example through migration to another country and formation of a 'hyphenated' identity, African-American or British-Asian (BrAsian). The creation of multi-ethnic families through cohabitation and intermarriage will also lead to the creation of subsequent generations that draw on mixed ethnic origins. Both these situations may therefore lead to the formation of new ethnicities. Secondly, instrumentalist approaches to ethnicity have been advocated, for example in Michael Banton's (1993) work on ethnic competition. Here ethnicity is seen as a social, political and cultural resource which can be used or drawn in competition for resources or motivation for conflict. This approach can be criticised for underplaying the strength of unchanging ethnic identities over time and space and the ways in which some ethnic groups maintain their cohesion and character over millennia despite sometimes intense assault and attempts at assimilation, e.g. the Roma in post-Communist Central and Eastern Europe, or Aborigines in Australia.

Distinguishing between ethnicity from culture can be analytically useful, rather than seeing these two concepts as interchangeable. The 'transactionalist' mode of enquiry advocated by Fredrik Barth (1969: 15) is seen as making a vital contribution to this field in arguing that 'the critical focus of investigation from this point of view becomes the ethnic boundary that defines the group, not the cultural stuff which it encloses'. In other words, ethnic groups are not hermetically sealed cultural entities, boundaries are porous and subject to negotiation. Ethnic boundaries are established through social interaction and may for example become fixed whilst cultural patterns within those boundaries may be rapidly converging. Young Sri Lankan Tamils in the UK may be inhabiting the same cultural world of clothes, dress, music, etc., as young white Britons, but at the same time retaining a strong feeling of belonging as members of this ethnic group. So, examining how ethnicity works and how lived-in dynamic cultures work can be seen as different tasks.

Ethnicity is also analytically different to the notion of a nation as Weber argued (see Chapter 3). Both ethnicity and nation do refer to groups of people with common descent, a common culture and a shared sense of homeland/territory. But what differentiates a nation from an ethnic group is the construction of the former as a state or a state-like political form. Also, ethnic groups are more frequently conceived as a type of sub-set of the nation state, particularly where states are very rarely of a pure mono-ethnic form. Irrespective of the level of ethnic diversity existing in a particular region, there have been many strong forms of mono-ethnic nationalism which have sought to claim the right of each ethnic group to autonomous self-determination. Ethnically exclusive forms of citizenship may be used, as in Germany for example, to build ethnic nationalism. It may also be used as the justification for genocide, as explored below in the case of Rwanda.

Race, as with ethnic group and nation, also refers to groups of common descent and culture but with explicit reference to physical or visible difference. The conceptual relationship between race and ethnicity has two particular forms. Firstly, race may operate as a sub-set of ethnicity, being one of the many markers used to differentiate a particular ethnic group. So, for black Caribbeans in the UK race may be one marker of ethnic identity, but in comparing Scottish and Welsh ethnicities there would be no racial markers of difference given their whiteness. Secondly, ethnicity may operate as a sub-set of race, where this racial identity may be seen as encompassing, or erasing, a multiplicity of different ethnic groups, for example black Caribbeans, where different island ethnicities, cultures and languages are erased. Analysis of specific cases illustrates the problems associated with operationalising ethnicity as the next section shows.

Explaining the role of ethnicity in genocide: the case of Rwanda

The Rwandan genocide resulted in the systematic massacre of 800,000 Tutsis and moderate Hutus in 100 days. Prior to considering the contribution of theories of ethnicity to our understanding you may wish to explore www.rwanda-genocide.org/ for multi-media resources and documents, and Human Rights Watch (1999) to identify key events, timelines and historical background. Most recently, an independent Rwandan commission has accused France of playing an active role in this genocide, with French troops being directly involved in the killings and in helping to train the ethnic Hutu militia who were responsible for these deaths (BBC News, 5 August 2008). The following extract introduces this horrific set of events.

Leave none to tell the story: Genocide in Rwanda

'When I came out, there were no birds', said one survivor who had hidden throughout the genocide. 'There was sunshine and the stench of death.'

The sweetly sickening odor of decomposing bodies hung over many parts of Rwanda in July 1994: on Nyanza ridge, overlooking the capital, Kigali, where skulls and bones, torn clothing, and scraps of paper were scattered among the bushes; at Nyamata, where bodies lay twisted and heaped on benches and the floor of a church; at Nyarubuye in eastern Rwanda, where the cadaver of a little girl, otherwise intact, had been flattened by passing vehicles to the thinness of cardboard in front of the church steps; on the shores of idyllic Lake Kivu in western Rwanda, where pieces of human bodies had been thrown down the steep hillside; and at Nyakizu in southern Rwanda, where the sun-bleached fragments of bone in the sand of the schoolyard and, on a nearby hill, a small red sweater held together the ribcage of a decapitated child.

In the 13 weeks after 6 April, 1994, at least half a million people perished in the Rwandan genocide, perhaps as many as three-quarters of the Tutsi population. At the same time, thousands of Hutu were slain because they opposed the killing campaign and the forces directing it.

The killers struck with a speed and devastation that suggested an aberrant force of nature, 'a people gone mad', said some observers. 'Another cycle of tribal violence', said others. The nation of some seven million people encompassed three ethnic groups. The Twa were so few as to play no political role, leaving only Hutu and Tutsi to face each other without intermediaries. The Hutu, vastly superior in number, remembered past years of oppressive Tutsi rule, and many of them not only resented but feared the minority. The government, run by Hutu, was at war with the Rwandan Patriotic Front (RPF), rebels who were predominantly Tutsi. In addition, Rwanda was one of the poorest nations in the world and growing poorer, with too little land for its many people and falling prices for its products on the world market. Food production had diminished because of drought and the disruptions of war: it was estimated that 800,000 people would need food aid to survive in 1994.

But this genocide was not an uncontrollable outburst of rage by a people consumed by 'ancient tribal hatreds'. Nor was it the preordained result of the impersonal forces of poverty and over-population.

This genocide resulted from the deliberate choice of a modern elite to foster hatred and fear to keep itself in power. This small, privileged group first set the majority against the minority to counter a grow-

→

ing political opposition within Rwanda. Then, faced with RPF success on the battlefield and at the negotiating table, these few power-holders transformed the strategy of ethnic division into genocide. They believed that the extermination campaign would restore the solidarity of the Hutu under their leadership and help them win the war, or at least improve their chances of negotiating a favourable peace. They seized control of the state and used its machinery and its authority to carry out the slaughter. (…).

Policymakers in France, Belgium, and the United States and at the United Nations all knew of the preparations for massive slaughter and failed to take the steps needed to prevent it. (…).

Source: Human Rights Watch and Fédération Internationale des Ligues des Droits de l'Homme, *Leave None to Tell the Story: Genocide in Rwanda*, © 1999 by Human Rights Watch. (Edited extract, pp.1–2).

Competing sociological theories of ethnicity have been successfully classified and critically differentiated by Siniša Malešević(2004). Classical sociology, neo-Marxism, functionalism, symbolic-interactionism, socio-biology, rational choice theory, elite theory, neo-Weberian approaches and anti-foundationalist positions have all been used to theorise ethnicity. Malešević illustrates how each position can be used to provide an explanation of Rwandan genocide and highlights key epistemological tensions.

Differing approaches would prioritise differing determining factors and this illustrates the difficulty of applying theoretical frameworks to particular case studies. Simple synthesis does not suffice and analysis of the Rwandan case continues. Table 4.1 identifies how sociological theories, the main factors that each position would prioritise in explaining these events and the main criticisms of each account.

Malešević favours a combination of the neo-Weberian macro historical approach and elite theory which would provide a coherent macro historical account and focus on the key role of elites in manipulating and exacerbating ethnic hostilities. In examining this case Mann (2005) has identified four important conclusions. Firstly, profound bi-ethnic rivalry, drawing on old ethnic hatred and modern escalation which focussed on constructing the respective states of these two groups in the same territory, was central to this genocide. Secondly, economic, political and military power was used to re-focus consciousness of exploitation and poverty into ethnic rage drawing on the emotional drivers of kin loyalty, patriotism and masculinity. Thirdly, the state was not in this case cohesive and totalitarian but was highly factionalised and within it radicals killed their moderate opponents and then turned to kill others in defence of their power. Fourthly, perpetrators' motives were highly varied, often mixing material and ideological goals with ordinary human emotions encompassing paramilitaries, embittered refugees, ex-soldiers, young men and democratic moderinisers who were effectively organised and not 'backward or simple'. (An examination of perpetrators' motives for racist violence in contemporary Europe is provided in Chapter 6, drawing on Mann's typology.) More generally, central factors in similar cases also include, as Helen Fein (1993) has argued in relation to the Armenian genocide and the Holocaust, the rise of new elites in declining states who see their idealised political vision as exclusive, positioning other minorities as outside moral obligation and where extermination is less visible and operates with little fear of sanction.

Table 4.1 Sociological explanations of the Rwandan genocide

Theory of ethnicity	Main explanatory factors	Key theoretical problems
Neo-Marxism	German and Belgian colonial divide and rule policies between proletarian Hutus and bourgeois Tutus, and the downfall of the Rwandan economy leading to impoverishment	Lack of correspondence between economic conditions and ethnic hostility
Functionalism	Weakness of Rwandan national identity and a common cultural system, resulting from Belgian institutionalisation of unequal ethnic status using an identity card system, which categorised every adult in 1933 as Tutsi (privileged), Hutu or Twa	Ignores stratification within ethnic groups, unable to explain ethnic group mobilisation
Symbolic-interactionism	Conflicting individual and group perceptions of inter-group reality, Hutus coming to perceive Tutsis as 'dangerous and bloodthirsty cockroaches'	Failure to theorise macro-context
Socio-biology	Ethnic groups are kinship groups seeking to preserve and extend the domination, fitness and reproduction of their group by killing and raping the others	Naturalises ethnic conflict as rooted in human nature and genetics and hence unavoidable
Rational choice	Individual self-interest: provision of food, drink, alcohol, cigarettes, housing and land to poor homeless, hungry Hutu youths	Inability to account for durable persistent ethnic bonds
Elite theory	Motives and behaviour of Hutu elite in a highly centralised state using propaganda, radio and provision of weapons and leadership to produce ethnic mobilisation	Poor conceptualisation of the masses/non-elites and poor attention to historical context
Neo-Weberian	Status differentiation between Tutsi aristocracy and Hutu farmers deriving from unequal feudal patterns of economic exchange. Monopolistic social closure of Tutsis over Hutus in pre-colonial and colonial periods, and reversal of domination in post-colonial period	Incomplete synthesis of macro-historical and micro-action dimensions of social reality
Anti-foundationalist	European colonial imposition of order on difference (or chaos) exacerbating Tutsi/Hutu distinctions and use of means of modernity to implement genocide	Failure to address cultural relativism, Eurocentric analysis and weakness of conceptualisation of identity

Source: material drawn from Malešević 2004.

Ethnic relations

Ethnic relations across the globe encompass highly varied, complex forms of social relations where attachment to cultural difference is paramount. Analysis of differing categories of ethnic relations have been helpfully identified by Milton Esman (2004).

Exclusionary domination involves enforcing unequal ethnic stratification of rights, status and opportunities. This was common in European colonial societies on all continents, apartheid South Africa and in many of the more extreme cases previously noted.

Inclusionary domination or assimilation involves dismantling ethnic cultures, languages and attachments by facilitating acculturation to the nation. The classic French republican model of aggressive assimilation, Thai government approaches to its Chinese minority and the Turkish government's approach to the large Kurdish minority are all examples of this form of ethnic relations.

Granting minority rights can also ensure domination. Limited rights have been granted to Arab-Palestinian citizens in Israel but this confirms their second-class status and there remains entrenched opposition to equal rights with Jewish Israelis. In Malaysia, domination with significant but unequal rights for Chinese and Indian citizens is well established.

Power-sharing solutions have been developed in many national contexts where ethnic divisions have not produced conflict or separation. Belgium, India and Switzerland provide examples where forms of federalism and consociationalism have enabled the establishment and development of multi-ethnic states. This approach supports ethnic pluralism while the final position, integration, foresees its decline with the gradual building of social and cultural cohesion.

Integration, as opposed to inclusion, is a political priority in virtually every European state. Integration policies tend to assume that ethnic minorities are culturally different and need to undergo some degree of acculturation. The hopes related to such (typically simplistic) normative conceptualisations, however, often remain unfulfilled. Integration policy is also strongly advocated in the UK where 'multiculturalism' has been officially abandoned. Here integration is seen as encompassing the goals of ethnic equality and ethnic interaction with strong concern over ethnic groups leading socially damaging 'parallel' and 'separated' lives. A fuller discussion of the UK migration/ethnicity/racism context and policy debates is given in Chapter 5.

Sources of ethnic conflict: a European view

In 2003 the Declaration on Intercultural Dialogue and Conflict Prevention (Conference of the European Ministers of Culture 2003) confirmed that new forms of conflict increase the difficulties of dialogue between cultures and that this may be used by certain groups with the avowed or unstated aim of fuelling hatred, xenophobia and confrontation between different communities. It was argued that cultural 'impoverishment' and marginalisation, on the one hand, and prejudice and ignorance, on the other, are among the prime causes of increasing violence and stereotypes of others. Here, conflict refers to (real or masked) disagreement giving rise to resentment and violent behaviour or even injustice which may culminate, at the most exacerbated stage, in destructive and uncontrolled violence. Ethnic conflict is seen as resulting from opposition to the recognition of difference and multiplicity in the world in which we live, with a refusal to acknowledge cultural diversity and democratic openness. The causes of intercultural conflict are identified as complex and multiple, with political, economic and social drivers being identified. The European project confronts the question of how deep-rooted, territorially located national, cultural, regional and religious identities, which are embedded in people's memories, everyday lives and in wider power relations, can be opened up and woven together (Beck 2006: 134).

Drivers of ethnic conflict

Political sources of ethnic and intercultural conflict are often centred around contested control of territory, whether in Northern Ireland, Belgium or the West Bank. Economic sources of conflict include disputes over access to, and control over, particular resources. These may include who gets access to higher education, government jobs, civil, military and government contracts and capital and credit. This raises the issue of what is fair and appropriate in determining the allocation of resources. Worsening economic conditions may also heighten intercultural hostility when perceived as being linked to increases in the fear of unemployment and the erosion of welfare. Economic migration policies that open up countries to upper professional circuits of global capital and tend to close down opportunities for what Sassen (2005) has called the new global class of disadvantaged workers including transnational immigrant communities and households may also provide a key structural context for conflict. The intensification and multiplication of regional economic inequalities may also be driving both long-established and newly articulated claims for redress and redistribution. Cultural sources of conflict often revolve around issues of language and religion. Which language is used for instruction in schools or universities, in entrance exams or civil service exams, the language of command in the military and communication in government will symbolise and institutionalise unequal power relations between cultural, ethnic and linguistic groups. Religious identities have in many countries and regions been a long-standing key site and source of disputes between differing groups.

Triggers of ethnic conflict

Many different cultural and ethnic groups live in peaceful coexistence, yet at certain points conflict will erupt. Esman (2004) identifies three key factors which may precipitate conflict. Firstly, perceived affronts to a community's honour or dignity, such as the Jyllands-Posten Muhammed cartoons controversy in September 2005 when a great many Muslims were angered by the publication of what they considered offensive images, or the French headscarf controversy in 2004. A further example is when in Sri Lanka the Sinhalese-dominated government decreed that all tests for university entrance and exams for civil service positions were to be conducted only in the Sinhalese language, which members of the Tamil minority interpreted as a lack of cultural respect and a form of economic and educational discrimination. Secondly, tangible threats to the vital interests of a cultural or ethnic group. Here in Europe many working class communities perceive non-white or non-European migrants as a threat to their homes, neighbourhoods, jobs, their schools and the safety of their families, resulting in attacks and violence together with demands for increased control, regulation and exclusion. The encroachment of Jewish settlements onto lands which the Palestinians regard as theirs by right is a further example. Thirdly, fresh opportunities to gain advantages or redress grievances where an unsatisfactory state of political and social relations becomes open to action and intervention, for example the collapse of the Soviet Union and the post-Soviet transition.

But the strength of ethnic loyalties and their practical adequacy for many people in making sense of their position in the world in pre-modern, modern and contemporary times indicates the likelihood that ethnic conflict will continue, despite international declarations and interventions, creative national policies and inter-ethnic mixing. It is 'a world-wide phenomenon that has become the leading source of lethal violence in international affairs' (Esman 2004: 26). In the context of insecure national states and global inequalities, population mobility and international migration will lead to greater cultural diversification of national populations. New technologies and changing patterns of consumption are driving the construction of larger regional and global cultures. These globalising, cosmopolitan forces are also stimulating new forms of ethnic defensiveness and hostility to migrants, e.g. in the USA, and towards long-established minorities, as evident in the development of anti-semitic movements and in anti-minority hate speech in Russia. Social science failed to predict the demise of apartheid in South Africa, as John Stone and Rutledge Dennis (2003) remind us, and this indicates the importance of theorising and understanding the potential for constructive conflict resolution and calculation of the role that ethnicity plays. We now turn to a closer investigation of ethnicity in the UK to examine this key social dimension further.

Ethnicity in the UK

What is Englishness?

Ethnic identities are social not natural constructions often arising through the political mobilisation of groups drawing on a myth of common ancestry and common origin in a time and place, shared historical memories of a common past, symbolic attachment to ancestral lands and a common identifying name. These features of ethnicity (Hutchinson and Smith 1996) have to be elaborated in order to understand what constitutes Englishness. There has been much attention given to the experiences of ethnic minorities in the UK and what it means to be black or Muslim in this country, but Englishness itself is rarely defined as a form of ethnicity. The end of Empire, the growth of ethnic diversity in the UK, the process of Europeanisation and devolution of power to Scotland, Northern Ireland and Wales have all led to increasing uncertainty over what it means to be English and what exactly English ethnicity is. In many political and cultural spheres this debate is about a particular 'embattled, hegemonic conception of Englishness' (Hall 1996: 170) which has been articulated through key linkages with nationalism, imperialism and racism. In a recent study Robert Young (2008), a leading cultural theorist, seeks to answer the question: what is Englishness? Young begins by exploring the myths of common English ancestry. We cannot expect to find a real, unified, unchanging group of ethnic English through archaeological and historical study, but we can find a series of dominant and powerful myths. What these fields of study can tell us is that English ethnicity was invented from the binding together of a range of disparate peoples and threads of meaning. The 'English' were a highly diverse group of people that arrived in Britain at the end of Roman rule and made up the English-speaking bloc of the peoples of Britain and are frequently referred to as Anglo-Saxons, coming from the coastlands of Northern Europe including the Elbe and Weser estuaries, Jutland, Schleswig Holstein, Friesland, the area between the northern coast and the Rhine, some Franks and others including the Suebi (Todd 2008). These people arrived in mixed groups and were not distinctive ethnic communities. Young's analysis of myths of Englishness begins with a focus on Saxonism.

Saxonism developed in the late seventeenth century and was the idea that the English were Saxons or Teutons, with an identity that was firmly rooted in German national character, markedly different to the ancient native Britons (Celts) who had been driven to the fringes of Scotland, Wales, Ireland and Cornwall. Ethnic violence was essential, then, to the formation of Englishness. Saxons were seen as arriving in Britain from 440 onwards and were personified in King Alfred (c.870). Writers, historians, essayists and novelists were largely responsible for the popularisation and emergence of English identity as 'Saxon', which through the Victorian period was expanded to 'Anglo-Saxon'. The characterisation of the English/Saxons in Scott's *Ivanhoe* (1819) linked together notions of ethnicity, blood lines, and language to produce a composite popular understanding of the 'English race'. Saxonism has always been closely identified with Protestant values from the Reformation onwards and underlay a range of bonds and solidarities with other white Protestant groups in the US and elsewhere associated with the emerging notion of an Anglo-Saxon diaspora. In the mid-1800s with the rise of racial science and modern nationalisms usage of the term 'Anglo-Saxon race' became more prevalent and came to refer to the English as not only at home but also those abroad, English people of any kind in any place: the unmarked, superior, diasporic English. The globalisation of Englishness was inextricably bound up with colonial settlers, imperialism and the expansion of trade, communication and migration in the ninteenth century. De-localised English, Anglo-Saxon ethnicity with its vague values, institutions and common language expanded to encompass and include increasing internal diversity and diasporic culture, illustrating what Young (2008: 236) describes as the 'curious emptiness of Englishness' arising from its many varieties in different national contexts, e.g. Canada or Australia. In the twentieth century, the extent to which Englishness has changed its character, from a Saxonist doctrine of exclusive racial superiority to a flexible and inclusive umbrella for a 'syncretic community of minorities', is highly contested, as Billy Bragg's recent book indicates.

Questioning Englishness: exclusive or inclusive?

- What does it mean to be English? What does it mean to be British?
- Does the rise in popularity of the St George's flag represent a new beginning or symbolise the return of the far right?
- Is the Union Jack too soaked in the blood of empire to be the emblem of a modern multicultural state?
- In a country in which all of us are born under two flags, what does it mean to be a patriot?

Source: Bragg 2007.

From ethnic diversity to super-diversity

The UK has always been ethnically diverse with a population developing from complex historical migration patterns and periods of conflict, conquest, state formation, empire and de-colonisation. Specific movements relevant here include sporadic in-migration of Gypsies and the importation of African slaves and servants from the sixteenth century onwards, mass migrations of Irish and Jewish people in the nineteenth century and post-war economic migration to Britain from the Caribbean, the South Asian subcontinent, China and Africa (Shyllon 1977, Okely 1983, Holmes 1988). In the post-war period there is both increasing mixing of ethnic groups and 'super-diversity' (Vertovec 2006, see below) which have created an ethnically complex society. The UK is also undergoing substantial social and cultural change due to globalisation, Europeanisation, devolution, the end of Empire, social pluralism and the acceleration of migration (Parekh 2000, Loury et al., 2005). As Ulrich Beck reminds us, the increasing development of inter-cultural and inter-ethnic social relations across modern societies has been identified by a range of intellectuals and scholars including Immanuel Kant, Johann Wolfgang von Goethe, Karl Marx and Georg Simmel, who all saw the modern period as the product of a transition from 'early conditions of relatively closed societies to "universal eras" [universellen Epochen] (Goethe)' (Beck 2006: 9) of societies marked by economic and social interdependence, together with increasingly complex patterns of movement and cultural interaction. The resulting swirl of social change has brought into being two opposing positions. On the one hand, cosmopolitanism brings with it an emphasis on openness to others, recognition and acceptance of difference and the universalist view that all are equal and everyone is different. Whereas anti-cosmopolitanism, which can be found across all political camps, organisations and countries, emphasises hostility to cultural and linguistic differences, and promotes exclusion of and contempt for racial, ethnic or cultural groups who are perceived as threatening in some way. The role of news media in promoting anti-cosmopolitan ideas, such as race hate speech by journalists in Russia, is examined in Chapter 8. In the UK most migrant groups have been subject to racism, xenophobia, hostility, violence and practices of restriction and exclusion during the process of migration and settlement in the UK (Holmes 1991, Panayi 1993). They have also been subject to varying levels of political and cultural recognition, acceptance of racial and ethnic difference, inter-ethnic marriage and cohabitation and incorporation into political, economic, cultural and social spheres of activity.

The post-war period saw a sustained level of inward migration from Commonwealth or former Commonwealth countries to supply labour. Migration from the Caribbean was followed by that from India and Pakistan and subsequently Bangladesh. Although much primary migration was male, with family re-unification (that is, applying for dependants from abroad to join them here) being a subsequent step, this was not the case for Caribbean immigration where there were large numbers of women among primary migrants who came, for example, to take up work in the health service. These groups were from former British colonies, with people subject to initial rights of entry that were gradually restricted during the 1960s and early 1970s until only families of settled migrants could enter. Citizenship and all the civil, political and social rights associated with it were held by most under post-colonial arrangements (Hansen and Weil 2001). Large and eventually well-organized communities were formed, particularly through the establishment of community associations and places of worship (Vertovec 2006). Expulsion also resulted in settlement by numbers of Vietnamese and East African Asian families around 1970. Since 1970, most primary immigration for employment has been at a standstill, with family re-unification and fertility being the routes through which minority groups have expanded. Refugees have also contributed to a diverse minority group population, a recent phenomenon being the arrival of asylum seekers from within Europe as well as from further afield.

The differentiation in economic position, migration history, political participation and perceptions of social citizenship are significant across minority ethnic groups in the UK and they are becoming increasingly evident. Recent debate has highlighted the problem of hyper- or super-diversity where professionals and managers face substantial dilemmas in responding to the needs of culturally complex societies, for example in education provision (see debate on exclusion in Chapter 7) (Vertovec 2006, Mir 2007). Hence understanding and taking account of increasing ethnic and cultural diversity is an increasing challenge. Vertovec argues that the new context of super-diversity in the UK arising from the 1990s onwards requires consideration of the following factors:

- country of origin (comprising a variety of possible sub-set traits such as ethnicity, language[s];
- religious tradition, regional and local identities, cultural values and practices);
- migration channel (often related to highly gendered flows and specific social networks);
- legal status (determining entitlement to rights);
- migrants' human capital (particularly educational background);
- access to employment (which may or may not be in immigrants' hands);
- locality (related especially to material conditions, but also the nature and extent of other immigrant and ethnic minority presence);
- transnationalism (emphasising how migrants' lives are lived with significant reference to places and peoples elsewhere);
- uneven responses by local authorities, services providers and local residents (which often tend to function by way of assumptions based on previous experiences with migrants and ethnic minorities).

There is a complex system of citizenship rights, forms of membership and restrictions and exclusions which cross-cut differing categories and groups of migrants to the UK. This produces an ad hoc and variable pattern of denial of service and responses to individual needs so that people in the same migrant category may receive different services and entitlements. This produces a situation where 'neither service providers, advice-givers nor migrants themselves are clear as to what services they might be entitled' (Morris 2002, 2004, Arai 2005, Vertovec 2006). The migration and exclusion of three ethnic minority groups in the UK is considered below to assess the differing intersections of ethnicity, migration and racism and patterns of inclusion and exclusion.

Minorities in the UK: differing histories and trajectories

This section provides a comparative overview of three ethnic minority groups in the UK: Gypsies and Travellers, black Caribbeans and Bangladeshis and considers their relative positions. These groups settled in the UK in different periods and have been chosen here to indicate that despite commonalities of experience there are marked dissimilarities in processes of migration, settlement and inclusion. Gypsies and Travellers arrived in the sixteenth century yet remain in the most marginalised position, whereas the other two groups are primarily post-war migrants with varying forms of exclusion/inclusion. The black Caribbean population tends to be economically disadvantaged and socially assimilated, in terms of cohabitation and marriage patterns, and with some significant degree of political incorporation.

The Bangladeshi population tends to be in a position of greater economic marginality and poverty, with more social distinctiveness, due partly to social closure, and less political incorporation (Peach 2005, Modood 2005b). Both of these groups had the right to settle in the UK, to acquire citizenship and participate in electoral politics due to previous British colonial relations and obligations (Robinson and Valeny 2005). The Gypsy and Traveller population appears to be in the most vulnerable position of economic, political and social marginality of any these groups, although data for this group is much more limited (Cemlyn and Clark 2005).

Gypsy/Roma/Traveller (GRT) people

Gypsies are believed to have moved into the UK from Europe from the sixteenth century onwards, with a significant community being established around London by the eighteenth century, often being subject to oppressive vagrancy legislation. There has been a history of conflict between this group and the state particularly in relation to the enforcement of planning and land control laws which has affected family travel and mobility (Morris and Clements 1999). Welfare outcomes are particularly poor for this group (Cemlyn and Clark 2005), for example they have higher levels of infant mortality and lower life expectancy due to difficulties in accessing health services than most other groups (Morris and Clements 2001), life expectancy for men and women is 10 years lower than the national average and Gypsy and Irish Traveller mothers are 20 times more likely than mothers in the rest of the population to have experienced the death of a child (Van Cleemput *et al.*, 2004). In education, as well as some of the lowest levels of educational attainment (DCFS 2008), some schools are refusing to admit children from this group, imposing discriminatory conditions on admission or delaying registration (Clark 2004). Also a recent study found that of those that do get access to education, at least half of Gypsy and Traveller children in England and Wales drop out of school between the ages of 8 and 16 and the same study also showed very high rates of exclusions (DfES 2005). Furthermore, there is increasing evidence of almost total failure of access to higher education for this group (Clark 2004).

This group has much diversity within it and is estimated to include 200,000–250,000 people (Morris 2003, Clark 2004, Clark and Greenfields 2006). In Britain there are UK Irish Travellers, Scots Travellers (Nachins), Welsh Gypsies (Kale) and English Gypsies (Romanichals) among others. There are also Travelling Showpeople (Fairground Travellers), Boat Dwellers (Bargees) and Circus Travellers. Ethnic identifiers, including language, identity, names and traditions, vary across these sub-groups, and many can opt to conceal their ethnicity as phenotypical characteristics are more difficult to use to mark out this group. They are therefore on the margins of racial visibility, but they are clearly socially and ethnically identifiable, particularly in terms of a long shared history, of which the group is conscious as distinguishing it from other groups, and the memory of which it keeps alive; and a cultural tradition of its own, including family and social customs and manners. In the decennial census of population these groups, where enumerated, are included in the 'White' category.

Appleby Fair Gypsies
Around 10,000 gypsies and travellers gather annually for the Appleby Horse Fair in Cumbria,
www.applebyfair.org
Source: © Annie Griffiths Belt/Corbis

Gypsy/Roma and Travellers of Irish Heritage are identified as racial groups and covered by the Race Relations Acts as legitimate minority ethnic communities. Gypsy/Roma people have been recognised as a racial group since 1988 (*CRE v Dutton*). Travellers of Irish heritage received legal recognition in law as a racial group in 2000 (*O'Leary v Allied Domecq*). Gypsy, Roma and Traveller communities frequently experience social exclusion and discrimination which can be intentionally or is unintentionally racist in character on account of the lack of knowledge by the perpetrator(s) of their legal minority ethnic status. Since 2003 Gypsy/Roma and Travellers of Irish heritage are two distinct ethnic group categories within the School Census. These two groups are defined as follows:

Gypsy/Roma: This category includes pupils who identify themselves as Gypsies and or Romanies, and/or Travellers, and/or Traditional Travellers, and/or Romanichals, and/or Romanichal Gypsies and/or Welsh Gypsies/Kaale, and/or Scottish Travellers/Gypsies, and/or Roma. It includes all children of a Gypsy/Roma ethnic background, irrespective of whether they are nomadic, semi-nomadic or living in static accommodation.

Traveller of Irish Heritage: A range of terminology is also used in relation to Travellers with an Irish heritage. These are either ascribed and/or self-ascribed and include: Minceir, Travellers, Travelling People, and Travellers of Irish heritage. Travellers of Irish heritage speak their own language, known as Gammon, sometimes referred to as 'Cant', and which is a language with many Romani loan-words, but not thought to be a dialect of Romani itself.

The School Census categorisation does not include Fairground (Showman's) children; the children travelling with circuses; or the children of New Travellers or those dwelling on the waterways unless, of course, their ethnicity status is either of those mentioned above. Although most of these people have full citizenship rights, this category of Gypsy/Roma will also include people whose immigration status will be either asylum seeker or refugee, and/or migrant workers who have moved to the UK more recently from other EU states. The most recently arrived Roma in the UK have been subject to highly visible media hostility and vilification (Craske 2000).

Black Caribbean people

There is extensive historical evidence of the establishment of black communities in selected British cities from the seventeenth century onwards, often remaining a key focal point for people of African descent in the UK for centuries (Walvin 1973, Law 1981). There is also extensive historical evidence of both the depth and pervasiveness of anti-black racism and associated violence, discrimination and hostility, as well as more positive forms of social interaction, including inter-racial marriage and cohabitation with white people which has increasingly formed a large mixed population.

Black Caribbeans are people of African descent who were born in the Caribbean or who come from families which include people born in one of the Caribbean islands. In the post-war period this group mainly arrived in the UK during the 1950s and 1960s from Jamaica and other islands including Barbados, Grenada and Trinidad and Tobago, in response to demand for labour in the UK due to post-war reconstruction and economic growth (Peach 1996, Robinson and Valeny 2005). This group generally came as families and by 2001 constituted about 1 per cent of the UK population, about half a million people (566,000). The black Caribbean group are now mainly British born and of Christian religious background. In comparison to the White British population they tend to have a younger age profile, a broadly similar socio-economic profile with, unusually, men tending to fare less well in both education and employment than women (ONS 2006).

In 2001, in recognition of the increasingly mixed heritage of certain groups of people, four new mixed categories were included in the national Census, one of these was mixed white and black Caribbean. This group was the largest of the mixed categories, comprising about 237,000 people who were largely born in the UK (94 per cent), it also was the youngest of these mixed groups, with 58 per cent being under 16 and the one with the lowest socio-economic profile and high levels of unemployment and poor educational outcomes. Also 25 per cent of economically active younger people from this group were unemployed, with an average of 16 per cent overall for this group, and 25 per cent had no educational qualifications at all (Bradford 2006). Black Caribbean and mixed white/black Caribbean young men are increasingly subject as a group to internal socio-economic polarisation, as they are increasingly found both amongst the ranks of those with higher incomes and amongst the long-term unemployed (Berthoud 1999).

Bangladeshi people

Of the three minorities under consideration here this group has been the most recent to settle in the UK, with migration beginning in the 1950s. Men from Bangladesh (then East Pakistan, Bangladesh was established in 1971) came as economic migrants in increasing numbers in the 1960s and 1970s, with further rapid expansion through family reunification through into the 1980s. There were 100,000 Bangladeshis in Britain by 1985 and three key problems were highlighted for this group; recent arrival from a rural peasant society lacking skills to access well-paid employment, poor command of English and racial discrimination in housing and employment (Home Affairs Committee 1986). In education at that time, 74 per cent of 15-year-old Bangladeshis were not fluent in English, being described as an 'educational and social disaster of profound significance' (HAC 1986: xiii). Other key causes of educational under-achievement identified were low teacher expectations, racial hostility in school and community contexts, deprivation of home background, poor educational provision in Bangladesh and missed schooling after arrival in the UK. Cultural differences were also seen as posing severe difficulties for schools in respect of halal food, sex education, religious education and uniforms. Social services were described as 'hostile and invasive' by Bangladeshi organisations and poor housing and material conditions led to high incidence of ill-health.

Over the last two decades there has been both substantial change in some aspects of life, for example a rapid improvement in educational achievement at school and declining unemployment, whereas in terms of housing, poverty and incomes there have been highly durable persisting inequalities for this group. In 2001 this group constituted 0.5 per cent of the UK population at about 283,000 people, with almost half being born in the UK. Significant characteristics of this group are that over 90 per cent are Muslims, although there is also a sizeable Bangladeshi Hindu community in the UK. This population group also has a much younger age structure with a particularly high proportion of children under 16 (38 per cent) and generally larger families with an average household size of 4.5 people (compared, for example, to 2.3 people for black Caribbean and white British households). They tend to occupy the worst and most overcrowded housing; 10 per cent of Bangladeshi households contain an extended family and this is one cause of overcrowding, with 44 per cent being in this category compared to 18 per cent of black Caribbeans and 6 per cent of white British. Due to high birth rates and net international immigration the Bangladeshi group grew faster than most other minority groups, by 74 per cent between 1991 and 2001. There is greater linguistic differentiation for this group, with Bengali and Sylheti speaking pupils being the largest of all the minority groups, in secondary education, with 40,400 such speakers amongst London pupils in 2001. Bangladeshis also have high unemployment rates, particularly for women at 22 per cent, with employment rates for women being the lowest of any ethnic group in 2001. However, between 1991 and 2001 Bangladeshis experienced the largest reduction in male unemployment rates, from 31 per cent to 19 per cent, illustrating their position of economic vulnerability and the hypercyclical cause of this trend, being more severely affected by economic cycle changes than the majority. More women from this group are moving into higher education and the labour market. High levels of fertility are declining, with the rate of teenage motherhood falling from 61 per thousand in the mid-1980s to 38 per thousand in the mid-1990s, and along with declining family size there are indications of a convergence with white fertility rates

(Berthoud 2005). Bangladeshi families are moving through a period of change re-negotiating core values and converging on the wider patterns across the UK, whereas black Caribbean family structures are very different, moving away from standard white norms. This black group has an increasing number of unpartnered parents, over 50 per cent of families, a very low rate of marriage and a high proportion of white partners, over 25 per cent of families (Berthoud 2005: 236).

Ethnic minority political mobilisation

Ethnic minority political mobilisation in the UK has been characterised as 'without parallel in Europe' (Modood 2005a: 471) due to the strength of its ideological assertiveness, prominence and civic impact. This has been due to an interacting set of key elements including the strength of British colonial and imperial relations whereby migrants had automatic British citizenship, political rights and strong perceptions of the right to be in the UK together with emulation of large scale anti-racist struggles, particularly in the USA and South Africa. Black Caribbeans (formerly West Indians), seeing themselves as British in many respects, were at the forefront of these struggles which drew on post-colonial and American ideas, producing the British 'race relations' framework referred to above. They have been politically very active and have secured a defining place in street-orientated British youth culture (Hall 1998: 40) and have established themselves in a variety of social contexts including sport, entertainment and media. Caribbeans have primarily mobilised around a colour identity, and paradoxically they have played a leading role in social mixing and cultural hybridity. In contrast, South Asians (Indians, Pakistanis and Bangladeshis) have tended to mobilise around religious, national and ethnic identities. So, clearly, British ethnic minorities have not united around a single identity. But alliances have been built, although often very fragile; Muslim organisations like the Muslim Council of Britain and the Forum Against Islamophobia and Racism have campaigned with groups like the National Assembly of Black People to oppose racism in various forms. Plural ethnic assertiveness and intense community and local forms of mobilisation continue to proliferate in the UK. The Ethnic Minority Foundation identifies 6285 independent minority ethnic organisations in the UK (www.ethnicminority-fund.org.uk) and the Council of Ethnic Minority Voluntary Organisations (CEMVO) identifies the inability of many of these groups to effect any change at national level due partly to their limited local coverage and lack of resources. These organisations do however make a major contribution to the material welfare of minority ethnic communities, often drawing on a wide range of funding sources from central and local government. The rise of Muslim political agency and its challenge to British multiculturalism has been accompanied by adaptation of Muslim demands to the national context and the construction of legal and institutional compromises in the governance and management of the British state. For example, demand for Muslim schools was rejected through the 1980s and 1990s and finally became accepted in government policy in 1997, a further example would be the gradual introduction of halal food in school meals despite vocal opposition from some parents (Times Online 9 Jan. 2008). This indicates the (limited) extent to which state policy, and specifically education policy, has been contested and revised to accommodate minority ethnic demands. This has been defined as 'moderate egalitarian multiculturalism' by Modood (2005a), who acknowledges its importance as a process that has been gradually established in the UK with the accommodation of Muslim demands through negotiation and consensus despite the events of 9/11 and 7/7. There are a number of well-established groups at the national level including the Council of Mosques, UK and Eire and the Union of Muslim Organisations and the more high-profile Muslim Council of Britain (MCB), which has been successful at lobbying at national level since the demise of the much more radical Muslim Parliament (Garbin 2005). There are also well-established youth groups, such as the Young Muslim Organisation (YMO), which is affiliated to the Islamic Forum Europe (IFE) and an expanding number of Muslim professional groups. There is however sometimes little contact with local Muslim activists. In local areas such as Bradford, Oldham, Birmingham and London, initiatives may be taken forward by, for example, a group attempting to coordinate action between mosques such as the Bradford Council of Mosques, campaigning for the provision of halal food in schools, or over conflict in the Middle East, Iraq, Chechnya and Afghanistan (Garbin 2005).

There has been increasing national mobilisation of Gypsy and Traveller organisations in the UK, with a primary concern to campaign for law reform in a variety of fields including housing, planning and education, particularly calling for access to land for caravan sites, and access to schooling. The Gypsy and Traveller Law Reform Coalition (G&TLRC) was an alliance of Gypsies, Irish Travellers, New Travellers and other travelling groups which came together to promote the Traveller Law Reform Bill and policies to increase and improve site provision. This coalition consisted of all the national Traveller groups including the Gypsy Council, the National Travellers' Action Group, the UK Association of Gypsy Women and the Irish Travellers Movement, the Advisory Committee for the Education of Romanies and Travellers (ACERT) and a range of other related organisations including Gypsy and Traveller support groups and units. This was disbanded (the reasons for this require further research) in 2006 and Friends Families and Travellers, the Gypsy Council, the Irish Travellers Movement and the London Gypsy and Traveller Unit sought to establish a way of continuing the valuable work on law reform achieved by the Coalition. These four organisations agreed to set up the Traveller Law Reform Project (TLRP) www.travellerslaw.org.uk/index.htm which primarily aims to bring about positive changes in the law in relation to the rights and needs of all the Gypsy and Traveller communities. At national level, as with other minority groups there is an all-party parliamentary group of MPs and others to advocate these concerns. They work closely with members and representatives of these minority groups but speak on their behalf. The APPG (All Party Parliamentary Group) Gypsy and Traveller Law Reform is a parliamentary group committed to raising the social inclusion of Travellers and improving relations between the settled and Traveller community.

Researching ethnicity

British sociology and the 'turn to ethnicity'

In Chapter 3 the development of the British sociology of race relations was outlined which prioritised a focus on black/white divisions in British society and related patterns of race relations, conflict and discrimination. As the section above shows, the importance of understanding and analysing ethnic differences is also highly relevant. In a recent examination of ethnicity and public policy Ceri Peach (2005) identifies this 'turn to ethnicity' in British academic work, which has been partly driven by some key intellectual concerns with work on the sociology of race relations, including a historic neglect of gender and a failure to address intersectionality and racial, ethnic and cultural homogenisation and essentialism:

> Challenging the dominant British discourse on racial discrimination and race relations have been scholars concerned to unpack racial categories and develop a more nuanced account of ethnic differentiation, gender differences and generational differences.
>
> (Peach 2005: 179, Modood *et al.*, 1997)

Interestingly, this set of theoretical critiques has also been elaborated by scholars who place their work within Critical Race Theory, such as David Gillborn (2008: 36–41; see discussion on race and education in Chapter 7). Theorists from this school of thought, drawing on the intellectual legacy of Du Bois and Cooper, suggest that the problems exemplified in the sociology of race relations can be overcome by re-thinking race and intersectionality, rather than replacing the focus on race with a focus on ethnicity.

Ethnicity has been a long-standing but marginal theme in British social science since the late 1960s. In recent years, events that have highlighted the importance of ethnic and racial divisions include the report of the Macpherson inquiry into the investigation of the murder of Stephen Lawrence, the urban disturbances of 2001 and 2005, and the growing controversy over asylum seekers and refugees. In addition, the events of 9/11 and 7/7 brought to the surface already emergent tensions around the situation of Muslim communities and served, simultaneously, to highlight the intersection of global and local issues that had always been central to Britain's emergent multi-ethnicity (Mason 2003).

The leading contribution of Tariq Modood's work on ethnicity is widely acknowledged and his theoretical position is located as a bridge between political theorists of multicultural citizenship including Bhiku Parekh and Will Kymlicka and the long-established tradition of sociological investigation of post-imperial migrant settlements highlighted above. His emphasis on the need for 'context-sensitive' theory and inquiry is seen as leading to theories of multiculturalism that fit specific national societies prior to systematic comparative inquiry (Modood 2005a: 189). He does not offer a comprehensive theory but emphasises five key dimensions of ethnic difference. These include:

Dimensions of ethnic difference

1. cultural distinctiveness (norms and practices such as arranged marriage),
2. identity (affective meanings that may motivate or demotivate),
3. strategy (differential responses to a set of circumstances that may contribute to group consciousness),
4. creativity (group innovations, e.g. clothing styles) and,
5. disproportionality (differential structural characteristics, e.g. unemployment).

The purpose here is to capture both the subjective and objective features of a group defined by descent. As with Richard Jenkins (1997), David Mason (2003) and Heidi Mirza (2000), there is a central concern here to explore why certain social contexts either over-determine or reduce the significance of ethnicity. The increasing recognition of both the highly durable nature of both racism and ethnicity and their complex and dynamic character is driving continued intellectual work in these fields.

Six 'leading-edge' research programmes on ethnicity in the UK

What constitutes leading-edge research in this field, who funds it and where can we find out what is being done? In order to understand the 'state of the art' regarding current academic research on ethnicity this section identifies six of the most significant research programmes, currently running in the UK and identifies some exemplar projects. There is a wealth of material and output from these programmes, which are too extensive to examine here (for further information see the relevant websites). Despite the expansion and significance of the output from the programmes shown below, a number of key problems remain in our understanding of how ethnicity works, and these are examined in the section below.

1. The Arts and Humanities Research Board, *Diaspora, Migration and Identities* programme (2005–2009) is concerned to develop our historical and cultural knowledge on aspects of diasporas, migration and identities, which includes the spheres of languages, religions, literature, material culture and the visual or performing arts. This seeks to explore the role, modes and stages of migration in human history, the transnational and cross-cultural interconnections that contribute to the formation of subjectivity and identity, and the representation and performance of these interconnections and points of contact). One exemplar case study from the programme explores the experiences of belonging, place and diaspora of South Asian children in East London, many of whose families retain close transnational links with their places of origin. It identifies how these children (aged 8–13 years) experience and represent 'transnational lives', whether this involves travel to 'the homeland', or being part of families and communities in which people constantly move. It seeks to ground analysis of cultural hybridity and involves close collaboration with local communities and arts groups (www.diaspora.ac.uk).

2. The Economic and Social Research Council, *Identities and Social Action* programme (2004–2008) funded 25 projects examining the construction of identity, the relationship between identities, social exclusion and conflict. It explores who we think we are, and how identity can determine who people argue with, distance themselves from, embrace, marginalise, include or exclude. One exemplar case study examines identities, educational choice and the white middle class and one key finding was the persistence of racial segregation *within* urban socially diverse secondary schools with white middle class children clustered in top sets, often benefiting from 'Gifted and Talented' schemes, with little interaction with children from other backgrounds. These children rarely had working class friends and their few minority ethnic friends were predominantly from middle class backgrounds. It was clear that there was little evidence of social mixing despite the ethnic mix of the school as a whole, confirming the persistence of embedded ethnic and racial divisions (www.identities.org.uk/).

3. The Leverhulme Trust, *Migration and Citizenship* research programme (2003–2008) led by Modood (see section above), consisted of eight projects and is concerned to examine the management of diverse and complex migration movements and the management of cultural, ethnic, religious and 'racial' differences. One specific project is examining patterns of racial and ethnic segregation with a specific focus on education. In the UK the residential segregation of ethnic minorities results in educational segregation, and this project seeks to examine the educational performance of minority students and to what extent educational segregation restricts or reinforces their attainments, particularly as education is a key factor in the transition to employment. (www.bristol.ac.uk/sociology/leverhulme/details.html#segregation).

4. The Gender, Social Capital and Differential Outcomes project, which is part of the Leverhulme Programme on *Migration and Citizenship* (2003–2008) has been researching how similar migrant groups may achieve divergent economic, educational and cultural outcomes. This project examines Asian Muslims in two communities of Pakistani heritage in Manningham in Bradford, and in Slough in three ways. It employs the notion of social capital to examine how community values, norms and structures may determine which ethnic groups achieve economic social mobility, and explores questions of social capital through a gendered and generational analysis, asking how men and women may enact community values differently (www.bristol.ac.uk/sociology/leverhulme/ethnicitycitizenship/leverhulme/).

5. The *Families and Social Capital* research group (2002–2006) at London South Bank University explored the relationship between ethnicity and social capital and identified that minority ethnic communities draw on social capital in their families and communities, for example young black Caribbeans use aspects of their bonding social capital heritage to respond to social exclusion (www.lsbu.ac.uk/families/ESRC_Group_report.pdf).

6. There is increasing research interest in challenging the conventional use of ethnic categories through exploration of diversity within and between ethnic communities as society is becoming more diverse due to changing patterns of migration and globalisation. This is exemplified in the new series of *community studies* being carried out by the *Runnymede Trust* which continue a long tradition in British sociology. This latest series has explored the lives of Bolivian, Ecuadorian, South African, Cameroonian, Vietnamese, Nepalese, Thai and Romanian migrants to the UK (www.runnymedetrust.org/projects/communityStudies/reports.html). These reports highlight widely differing experiences and community contexts and no meta-analysis of the output from these varying studies has yet been made. The reports highlight differing patterns and experiences of migration to the UK, establishment of informal and formal community networks, and labour market experiences, for example racial discrimination reported by Cameroonians and difficulty in getting their qualifications recognised by employers in the UK forcing them to start their education from scratch. Many of the reports deal specifically with community experiences in London.

Ethnicity: four sets of research questions

This section brings together a range of contemporary research agendas and under-investigated issues and presents a range of questions that remain unanswered. It is just as important to know what we do not know, as it is to know what we know. This section presents four sets of unanswered research questions relating to the operation of ethnicity in everyday contexts, social identities, governance and citizenship and cross-national comparisons.

The significance of ethnicity in differing everyday contexts e.g. home, work or education

How do claims and attributions of ethnicity play out in the everyday lives of individuals and institutions? What governs claims and attributions of ethnicity? What is the significance of our inherited categorisation and measurement practices? How, and under what circumstances, are distinctively ethnic groupings formed? How do such groupings relate to religious and faith communities? Under what circumstances do asylum seekers utilise the ethnic route to regaining a sense of social positioning? Similarly new patterns of belonging and cultural hybridity engendered by generations of mixing and movement offer creative solutions, demonstrating the possibility for anti-racist solidarity and an holistic multiculturalism for all. Yet little is known about socially situated patterns of social change and transformation.

The significance of ethnicity for social identities

To what extent are ethnic identities of primary significance when ethnic differences appear to be present? To what extent are identity choices structurally constrained by processes of exclusion, of racialisation and, perhaps, even by measurement systems designed to address exclusion? Why are some differences defined as ethnic and others not? What implications do these definitions have for our understanding of majority ethnicities? How does ethnicity relate to 'race'? Can the answers help us to problematise and deconstruct 'whiteness'? How are we to analyse the place of sub-national (or state) communities such as the Scots, Welsh and Irish? What light can be thrown on this by comparative analyses of sub-state (or national) communities elsewhere in the world – such as the Balkans?

The significance of ethnicity for governance and citizenship

What are the implications of these issues for governance and government? How do they relate to the legal dimensions of citizenship and social participation? Most analyses of citizenship in the context of ethnicity focus on the processes by which minorities are excluded from access to full citizenship rights – either formally or substantively. However, in legal and political terms, citizenship is characteristically seen as embodying a complex of rights and duties. What implications would voluntary exclusion – for example from the armed services – have for a model of citizenship that emphasises duties as well as rights? Why should this be regarded as a problem for minority ethnic groups but not for the bulk of the majority population that exercises a similar choice? To what extent, then, are political and legal conceptions of citizenship also implicitly assimilationist? What level of normative and value diversity within a multi-ethnic society is consistent with the minimal level of cohesion necessary for us to speak of a society (or national community) at all? How do collective rights play against individual rights? What role can the concept of human rights play in reconciling differences of emphasis? How will human rights, race relations legislation, equality and rights commissions at regional and national levels affect racial and religious equality? How do we achieve mainstreaming of multicultural, anti-racism and racial equality issues and facilitate joined up thinking in government policy? (Mirza 2000, Mason 2003).

Racism and ethnicity in global and comparative contexts

Taking the highly durable nature of racism and ethnicity seriously in sociological thinking and interrogating the ways in which social, cultural and political significance is given to these ideas in widely differing places and times is a fundamental task. Rather than abandoning a general theory of how these operate, as many commentators have suggested (Modood 2005a) because of the difficulties in grasping the totality of the ways and means by which they operate, it is argued that such a theory requires a global approach, avoiding the pitfalls of generalising from regional or national standpoints. These issues, and the development of global approaches, are an increasing trend in this field (see, for example Bhattacharya *et al.*, 2002; Spickard 2005, Macedo and Gounari 2006). Globalisation also affects the local through the medium of direct and vicarious international contacts. Thus community reproduction is frequently mediated through marriage to partners from the country of 'origin'. Domestic politics in countries of origin and international events more widely can shape both intra- and inter-group relations in the countries of settlement. A sense of imagined community with the place of origin also helps to shape cultural reproduction and, more often than is typically recognised, processes of cultural innovation and renewal. Examples of these processes can be found in the realms of both religion and language (Mason 2003). What can we learn from comparative models of multiculturalism in Australia, New Zealand, Northern Ireland, Canada, USA, Malaysia, South Africa and the Caribbean and ethnicity across and within different regions of the world?

End of chapter activity

Have a look at the Arts and Humanities Research Board, *Diaspora, Migration and Identities* programme (2005–2009) which is concerned to develop our historical and cultural knowledge on aspects of diasporas, migration and identities, which includes the spheres of languages, religions, literature, material culture and the visual or performing arts (www.diaspora.ac.uk). Pick one of the research projects and assess the extent to which it adds to our knowledge of how ethnicity works and critique its limitations.

The Rwandan genocide resulted in the systematic massacre of 800,000 Tutsis and moderate Hutus in 100 days. Explore www.rwanda-genocide.org/ for multi-media resources and documents, and Human Rights Watch 1999, www.hrw.org/reports/1999/rwanda/ to identify key events, timelines and historical background. What was its role and how important was ethnicity in explaining these events?

Further reading

Hutchinson, J. and Smith, A. D. (eds.) (1996) *Ethnicity, a reader*, **Oxford: Oxford University Press**. A valuable collection of classis and contemporary readings on ethnicity.

Jenkins, R. (1997) *Rethinking Ethnicity*, **London: Sage**. A sound and clear account of social anthropological approaches to ethnicity.

Vertovec, S. (2006) *The Emergence of Super-Diversity in Britain*, **Centre for Migration, Policy and Society, Working Paper No. 25, Oxford: University of Oxford**. A seminal paper which examines the dimensions of super-diversity in the UK.

Office for National Statistics (ONS) (2006) *Focus on Ethnicity and Religion*, **Basingstoke; Palgrave Macmillan**. Accessible overview of 2001 Census data on ethnicity.

Clark, C. and Greenfields, M. (2006) *Here to Stay: the Gypsies and Travellers of Britain*, **Hatfield: University of Hertfordshire Press**. This critical and comprehensive text provides an excellent foundation for understanding the overall social context for this group.

Modood, T. (2005) *Multicultural Politics, racism, ethnicity and Muslims in Britain*, **Edinburgh: Edinburgh University Press**. A leading voice in the field draws together a lifetime of work on Muslims in the UK.

Modood, T., and Teles, S. M. (eds) (2005) *Ethnicity, Social Mobility and Public Policy,* **Cambridge: Cambridge University Press.** An extremely valuable set of essays which address political mobilisation, family dynamics, educational attainment, employment and other spheres for ethnic minorities in the UK and draws systematic comparison with the USA. This may be the best place to start for an assessment of ethnicity in the UK.

References

Arai, L. (2005) *Migrants and Public Services in the UK: A review of the recent literature,* Oxford: ESRC Centre on Migration, Policy and Society (COMPAS), www.compas. ox.ac.uk/publications/Resources_Lit_Review_1205.shtml.

Barth, F. (ed.) (1969) *Ethnic Groups and Boundaries: the social organisation of cultural difference,* London: Allen and Unwin.

Banton, M. (1993) *Racial and Ethnic Competition,* Cambridge: Cambridge University Press.

Beck, U. (2006) *The Cosmopolitan Vision,* Cambridge: Polity.

Berthoud, R. (1999) *Young Caribbean Men and the Labour Market,* York: Joseph Rowntree Foundation.

Berthoud, R. (2005) 'Family formation in multicultural Britain', in G.C. Loury, T. Modood and S. M. Teles (eds) *Ethnicity, Social Mobility and Public Policy,* Cambridge: Cambridge University Press.

Bhattacharya, G., Gabriel, J. and Small, S. (2002) *Race and Power, global racism in the twenty-first century,* London: Routledge.

Bradford, B. (2006) *Who are the Mixed Ethnic Group?,* London: Office for National Statistics.

Bragg, B. (2007) *The Progressive Patriot, a search for belonging,* Illinois: Black Swan.

Cemlyn, S. and Clark, C. (2005) 'The social exclusion of Gypsy and Traveller children', in G. Preston (ed.) *At Greatest Risk: the children most likely to be poor,* London: CPAG.

Clark, C. (2004) '"It's possible to have an education and be a Traveller", education, higher education and Gypsy/Travellers in Britain', in I. Law, L. Turney and D. Phillips (eds) *Institutional Racism in Higher Education,* Stoke-on-Trent: Trentham Books.

Clark, C. and Greenfields, M. (2006) *Here to Stay: the Gypsies and Travellers of Britain,* Hatfield: University of Hertfordshire Press.

Commission for Racial Equality v Dutton [1989] 1 QB 783, CA, http://83.137.212.42/ sitearchive/cre/legal/indirect/case_ØØ1dutton.html.

Conference of the European Ministers of Culture (2003) *Declaration on Intercultural Dialogue and Conflict Prevention,* www.coe.int/T/E/Com/Files/Ministerial-Conferences/ 2003-Culture/declaration.asp.

Craske, O. (2000) 'Breathing uneasy sighs of relief', *Central European Review,* 2., 27, July, www.pecina.cz/files/www.ce-review.org/00/27/craske27.html (accessed 6 Aug. 2008).

DCSF (Department for Children, Schools and Families) (2008) *The Inclusion of Gypsy, Roma and Traveller Children and Young People,* London: DCFS.

DfES (Department for Education and Skills) (2005) *Ethnicity and Education: the evidence on minority ethnic pupils,* London: DfES.

Esman, M. J. (2004) *An Introduction to Ethnic Conflict.* Cambridge: Polity.

Fein, H. (1993) *Genocide: a sociological perspective,* London: Sage.

Garbin, D. (2005) *Bangladeshi Diaspora in the UK: some observations on socio-cultural dynamics, religous trends and transnational politics*, Guildford: CRONEM, University of Surrey.

Gillborn, D. (2008) *Racism and Education, confidence or conspiracy*, London: Routledge.

Hall, S. (1996) *Stuart Hall: critical dialogues in cultural studies*, Routledge: London.

Hall, S. (1998) 'Aspirations and attitude: reflections on black Britain in the nineties', *New Formations*, 33, pp. 38–46.

Hansen, R. and Weil, P. (2001) *Towards a European Nationality: citizenship, immigration and nationality law in the EU*, New York: Palgrave.

Holmes, C. (1988) *John Bull's Island: immigration and British society, 1871–1971*, London: Palgrave Macmillan.

Holmes, C. (1991) *Tolerant Country: immigrants, refugees and minorities*, London: Faber and Faber.

Home Affairs Committee (1986) *Bangladeshis in Britain*, London: HMSO.

Human Rights Watch and Fédération Internationale des Ligues des Droits de l'Homme (1999) *Leave None to tell the Story: Genocide in Rwanda*, Washington DC: Human Rights Watch.

Hutchinson, J. and Smith, A. D. (eds) (1996) *Ethnicity, a reader*, Oxford: Oxford University Press.

Jenkins, R. (1997) *Rethinking Ethnicity*, London: Sage.

Kymlicka, W. (2007) *Multicultural Odysseys, navigating the new international politics of diversity*, Oxford: Oxford University Press.

Law, I. with Heuf, J. (1981) *A History of Race and Racism in Liverpool, 1660–1950*, Liverpool: Merseyside Community Relations Council.

Loury, G. C., Modood, T. and Teles, S. M. (eds) (2005) *Ethnicity, Social Mobility and Public Policy*, Cambridge: Cambridge University Press.

Macedo, D. and Gounari, P. (eds) (2006) *The Globalisation of Racism*, Boulder, CO: Paradigm.

Malešević , S. (2004) *The Sociology of Ethnicity*, London: Sage.

Mann, M. (2005) *The Dark Side of Democracy, explaining ethnic cleansing*, Cambridge: Cambridge University Press.

Mason, D. (2003) *Ethnicity, the need for a programme*, Unpublished paper.

Mir, G. (2007) *Effective Communication with Service Users*, London: Race Equality Foundation.

Mirza, H. (2000) *Key issues for race and diversity research*, Unpublished ESRC paper.

Modood, T. (2005a) *Multicultural Politics, racism, ethnicity and Muslims in Britain*, Edinburgh: Edinburgh University Press.

Modood, T. (2005b) 'Ethnicity and political mobilisation in Britain,' in G. C. Loury, T. Modood and S. M. Teles (eds) (2005) *Ethnicity, Social Mobility and Public Policy*, Cambridge: Cambridge University Press.

Modood, T., et al. (1997) *Ethnic Minorities in Britain, diversity and disadvantage – Fourth National Survey of Ethnic Minorities*, London: psi.

Morris, L. (2002) *Managed Migration: civic stratification and rights*, London: Routledge.

Morris, L. (2004) *The Control of Rights: the rights of workers and asylum seekers under managed migration*, London: Joint Council for the Welfare of Immigrants, Discussion Paper.

Morris, R. (2003) *Factsheet: Travelling People in the United Kingdom*, www.cf.ac.uk/claws/tlru/ Factsheet.pdf (accessed August 2008).

Morris, R. and Clements, L. (eds.) (1999) *Gaining Ground: law reform for Gypsies and Travellers*, Hertford: University of Hertfordshire Press.

Morris, R. and Clements, L. (2001) *Disability, Social Care, Health and Travelling People*, Cardiff: Traveller Law Research Unit.

Office for National Statistics (ONS) (2006) *Focus on Ethnicity and Religion*, Basingstoke; Palgrave Macmillan.

Okely, J. (1983) *The Traveller Gypsies*, Cambridge: Cambridge University Press.

O'Leary v Allied Domecq, 29 Aug. 2000, CL 950275.

Panayi, P. (ed.) (1993) *Racial Violence in Britain in the Nineteenth and Twentieth Centuries*, Leicester: Leicester University Press.

Parekh, B. (2000) *The Future of Multi-Ethnic Britain*, London: Profile Books.

Parekh, B. (2002) *Rethinking Multiculturalism: cultural diversity and political theory*, London: Palgrave Macmillan.

Peach, C. (1996) *Ethnicity in the 1991 Census, Vol. II: The Ethnic Minority Populations of Great Britain*, London: HMSO.

Peach, C. (2005) 'Social integration and social mobility: spatial segregation and inter-marriage of the Caribbean population in Britain', in G. C. Loury, T. Modood and S. M. Teles (eds) *Ethnicity, Social Mobility and Public Policy*, Cambridge: Cambridge University Press.

Robinson, V., and Valeny, R. (2005) 'Ethnic minorities, employment, self-employment and social mobility in postwar Britain', in G. K. Loury, T. Modood and S. M. Teles (eds) *Ethnicity, Social Mobility and Public Policy*, Cambridge: Cambridge University Press.

Sassen, S. (2005) 'New global classes: implications for politics', in A. Giddens and P. Diamond (eds) *The New Egalitarianism*, Cambridge: Polity.

Shils, E. (1957) 'Primordial, personal, sacred and civil ties', *British Journal of Sociology*, 8, 2, pp. 130–145.

Shyllon, F. (1977) *Black People in Britain 1555–1833*, Oxford: Oxford University Press.

Spickard, P. (ed.) (2005) *Race and Nation, ethnic systems in the modern world*, London: Routledge.

Stone, J. and Dennis, R. (eds) (2003) *Race and Ethnicity, comparative and theoretical approaches*, Oxford: Blackwell.

Todd, M. (2008) *Anglo-Saxon Origins: the reality of the myth*, www.intellectbooks.com/nation/html/anglos.htm (accessed Sept. 20 2008).

Van Cleemput, P., et al. (2004) *The Health Status of Gypsies and Travellers in England*, Sheffield: University of Sheffield.

Vertovec, S. (2006) *The Emergence of Super-Diversity in Britain*, Centre for Migration, Policy and Society, Working Paper No. 25, Oxford: University of Oxford.

Walvin, J. (1973) *Black and White: the negro and English society, 1555–1945*, London: Allen Lane, the Penguin Press.

5

Migration, ethnicity and racism: frameworks and formations

Key issues in this chapter:

- Global patterns of migration

- The nature of modern slavery

- Regional racisms

- Racial domination in Palestine and Tibet

- Immigration and racism in the UK

At the end of this chapter you should be able to:

- Understand the linkages between ethnicity, migration and racism

- Identify the main types of post-war migration flows

- Assess the relationship between migration and racial domination in specific contexts including Palestine, Tibet and the UK

- Evaluate the policy implications of these relations in the UK

Introduction

The purpose of this chapter is to explore the inter-relation between structures of racism, ethnicity and migration and to develop a global framework for examining some of the many different contexts and ways in which these relations operate in different societies. Earlier chapters have mapped out some of the key features of patterns of racism and ethnicity and this chapter brings together some of the key arguments introduced so far with a particular focus on the role migration plays in the development of racialised situations and patterns of ethnic relations. There have been various attempts to develop global typologies of ethnicity including those by Thomas Eriksen (1993) and Stephen Castles (2000). These types include *indigenous peoples* dispossessed and overwhelmed by colonisers. The USA, Canada, Australia and New Zealand have similar histories in this respect and contain indigenous minorities: Aborigines, Maoris, Native Americans and Native Canadians who remain in unequal marginalised positions. Indigenous groups are also found in Latin America, where there have been massacres, for example in Guatemala, and in most Asian countries where they may be categorised as 'tribal peoples' or 'hill tribes' (Castles 2000). Other categories and contexts include *migrant workers* and their descendants forming strong ethnic communities, for example Turks in Germany or Pakistanis in the UK; *ethno-nations*, for example Quebecois in Canada or Basques in Spain with regional ethnic groups contesting national control; and also *post-slavery* (Brazil, USA and the Caribbean) and *post-colonial/post-communist contexts* (Uganda, Zimbabwe, Chechnya or former Yugoslvia) where ethnic loyalties have had grave consequences in terms of conflict and violence. In all these contexts migration processes and flows have been highly significant (Duvell and Jordan 2003). The study of international migration does not only concern itself with the incorporation of migrants and minorities into receiving societies but also with the longer term issues of national identity, citizenship and government policy. Examining migration also involves the study of mobility, with a focus on the determinants, patterns and dynamics of migration flows and this is examined more closely in the next section.

Migration

We are all migrants, as highlighted in Chapter 1 humans have migrated throughout the world from their origins in Africa, and today continuing emigration has led Africa to be the global region with the highest proportion of countries with policies seeking to limit or reduce emigration. The movement of people, whether out of choice or from economic or political necessity or for any other reason constitutes migration and it is a fundamental human characteristic which was recognised as one of the key fundamental human rights by the United Nations in 1948. Migration is a global phenomenon with about 175 million people, or 3 per cent of the world's population, living in a different country to the one where they were born. Migration is also accelerating: the number of migrants has more than doubled since 1970, and the number of migrants increased by 21 million in the decade up to 2000. However, the rate of migration in relation to total population may well have been higher in previous historical periods (Hayter 2004). Irrespective of the long-standing social nature of human migration, migrants are now subject to increasingly high levels of control and regulation. Growing national concerns with the economic, political and social consequences of immigration have increasingly led to attempts to lower and restrict inflow of migrants, with such policies now in place in 44 per cent of developed countries and 39 per cent of developing countries. Whereas 20 per cent of all countries have opposite policies, seeking to limit or reduce emigration, for example Mozambique, Nepal, Rwanda, and Zambia (United Nations 2002).

In examining historical global patterns of migration, four major phases have been identified as occurring since the sixteenth century (Hayter 2004). These are:

- Forced transportation of between 10 and 20 million slaves from Africa to North and South America and the Caribbean;
- Partially forced migration of indentured or bonded labour (temporary slaves) from India to the mines and plantations of, e.g. South Africa, Burma and Guyana, and from China to South Africa, the Caribbean and South East Asia;
- Voluntary migration of Europeans to North and South America, Central and Southern Africa and Australasia with the formation of colonial empires;
- Post-war migration of a variety of types from the Third World to industrialised countries, 35 million between 1960 and 1990 (see below).

Each of these migrations is intimately associated with key elements of the construction of racism in slavery, colonial and post-colonial contexts. Ethnic relations have also been centrally determined by patterns of migration, whether the overwhelming of indigenous peoples by colonisers, or the ethnic differentiation of peoples in former colonial contexts and in European societies.

In examining contemporary global patterns of migration the UN has grouped countries into six major areas: Africa, Asia, Europe, Latin America and the Caribbean, Northern America, and Oceania, and within these areas smaller regions have been classified as either more developed or less developed. The more developed regions comprise Australia/New Zealand, Europe, Northern America and Japan. The less developed regions include all the regions of Africa, Asia (excluding Japan), and Latin America and the Caribbean, as well as Melanesia, Micronesia and Polynesia.

Global patterns of migration: some key indicators

- Global migrants tend to live in more developed regions (60 per cent)
- Europe has the largest number of migrants (56 million)
- In less developed regions the number of migrants fell by 2 million in 1990-2000
- Top three countries with the largest *number* of migrants: US (35 million), Russian Federation (13 million), Germany (7 million)
- Top three countries with the largest *proportion* of migrants are all in Western Asia: United Arab Emirates (74 per cent), Kuwait (58 per cent) and Jordan (40 per cent)
- In 2000, there were about 16 million refugees in the world with most being in less developed regions

Source: United Nations 2002.

The United Nations' overview of migration (2002) provides a detailed examination of the main types of post-war migration flows and these are explored and summarised in the section below. Four types of migrant flows have been the particular focus for national governments:

- Labour migration;
- Immigration of family members (re-unification);
- Refugees and asylum seekers;
- Undocumented migrants and contemporary slaves.

Labour migration

Labour migrants have faced growing restrictiveness and selectiveness in their admission both in developed and developing countries together with increasing recognition that the rights of migrant workers and their families need to be protected along with the adoption of regional agreements facilitating free movement. The development of immigration controls from the 1970s in many countries led to a major reduction of this form of migration. In Western and Northern Europe, the recruitment of regular migrant labour practically ceased, with many governments also implementing repatriation programmes that provided incentives for migrant workers to return to their home country, although with very limited success, as was the outcome for many immigration policies and programmes. Increasing restrictions on labour migration have paradoxically accompanied significantly increasing foreign populations in many countries due to other forms of migration including family re-unification and refugees. In a climate of growing policy restrictiveness, policies reflect a move towards greater selectiveness, favouring the admission of individuals and groups of people who meet specific labour needs, such as those in science and technology, those with skills considered in short supply in the labour market, and those who are able to bring in capital. By the early 1990s many of those countries affected by immigration had attempted to reduce this by passing legislation which specified skills as a regulator of entry, which has had some impact. For example, newly arrived immigrants in the United States are more likely to come from Asia and Europe, while in Canada and Australia the numerical weight attached to factors such as education, training, occupation and language skills has reduced the proportion of immigrants dependent on family relationships. There has also been ongoing concern with the brain-drain of skilled migrants from sending countries, particularly in the health and education sectors. Globally, despite attempts at restriction, many more countries are now drawing in foreign workers, such as the oil-producing countries of the Gulf region which have become the main destination for migrant workers from Asia, although this has been scaled back due to the Gulf War in 1990. Many governments of sending countries have been concerned about the mistreatment and abuse of their nationals employed overseas, and have become more actively involved in migration issues, such as Indonesia and the Philippines, which have adopted measures for the protection of their manpower abroad.

In Southern Europe, with economic growth, many traditional countries of emigration, such as Italy, Greece, Spain and Portugal, have become immigration countries. Migrant workers came to Southern Europe mostly from Northern Africa – Morocco, Tunisia, and Egypt – and tended to be concentrated in low-paying sectors such as construction, manufacturing and agriculture. In the

1990s, labour migration reflected former colonial links such as migrants from Latin America in Spain and Portugal. With increasing European integration, immigrant flows in the 1990s also included a mix of relatively high-income professionals from the EU, contract workers from Eastern Europe, as well as spontaneous movements of unskilled migrant workers from Northern Africa and Asia. There has also been a change in national contexts with a shift from unregulated migration to increasing attempts at restriction. In Eastern Europe, there has been an opposite shift in migration controls, with a move from severe restrictions on entry and departure of both citizens and foreigners to increasing de-regulation and official guarantees for the right to movement.

Family reunification

This has increasingly become a major source of legal immigration, particularly in Europe, where it has followed government attempts to stop migration flows, particularly of non-white migrants, through restrictions on primary labour migration. The opportunity for family reunification derives from national recognition of both the right to family life and the right to travel. Human rights considerations, concerns over migrant integration and concerns over the cost of providing migrants' dependants with health, education and welfare benefits, have been three key dimensions of political debates over this issue. Different national responses to this debate have led to many variations in definitions of the family, criteria for eligibility and rights accorded to migrants entering a country under family reunification procedures. In all countries, family reunification provisions apply to spouses and unmarried, dependent, minor children. But there is much difference in the treatment of the age of children, polygamous unions, un-married partners, homosexual partners and other relatives.

Refugees and asylum seekers

The attempts to increase migration restrictions in many countries has been accompanied by a surge in the number of refugees during the 1980s and early 1990s, resulting for example from the conflicts in the Horn of Africa and Afghanistan. Under the 1951 Geneva Convention, every person who claims that he/she has been persecuted in his/her country of origin for reasons of race, religion, nationality, membership in a particular group or political opinion has the right to seek asylum in a third country. Reluctance to grant asylum spread during the early 1990s when the Gulf Crisis, ethnic strife in Rwanda and the disintegration of the former Yugoslavia resulted in large and unexpected international displacements of population. For example, in the EU as a whole, recognition rates for asylum applications averaged only 11 per cent in both 2000 and 2001. The implicit assumption driving policy in many countries is that most asylum seekers are in fact economic migrants. Restrictive measures taken include visa requirements, sanctions against carriers, in-country processing (i.e., the requirement that asylum seekers submit their application at a consulate or embassy in their country of origin) and the adoption of the 'safe country' principle under which an asylum-seeker can be denied access to national asylum procedures and sent back to a safe third country, if they had travelled through such country prior to applying for asylum. Some countries such as Austria, Germany and Switzerland have gone one step further and have developed lists of 'safe countries of origin' the nationals of which will not be considered for asylum. In addition, many countries now resort to rapid asylum procedures for 'manifestly unfounded applications' and enforce removal decisions concerning rejectees, often by way of detention so as to facilitate deportation. Stricter control during the processing of applications has been in effect, ranging from finger-printing to quasi house arrest in reception facilities. One effect of such regulation is that displaced persons who have been forced to flee their homes, but who have not reached a neighbouring country, are on the rise, with about 20 to 25 million people in this group (United Nations 2002). Global recognition of the institution of asylum is hence under significant threat.

Undocumented migration and modern slavery

Undocumented migration, although very difficult to estimate, is rising due to increasingly restrictive controls on immigration in some countries and decreasingly restrictive emigration controls, for example in Eastern Europe. This has brought with it an increase in trafficking, which ranges from small-scale operators who provide transport across a border to, increasingly, international criminal networks that provide an entire range of services, including bogus documentation, transportation and assistance in crossing borders, places for transit and residence in receiving countries and illegal employment. A recent world survey of human trafficking summed up what this is and the extent of this phenomenon.

The scope and nature of modern-day slavery

The common denominator of trafficking scenarios is the use of force, fraud, or coercion to exploit a person for profit. A victim can be subjected to labour exploitation, sexual exploitation, or both. Labour exploitation includes traditional chattel slavery, forced labour, and debt bondage. Sexual exploitation typically includes abuse within the commercial sex industry. In other cases, victims are exploited in private homes by individuals who often demand sex as well as work. The use of force or coercion can be direct and violent or psychological. A wide range of estimates exists on the scope and magnitude of modern-day slavery. The International Labour Organization (ILO) – the United Nations agency charged with addressing labour standards, employment and social protection issues – estimates that there are 12.3 million people in forced labour, bonded labour, forced child labour and sexual servitude at any given time; other estimates range from 4 million to 27 million. Annually, according to US government-sponsored research completed in 2006, approximately 800,000 people are trafficked across national borders, which does not include millions trafficked within their own countries. Approximately 80 per cent of transnational victims are women and girls and up to 50 per cent are minors. The majority of transnational victims are females trafficked into commercial sexual exploitation. These numbers do not include millions of female and male victims around the world who are trafficked within their own

→

national borders – the majority for forced or bonded labour. Human traffickers prey on the vulnerable. Their targets are often children and young women, and their ploys are creative and ruthless, designed to trick, coerce and win the confidence of potential victims. Very often these ruses involve promises of a better life through employment, educational opportunities or marriage. The nationalities of trafficked people are as diverse as the world's cultures. Some leave developing countries, seeking to improve their lives through low-skilled jobs in more prosperous countries. Others fall victim to forced or bonded labour in their own countries. Women, eager for a better future, are susceptible to promises of jobs abroad as babysitters, housekeepers, waitresses or models – jobs that traffickers turn into the nightmare of forced prostitution without exit. Some families give children to adults, often relatives, who promise education and opportunity – but sell the children into exploitative situations for money. But poverty alone does not explain this tragedy, which is driven by fraudulent recruiters, employers, and corrupt officials who seek to reap unlawful profits from others' desperation.

Source: **Trafficking in Persons Report** (Office to Monitor and Combat Trafficking in Persons, US State Department, 4 June, 2008, USA), http://www.state.gov/g/tip/rls/tiprpt/2008/.

The intimate link between undocumented migration and contemporary patterns of slavery is well documented by both states and NGOs. The world's oldest human rights organisation is Anti-Slavery International founded in 1839 (www.antislavery.org/) which endeavours to expose and campaign against the many forms that contemporary slavery takes, for example they identify women from Eastern Europe who are bonded into prostitution, children who are trafficked between West African countries and men who are forced to work as slaves on Brazilian agricultural estates. They define a slave as someone who is forced to work through mental or physical threats, who is owned or controlled by an 'employer', usually through mental or physical abuse or threatened abuse, who is dehumanised, treated as a commodity or bought and sold as 'property' and who is physically constrained or has restrictions placed on his/her freedom of movement. Examples of slavery include bonded labour where millions of people around the world are taken or tricked into taking a loan for as little as the cost of medicine for a sick child. To repay the debt, many are forced to work long hours, seven days a week, up to 365 days a year. They receive basic food and shelter as 'payment' for their work, but may never pay off the loan, which can be passed down for generations. Three examples of the links between human trafficking and contemporary forms of slavery are given below.

Trafficking and slavery in Japan, China and Australia

Japan is a destination country for women and children who are trafficked from China, Southeast Asia, Eastern Europe, and to a lesser extent Latin America for sexual and labour exploitation. Many of the trafficking victims were coerced into commercial sexual exploitation in strip clubs, sex shops, hostess bars, private video rooms, escort services and mail-order video services. NGOs reported that in some cases brokers used drugs to subjugate victims. Women also voluntarily migrate to work in Japan but are later coerced into exploitative conditions. Women are usually held in debt bondage for $26,000 to $43,000 for their living expenses, medical care and other necessities.

→

Chinese women and children are trafficked for sexual and labour exploitation in Malaysia, Thailand, the United Kingdom, the United States, Australia, Europe, Canada, Japan, Italy, Burma, Singapore, South Africa and Taiwan. Many Chinese are recruited by false promises of employment and are later coerced into prostitution or forced labour. Children are sometimes recruited by traffickers who promise their parents that their children can send remittances back home. In poorer areas, most trafficked women are sold as wives to old and disabled unmarried men. In richer areas, most trafficked women are sold to commercial sex businesses, hair salons, massage parlours and bathhouses. Chinese children were also kidnapped and sold for adoption.

Australia is a destination country for victims trafficked from East Asia, South East Asia and Eastern Europe, particularly the People's Republic of China, the Republic of Korea and Thailand. There are several reports of migrants, particularly from India, the People's Republic of China and South Korea, who voluntarily migrate to work in Australia but are later coerced into exploitative conditions. The Australian Crime Commission reports that deceptive practices in contract terms and conditions appeared to be increasing among women in prostitution, while deceptive recruiting practices appeared to be decreasing.

For further information on these and other countries see www.humantrafficking.org/.

Source: www.humantrafficking.org

There are major differences between the Atlantic slave trade and modern slavery. Firstly, the role of racialisation is different. All peoples have been objects of modern slavery, unlike the Atlantic slave trade. Now women and children are its principal victims, those who are bought, sold and enslaved come from almost every continent and are sold into slavery in virtually every country. Secondly, the scale is different, it is estimated that there are over 27 million enslaved persons worldwide, more than double the number of those who were deported in the 400-year history of the transatlantic slave trade to the Americas. The increasing use of law to control, reduce and eliminate both forms of exploitation is however somewhat similar in that Atlantic slavery was legal for many years until abolition was secured. Human trafficking was also legal for many years until more recent moves to develop legislative interventions. However, the demand side of trafficking, which includes, for example, sweatshop or brothel owners, farmers, clients of sex workers, and people who hire domestic servants, is often neglected by trafficking prevention programmes. Activities tend to focus only on the supply side with a view to curtailing it, protecting victims and prosecuting the traffickers. While some of these individuals are fully aware of the mistreatment that occurs, many are ignorant of the severe abuse and exploitation involved in trafficking and are not aware that the majority of trafficking victims do not choose that lifestyle, but were forced or coerced into it (Humantrafficking 2006). Beyond organised crime trafficking syndicates and individual slave holders, states can also play a direct role, Burma, China, Mauritania and Sudan are some examples of countries where government regimes have in a variety of ways supported the enslavement of their own citizens, particularly through forms of forced labour. For example, China's *laogai*, or system of prison/work camps are exposed in the first-hand narrative of Harry Wu (see Chapter 5 of *Enslaved, true stories of modern day slavery*, Sage and Kasten 2006 and further information on www.laogai.org).

Approaches to an integrated analysis of migration, racism and ethnicity

The nature and complexity of relations between the movement of people (migration), the formation of boundaries between groups of people, who have shared cultural meanings, memories and descent (ethnicity) and the formation and negative treatment of racial groups (racism) is a key focus for this chapter and this section seeks to identify some of the main ways in which this occurs. There are a variety of approaches that have been used to examine these questions which include:

- regional accounts of dominant forms of relations as with the example of the United Nations account of migration (2002) in Africa, Asia, Europe, Latin America and the Caribbean, Northern America, and Oceania, explored above, Goldberg's account of racial regionalisation (2008) and Winant's account of racial formations (2001) discussed below;
- national country by country models and case studies, for example the study of race, ethnicity, migration and culture in Japan (Weiner 2004).

This section will examine these approaches and consider their value and pitfalls. Firstly, one of the main forms of contemporary racial governance, racial Palestinianisation, and its intimate relationships with processes of migration are examined. Also parallels between this context and Chinese racial domination of Tibet are explored. Secondly, following on and building from the account of ethnic diversity in the UK given in Chapter 4, the relationships between migration, racism and ethnicity are examined through a focus on policy contexts; immigration policy, race relations policy and English law.

Two leading race theorists David Goldberg (2008) and Howard Winant (2001) have set out to examine the historical and contemporary formation of race and racism through a focus on differing processes across varying regions of the world. Goldberg provides a new taxonomy of these regions identifying:

Golderg's forms of contemporary racial processes

- Racial Americanisation: historical processes of racial segregation, renewed 'born-again' racism and linkages to neo-imperialism
- Racial Palestinianisation: processes of occupation, partition and military domination
- Racial Europeanisation: renewed fixing of cultural and territorial boundaries with immigration the key racial threat
- Racial Latinamericanisation: social regulation, promotion and containment of racial mixture

→

- Racial Southafricanisation: move from repressive restrictions of apartheid to post-racial ambivalence
- (Cross-regional) Racial Neoliberalism: move from public/state racisms to remaking racial inequalities and divisions through privatisation, and a focus on security and control, e.g. of immigration

These vary from the sub-national to the continental in scope. Goldberg (2008: 87) identifies these as often 'interactive and overlapping landscapes' but argues for their racial distinctiveness in terms of history, conditions and articulation (2000). Winant's approach is driven by a concern to overcome the limitations of a focus on nation states as a primary unit of analysis by emphasising both the operation of a world racial system and national/regional case studies within which key dimensions of this system have been played out. Winant's national/regional cases include the United States, Europe, Brazil and South Africa.

The similarities between the choices made in these two accounts are clear and indicate some consensus about what are the most significant contemporary sites for analysing racism, but what is missing? Comparing this to the account of global migration given by the United Nations which examined trends in the six regions of Africa, Asia, Europe, Latin America and the Caribbean, Northern America, and Oceania, it is clear that Oceania is not considered and also large parts of Asia and Africa. In terms of population 8 out of the 10 largest countries in the world would not be considered here: China, India, Indonesia, Pakistan, Bangladesh, Nigeria, Russia and Japan. In terms of the top 10 principal agglomerations of people in the world, 6 would not figure in these analyses, including Tokyo (Japan), Seoul (South Korea), Manila (Phillipines), Mumbai and Delhi (India), and Shanghai (China). Migration has had a huge impact on all these countries and conurbations. They are all characterised by varying forms of ethnic diversity and differentiation. Race has also played a significant part in these contexts, as highlighted in the cases of China and Japan earlier in this book. These criticisms are broadly acknowledged by Goldberg and Winant and indicate the need to be cautious of unfounded generalisations and to continue building an integrated global account of these issues. In particular Goldberg flags up two further forms of racial region in his typology for further investigation: firstly, racial Asianisation, covering for example racism faced by Zainichi Koreans in Japan, together with Chinese and Indian forms of racial articulation, and secondly, racial Balkanisation which remains to be fleshed out. Aspects of the racialisation of Europe and America have been discussed previously and here one of the 'most repressive, most subjugating and degrading, most deadly' (Goldberg 2008: 106) examples of racialisation now is examined: racial Palestinianisation. There are similarities with a further example presented here, which is not addressed in these two global accounts: the case of Tibet, with its parallels of military occupation and racial regulation and control.

Racial Palestinianisation

The historical development of anti-semitism was introduced in Chapter 1, and later in Chapter 6 contemporary forms of anti-semitism and associated violence are examined. Given the nature and extent of anti-semitism, both historically and geographically, it appears paradoxical that Israel has been responsible for the creation of a new form of racial state. The purpose of this section is to examine this particular case, termed racial Palestinianisation by Goldberg (2008). The extent to which criticism of the Israeli state constitutes a new form of anti-semitism is also considered in Chapter 6.

The name Palestine refers to a region of the eastern Mediterranean coast from the sea to the Jordan valley and from the southern Negev desert to the Galilee lake region in the north. Regional affirmation of Palestinian identity was forged in response to both British and French colonialism in the early twentieth century and the founding of Israel. This latter event followed the ending of Ottoman-Turkish rule in 1917 and the establishment of the League of Nations' 'British Mandate for Palestine' in 1919 which recognised this region as the national home for Jewish people.

Goldberg acknowledges the key role that British modernisation played in transforming a complex cosmopolitan order into a more 'segregating, ethnoracially' divided set of communities. He makes a strong comparison between the formation of some key features of Israel with that of the apartheid state in South Africa, but seeks to shows that this was a different and new form of racial state. Migrations, expulsions, exiles and evictions were central to this process both for the movement of Jewish people into this region, and for the evictions and forced movement of Palestinians into defined and separate territories. The ending of British rule in 1948, the ensuing UN partition plan which set up separate Jewish and Arab states and the 1948 war led to the elimination of Palestine as a distinct territory and both a Palestinian exodus and a Jewish exodus from Arab land. The creation of Israel as an apartheid-like state in which Palestinians have reduced rights and power, exclusions from property ownership and material opportunities has followed. For Goldberg racial Palestinianisation is marked out by three key elements: land clearance justified by historico-moral claims and land reclamation through settlement, accompanied by processes of occupation and militarisation. The racial distinction between 'highly intelligent and enterprising' Jews and poor, indigenous culturally inferior Palestinians described by the British Peel Commission in 1937 in this region articulated long-standing racial categories which have been central in the formation of deep political and territorial divisions and related processes of racial domination. One key site of this conflict has been summed up in this way, 'Gaza is a classic case of colonial exploitation in the post-colonial era' (Shlaim 2009).

In 2001 the United Nations World Conference Against Racism (WCAR) identified, as part of its declaration on vulnerable groups and victims of racial discrimination, Palestinian people as a people under foreign occupation, and recognised their inalienable right to self-determination and the right of the refugees to return voluntarily to their homes and properties in dignity and safety. More recently, in October 2008 the Palestinian Boycott, Divestment, and Sanctions National Committee (BNC), which represents over 170 Palestinian civil society organisations, called attention to the fact that multiple examples of Israel's systematic and institutional discrimination against the Palestinian people constitute racial oppression. These include:

- The continued prevention of the return of the Palestinian refugees by means of force, law and court rulings;
- The confiscation of 3350 square kilometers (almost 60 per cent) of the West Bank for the purpose of Jewish colonisation, including ongoing settlement and attempts to isolate and segregate East Jerusalem and the Jordan Valley;
- Passage of discriminatory laws by the Israeli parliament to limit the fundamental human and civil rights of Palestinians;
- The siege of the Gaza Strip;
- The ongoing segregation and house demolitions of Palestinians in Israel, including Bedouin of the Negev;
- The expropriation of Palestinian-owned land inside Israel;
- Denial of due process and effective remedies for roughly 11,000 Palestinian prisoners held in Israeli jails, including those held in administrative detention that are vulnerable to torture and related forms of ill treatment. (http://electronicintifada.net/v2/article9987.shtml).

The highly politicised and contested context of the Arab–Israeli conflict is marked by claim and counter-claim and accusations of racism and repudiation of these accusations reverberate across international, national and local terrains (new forms of anti-semitism linked to this conflict are examined in the next chapter). In examining this region Goldberg makes a convincing case for the focus upon and interrogation of racial Palestinianisation and links this closely with his account of racial Americanisation. Without questioning Israel's right to exist, he challenges the operation of the Israeli state's marking of a population as 'excess, superfluous' and the enforcement of associated 'death and dominating destruction'. The recent conflict in Gaza in 2008/09 illustrates many of the key themes identified here and the vision of the creation of peaceful relations between two states seems, at present, unachievable. The two-state solution would give Arabs citizenship in the new Palestinian state with Palestinian refugees and Arab citizens of the current Israeli state being offered citizenship, although the latter would also have the opportunity to stay as Israeli citizens. However unlikely to occur, it does seem more probable than the creation of an independent Tibetan state where parallel racist logics of domination are at work.

Chinese racial domination of Tibet

The exposure of the origins, development and implications of racism in Tibet have been extensively set out (ICT 2000). As with the Palestinian case this has been made in the context of lobbying the WCAR both in 2001 and beyond. Tibet is a regional plateau in Central Asia roughly the size of Western Europe. Formerly an independent kingdom, it was invaded and occupied by the People's Republic of China (PRC) following the victory of the Communist Party of China in the Chinese civil war in 1949. This resulted in the death of over 1 million Tibetans, the destruction of over 6000 monasteries, nunneries and temples, and the imprisonment and torture of thousands of Tibetan people. China has maintained that racism is a Western phenomenon and that it does not exist in China. However, the origins of Chinese/Tibetan racism have been traced back to border conflicts between Tibetans and Chinese warlords, migration of Chinese settlers into border regions of Tibet and hostility arising from the conflicts between atheist Communist ideas and Tibetan Buddhism. So, as in other parts of the world an indigenous people began to be overwhelmed by settler colonialism with which there was profound cultural hostility. Chinese notions of cultural and racial superiority derived from Confucian ideas of the global centrality and importance of China and its people, and the impulse to either assimilate or eliminate foreign/barbaric/uncivilised people in and around its borders. Tibetans were seen in this way as backward, savage, superstitious, primitive people a view which was rehearsed, reworked and promoted in Chinese political and media discourse. In emerging Chinese political ideology, Tibetan identity was seen at best as one sub-section of Han national identity, and at worst as backward-looking 'false consciousness' which would dissolve with the recognition of the benefits of Chinese nationalism.

Jampa
The 1963 propaganda film *Serf* portrays the main character, Jampa, as dark, enslaved, dirty and uneducated prior to the 'liberation of Tibet' by China.

In 1949 Mao Zedong officially abolished the doctrine of race in China, just as Castro did in Cuba a decade later in 1959, and in the name of civilisation, liberation, enlightenment and modernisation the People's Liberation Army carried through racial subjugation of national minorities and the Tibetan people. The purpose here was to secure the unity of the *zhonghua minzu*. This is the term for the modern notion of the Chinese nation which encompasses both the Han Chinese, the largest ethnic group (92 per cent) and the other 56 officially recognised ethnic identities who comprise 105 million people including the Zhuang, Manchu, Hui,

Mongol and 5.4 million Tibetans. The claim of common ancestry for all these peoples and that Tibetans are part of the same race as Han Chinese is used to counter calls for ethnic self-determination. The ICT report (2000) highlights the parallels between Chinese colonialism and Western colonialism, identifying paternalism and the civilising mission as key articulations.

As with many other groups' colonialism has led to the formation of new diasporas. The Tibetan diaspora began with the failed uprising in March 1959 that led to the flight of the current Dalai Lama from Tibet to India. Rumours that the Chinese government was planning to abduct the Dalai Lama and spirit him from Lhasa precipitated a popular uprising, which ended in the death of thousands of Tibetans, and during which the Dalai Lama ultimately decided to flee. The Dalai Lama's escape from Tibet in 1959 was followed by the establishment of an exile government and diasporic communities in, for example, the USA and India (Hess 2006).

Illustrations of more everyday anti-Tibetan Chinese racism include passengers throwing Tibetans off Chinese buses, beatings and violence by police and others, refusal of service in hotels and restaurants, and discrimination and exclusion in accessing permits, contracts and housing. Discriminatory treatment of Tibetans in Tibet is very evident and occurs in relation to freedom of expression, freedom of movement and residence, the treatment of Tibetan religion and culture, employment practices, access to health services and to education and training, and other social and economic rights (ICT 2000: 70). At school Tibetan children are frequently ridiculed or beaten if they, or their parents, express interest in Tibetan religious beliefs, traditions or culture. Basic freedoms are denied and political imprisonment and torture continue. Denial of racism together with the racist foundations of Chinese nationalism with its belief in the superiority of the Chinese (Han) socialist revolution provide a powerful set of mechanisms for the continuing domination of Tibet.

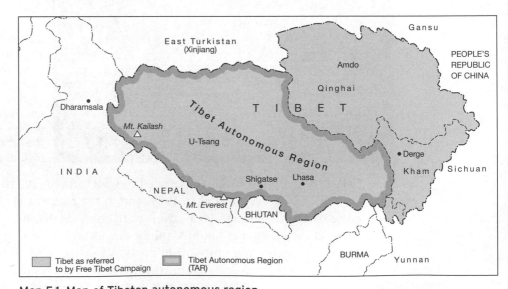

Map 5.1 Map of Tibetan autonomous region
The 'Tibetan Autonomous Region' (TAR) is not Tibet, nor is it autonomous. The Chinese government has divided historical Tibet into one region and several prefectures and counties, with the TAR encompassing only the central area and some eastern regions of Tibet. (Source: www.freetibet.org)

Migration, settlement and occupation are used as weapons of racial domination in Tibet. Han Chinese are encouraged to migrate and settle through a variety of initiatives including the establishment of large scale Chinese staffed construction, mining and hydroelectric projects, the appropriation of Tibetan land for agriculture, de-regulation of private enterprise and provision of loans to help Chinese migrants establish markets, clothes shops, hotels, discos and brothels and lastly the speeding up of migration through the opening of rail links with China. Government financial incentives also include higher wages and better housing for Chinese workers and their families, and this is accompanied by denial that it is practising a policy of population transfer. Currently Tibetans are a minority in 5 of the 10 areas of Tibet. In 2008 the worst violence in Tibet in 20 years together with international protests prior to the Olympic Games in Beijing brought renewed attention to these issues. However, the powerful political logics of Chinese occupation and modernisation have resulted in aggressive responses to these protests and underline the strength of racial domination, the increasing effectiveness of migration and occupation and entrenched hostility to ethnic, cultural, linguistic and religious difference.

The central importance of understanding the linkages between racism, migration and ethnicity is also necessary even where there have been many decades of initiatives aimed at addressing these issues. The problems the UK still faces 40 years after the first race relations legislation was passed include high levels of ethno-racial inequality and segregation, rising right-wing extremism and mass evidence of racial hostility and violence.

Regulating migration, racism and ethnicity in the UK

Immigration and exclusion

In a recent examination of racism, migration and welfare in the UK welfare Craig (2007) identifies that 'immigrants have been characterised as "cunning", "loathsome", "unprincipled" and likely to "swamp" British culture'. British state policy towards migrants and minorities demonstrates a 'long pedigree of racism' (Craig 2007: 605). Regulation to exclude 'aliens', denizens (permanent settlers without British nationality) and particular racialised categories of British citizens from access to welfare benefits is evident in immigration legislation and wider social policy reforms from the Victorian period onwards. Poor Law rules, pensions law, aliens legislation as well as national insurance criteria incorporated such practices (Williams 1989). The racialisation of the British welfare state drew on eugenic notions of the quality of the race and the nation in order to maintain imperialism, and to manage both the 'burden' of the black, Asian, Irish and Jewish poor and the perceived threat of such groups to the jobs and wages of those in the 'new' mass trade unions. The articulation of race ideas with those of breeding, motherhood, the family, dirt and disease and 'mental deficiency' shows the pervasive nature of racist discourse in policy and practice. Post-war welfare reforms and immigration legislation have continued to institutionalise racially exclusionary rules which determine eligibility to welfare benefits, these include residence tests, rules on 'recourse to public funds' and sponsorship conditions (Law 2008).

The two central planks of British government policy in relation to minority groups have been strong racialised immigration controls and weak protection against racial discrimination. The targeting of racial groups has been a constant feature of immigration policy in the UK, whether Jews, blacks, Asians or asylum seekers. More recently policy has been 're-racialised' as new EU citizens are substituted for workers from the developing world (Sales 2007: 158, Benyon 2006). Greater freedom of movement for EU nationals together with increasing restrictions on non-EU nationals means that it is people of colour from the regions subordinate in the global economic structure – those who would benefit most from being able to migrate to do unskilled as well as skilled work – who will continue to find their opportunities to migrate restricted out of proportion to their need to do so.

Four phases of immigration policy in the UK

- Controls on Jews and other 'aliens' arriving from Europe, 1905 onwards
- Controls on New (black and Asian) Commonwealth migrants, as opposed to Old (white) Commonwealth migrants, 1962 onwards with explicit distinctions being made
- Controls on the entry and rights of asylum seekers, 1980s onwards
- Managed migration and tighter more selective controls on labour migration, including some East European migrants such as Bulgarians and Romanians, 2000 onwards

Key source: Rosemary Sales (2007) *Understanding Immigration and Refugee Policy*, Bristol: Policy Press also see discussion piece by Benyon 2006

New Labour has continued and amplified previous Conservative policy in relation to welfare, immigration and asylum (Somerville 2007, Morris 2007), reducing the benefit rights of asylum seekers, tightening job search requirements and availability tests and tightening migration controls except for particular groups of skilled migrants. Immigration policy is being shaped both by concerns over the protection of welfare resources and labour market needs, as well as international conventions and trans-national rights. The resulting tensions lead to the deployment of ideological and organisational dimensions of welfare in the management of migration, for example in hostile media and political discourse and in new policy restrictions (Morris 2007, Daly 2003). Increasing differentiation and conditionality in access to welfare rights has been accompanied by both demonisation and hostility towards asylum seekers and concern that no one should be left destitute. There is fierce debate over the extent to which the government's view, that asylum seekers are 'pulled' to the UK by welfare benefits, is correct. This is contested by a group of researchers including Vaughan Robinson and Jeremy Segrott (2002), Alice Bloch and Lisa Schuster (2002), Alan Gilbert and Khalid Koser (2003) and Bill Duvall and Franck Jordan (2002). Other factors including the unregulated labour market and ineffective deportation and removal of illegal migrants from the UK to their country of origin are cited as significant in migration decisions. Also, Southern European states with lower levels of welfare have also experienced increasing asylum applications (Sales 2007).

Immigration law has interacted directly with social security to limit the possibilities for claiming for those in transitional status or seeking family reunification. The two main points of interaction have been the rules around recourse to public funds and the provisions for those seeking refugee status. The 1971 Immigration Act introduced the requirement that those seeking family re-unification – that is, applying for dependants from abroad to join them – should have no 'recourse to public funds' at the time of the application and until the dependants were granted residence. Thus applicants have to demonstrate that they can support their dependants; and should they make a claim following their arrival they risk their dependants' status. Immigration law has also inhibited family re-unification through visa requirements, that applications have to be made before departure. The geographical distance of immigration officers making visa decisions from British legal process can limit their accountability (Bevan 1986). A further obstacle was supplied by the former, notorious, 'primary purpose' rule, which required that a spouse's primary reason for immigration should not be to live in Britain.

Successive immigration rules since 1973 have required people, other than EEA (European Economic Area) nationals, seeking leave to enter or remain in the UK to show that they can adequately maintain and accommodate themselves and any dependants without recourse to public funds. This means they have to show that they have adequate means to support themselves, or be supported, without needing to claim benefits which are considered to be public funds. The meaning of 'public funds' was first defined in immigration rules in 1995. Since then the list of benefits defined as 'public funds' has grown steadily and in 2005 the immigration rules were further amended to add child tax credit, pension credit and working tax credit to the existing definition of 'public funds'. Public funds also includes social housing, but not schooling or healthcare. If a person with a public funds restriction claims a benefit the person's immigration position can be put at risk as the claim may affect her or his right to remain in the UK or to get an extension of stay. The restriction on access to public funds varies widely across migrant categories and is determined by the government. In recent years, benefit rules have been brought into line with immigration rules. Many benefits now have specific immigration conditions attached, which render a person ineligible purely because of their immigration status, for example social security and tax credits law categorises certain people as a 'person subject to immigration control' (PSIC) (Fitzpatrick 2005).

Some key moments in UK immigration policy

1948 British Nationality Act: enshrined right of all Commonwealth citizens to reside in the UK
1962 Commonwealth Immigrants Act: first legislation to restrict right of Commonwealth citizens to reside in the UK, it introduced a voucher system for primary immigration, where work vouchers for migrants were required
1971 Immigration Act: introduced recourse to public funds provisions; and notion of patriality, which favoured immigration by those from 'white' Commonwealth countries (e.g. Australia, South Africa, Canada) above that from other Commonwealth countries

➔

1993 Asylum and Immigration Appeals Act: introduced finger-printing and removed rights to public sector housing

1996 Asylum and Immigration Act: penalised employers who employed those without the appropriate documentation

1999 Immigration and Asylum Act: introduced vouchers for support and the dispersal and accommodation system devolved to National Asylum Support Service (NASS) who have a direct role in supporting asylum seekers only

2002 Secure Borders, Safe Haven White Paper: proposes phasing out of vouchers, but support and accommodation to remain with NASS

2002 Nationality, Immigration and Asylum Act: introduced new induction/accommodation/removal centres for asylum seekers which deal with deportations, withdrawal of support to individual asylum seekers who are 'late' applicants and unsuccessful applicants

2004 Asylum and Immigration (Treatment of Claimants Act): withdrawal of support from families with children under 18 in selected areas of the country, limited rights of appeal

2006 Immigration, Asylum and Nationality Act: introduces new asylum model giving greater control over asylum seekers with separate procedures for different nationalities

2007 UK Borders Bill: gives immigration officers further powers, decreasing the rights of those subject to immigration control and creating further duties and penalties for them; anyone subject to immigration control must have a biometric ID card

Labour followed the previous Conservative government in tightening restrictions on welfare for asylum seekers. The 1999 Immigration Act established the National Asylum Support Service (NASS) separate from Department of Social Security provision to arrange accommodation and provide cash vouchers (rather than actual cash) at 70 per cent of income support rates for adults (though 100 per cent for child dependants). Following a campaign led by Bill Morris, then General Secretary of the Transport and General Workers Union, cash replaced vouchers in 2002 but the provision of funds for basic support remains with NASS and distinct from social security though tied into income support rates. Also for those on Section 4 'Hard Case' support (failed asylum seekers who temporarily changed cannot be returned to their country of origin) vouchers continue to be used (Somerville 2007, CAB 2006). A concerted set of measures systematically reducing support for asylum seekers has been implemented including withdrawing support to 'late' applicants, unsuccessful applicants and some families. Also increasing exclusion of this group from work and public services including social housing, non-emergency healthcare and secondary healthcare for failed asylum seekers has led to widespread destitution, as identified by the UK parliamentary Joint Committee on Human Rights (2007). This has most recently been identified for those processed through the New Asylum Model (Lewis 2007, Somerville 2007).

> Destitute asylum seekers rely upon friends and charity from voluntary organisations and churches to try to meet their basic needs of shelter, food, health, income and safety. Others are forced to find undocumented work to survive. All sources of support are highly precarious. People remain in this vulnerable position for protracted

periods during which time they experience differing degrees of destitution that have an acute impact on their wellbeing, and can lead to self-harm and suicidal thoughts. Periods of rough sleeping are common for some.

(Lewis 2007: 1)

Here both Conservative and Labour migration policy has been demonstrated to generate increases in both child and adult poverty. Currently the new Borders Bill gives immigration officers further powers, decreasing the rights of those subject to immigration control and creating further duties and penalties for them, and proposes that anyone subject to immigration control must have a biometric ID card. In relation to welfare, the Refugee Council has welcomed the government's commitment to continue support to asylum seekers throughout the appeals process here, but they raise a central concern that when claims and appeal have been refused, 'people are not entitled to any housing and financial support and are left totally destitute – unless they fit the tight eligibility criteria for hard case support. Currently the UK is forcing people who have claimed asylum into destitution in the name of immigration control' (Refugee Council 2007). A recent report by the Scottish Refugee Council identified 'at least 154 asylum seekers, refugees and their dependants [including 25 children] were destitute in Glasgow between 30 January and 26 February 2006' (quoted in Lister 2007: 120).

Workers from new EU accession states are allowed entry only on terms that deny access to some benefit rights for the first year, whereas all other workers have no recourse to public funds until securing permanent residency. This includes those from the A8 states, the Czech Republic, Estonia, Latvia, Lithuania, Hungary, Poland, Slovenia and Slovakia, which joined the EU on 1 May 2004, and A2 nationals from Bulgaria and Romania. For these groups means-tested benefits are all subject to the habitual residence test, of which the right to reside test is one part. A2 nationals who are in authorised work are able to claim entitled benefits immediately, including housing benefit, council tax benefit, working tax credit and child benefit. However, if they become unemployed before completing a year of authorised work they lose their entitlement to benefit. After a year of authorised work they are to be treated in the same way as other EU nationals and will have access to any type of work and be able to claim benefits freely (Fitzpatrick 2007). The experiences of Central and East European migrants include low earnings, long hours, lack of contracts/sick pay and working illegally in breach of immigration status (Anderson *et al.*, 2006). On arrival in the UK almost half of migrants had no knowledge of the conditions attached to their immigration status or how to access healthcare, with fewer than 1 in 5 knowing where to go for advice (Spencer *et al.*, 2007).

The UK's approach to 'race relations' policy

The liberal policy framework which emerged in the UK in the mid-1960s has been analysed by Michael Banton (1985) and Shamit Saggar (1992). Four elements of this framework have been identified: the notion of racial harmony as a public good; the philosophy of community relations; attempts to de-politicise issues of racism and migration; and the notion of a multi-racial society. The notion of racial harmony was largely displaced by the focus on racial equality by the mid to late 1970s, and it was belatedly marked by the change in name of Community Relations Councils to Racial Equality Councils in the early 1990s. But peripheralisation of policy and management with respect to domestic racism, which was evident in the devolution of policy making to local authorities and community relations agencies, remains a persistent feature in Britain. The notion of a multi-racial society carried with it a range of dubious assumptions including the view that prior to the migration of colonial subjects from Asia and the Caribbean, after the Second World War, Britain was a nation with definable boundaries enclosing a culturally homogenous political unit. This 'coloured' migration was seen as fundamentally changing the nature of this political unit and hence a new multi-cultural society was being established which should be nurtured and fostered through policies of assimilation, integration and equal opportunity. This conception has been much criticised, but Miles (1993: 117–8) has usefully structured this criticism and has focused on three objections. Firstly, the making of the British nation state has always been partial and incomplete. The cultural integration of the British nation has never been achieved and, in that sense, the process of 'incomplete nationalisation' had therefore failed to deliver a unified British culture which could be counterposed to the 'culture' of Asian and Afro-Caribbean migrants. Secondly, previous migrations of groups had occurred, including Irish, Jewish, Chinese and African people who were seen as belonging to biologically and culturally determined 'races'. This was overlooked in the emphasis on the 'newness' of multi-culturalism. Thirdly, class divisions were perceived as having cultural and racial significance, with for example racialised notions of the poor as backward, uncivilised and living in the 'dark underworld' of Victorian inner cities and the ruling class as having different breeding and being a 'race' apart. Douglas Lorimer (1978) points to the convergence of discourse relating to class, sexuality and 'race' in the 1850s, and their subsequent elaboration in a wide variety of social contexts. These perceptions challenge the assumptions of cultural homogeneity.

Legal implementation of community relations policy and protection from racial discrimination began in 1965 and a summary is given below.

Community relations policy and race relations legislation

1943 – first Government consideration of racial discrimination legislation.

1962 – Government establishes non-statutory Commonwealth Immigrants Advisory Council (CIAC) with a focus on 'immigrant ' welfare and integration.

1964 – National Committee for Commonwealth Immigrants (NCCI) extends work of CIAC and supports establishment of a network of local committees.

1965 – *first Race Relations Act*
  – racial incitement a criminal offence, limited forms of direct racial discrimination a civil wrong, emphasis upon conciliation and friendly settlement through local conciliation committees and the Race Relations Board (RRB) – Act seen to have weak enforcement and needed to be extended.

→

1968 – *second Race Relations Act*
- direct racial discrimination provisions extended to cover public and private employment and housing, replacement of the NCCI with the Community Relations Commission (CRC) with task of encouraging 'harmonious community relations' through funding of local community relations councils (CRCs).

1968–75
- enforcement problems: discrimination difficult to prove, Act did not apply to effects of past discrimination or indirect discrimination, low number of complaints, no power to require evidence, cases took too long, were often not proven and remedies extremely limited. Limited success in influencing perceptions and behaviour through a declaration of public policy.

1976 – *third Race Relations Act*
- extension to cover indirect discrimination, sanction of promotional work on equal opportunities through codes of practice and investigations, encouragement of individual complaints by giving direct access to the legal process, provision for positive action in certain circumstances, Commission for Racial Equality (CRE) replaced RRB and CRC.

1976–90s
- problems: extension of law to cover indirect discrimination has not worked as the vast majority of cases heard are direct discrimination, long delays in CRE formal investigations due to poor planning, lack of focus and legal challenges, conflict between enforcement and promotional strategies in the CRE, individual complaints difficult due to lengthy procedures, low compensation and inadequately resourced legal representation.
- successes: increase in number of individual complaints substantial since 1976, CRE success in assisting complainants, evidence of widespread adoption of equal opportunity policies and practices in both the private and public sectors, particularly larger organisations, symbolic importance as a rallying point around which many campaigns have been organised and a measure for determining unacceptable behaviour.
- context: inadequate government funding, hostile judicial review (ruling out general investigations of specific bodies), culture (inside and outside the CRE) which attaches greater value to individual rights rather than to group/collective remedies.
- overall: failure to reduce real levels of racial discrimination irrefutable but the value of the Act in contributing to and stimulating policy development has been frequently cited.

2000 – *Race Relations (Amendment) Act* introduced a statutory obligation on all public agencies to eliminate racial discrimination and promote good community relations.

2003 – *Race Relations (Amendment) Act* introduced new definitions of indirect discrimination and harassment.[1]

2006
- *Racial and Religious Hatred Act* seeks to stop people from intentionally using threatening words or behaviour to stir up hatred against somebody because of what they believe.
- *Equality Act* Abolition of the Commission for Racial Equality and integration into the new Commission for Equality and Human Rights in 2007.

---

[1] This extended legal protection from racial harassment to school pupils amongst others, and widened the concept of indirect discrimination to include any policy or practice which puts racial or ethnic groups at a disadvantage.

In the UK the leading government agency concerned with antiracism, racial equality and multiculturalism, the Commission for Racial Equality, was abolished in 2007, in its final summing up of the state of inter-ethnic relations it said:

> Britain, despite its status as the fifth largest economy in the world, is still a place of inequality, exclusion and isolation. Segregation – residentially, socially and in the workplace – is growing. Extremism, both political and religious, is on the rise as people become disillusioned and disconnected from each other. Issues of identity have a new prominence in our social landscape and have a profound impact upon race relations in Britain. An ethnic minority British baby born today is sadly still more likely to go on to receive poor quality education, be paid less, live in substandard housing, be in poor health and be discriminated against in other ways than his or her white contemporaries. This persistent, longstanding inequality is quite simply unfair and unacceptable.
>
> (CRE 2007: 2)

It has been replaced by the new Commission for Equality and Human Rights with a much wider brief for different forms of social division. The Traveller Law Reform Project, along with many other organisations, thinks that the proposals will weaken existing protection for ethnic minorities, including Gypsies and Irish Travellers. They argue that Gypsies and Travellers benefited little from race equality legislation until the Race Relations (Amendment) Act was passed in 2000, that voluntary guidance does not work and that a focus on race equality is needed which may be lost in the harmonisation of equality legislation and agencies. In applying 'modernisation' and managerialist priorities to equality legislation, protection against discrimination and the statutory responsibilities of public authorities and agencies have been eroded through the principle of 'proportionality' (no need to take any action which might be disproportionate to the benefits of that action'). This is a move back to voluntarism, allowing public services to address issues of ethnicity, racism and related inequalities only as they see fit (Gillborn, 2008: 131–2).

English law and ethnicity

Sebastian Poulter (1986, 1992) has analysed the accommodation of ethnic minority customs and cultural pluralism in English law. In the context of law governing marriage and divorce, choice of school, court sentencing and prisoners' rights there is evidence of both separate and distinctive treatment and regulation being given to minority ethnic or religious groups, and situations where there is a refusal to recognise cultural diversity. Poulter (1992: 176) notes that English judges have emphasised that cultural tolerance is bounded by notions of reasonableness and public policy, and that minority customs and laws will not be recognised if they are considered repugnant or otherwise offend the conscience of the court. The adaptation of English law on an ad hoc basis leaves open the question as to where the limits of cultural diversity, for example on public policy grounds, are to be set. Poulter sets out a 'human rights' approach to such questions. The European Convention on Human Rights and the International Covenant on Civil and Political Rights provide a framework to assess whether demands for legal or public policy recognition of cultural practices are supported by an emphasis on general human rights, or whether such practices constitute a violation of human rights. The operation of Islamic personal law would then be resisted because of the risk that the rights of women would be violated through such practices as *talaq* divorces and forced marriages, whereas the unequal treatment of Muslim religion by blasphemy law could not be justified. International human rights law, it is argued, provides a basis for establishing the principles of both non-discrimination and differential treatment in that the latter can be justified by reference to genuine equality in the form of equal respect for religious and cultural values. Poulter recognises some of the problems with this approach including the level of generality which leads to difficulties in prescribing the limits of cultural pluralism in practice and the vulnerability to criticism of cultural bias from either those who favour assimilation or those who emphasise cultural relativity. The extent to which religious practices become controversial and are seen as appropriate for legal intervention is highly variable across religions. Where marginalised minority ethnic communities use religion to express their identity there is much greater likelihood that wider conflicts will be played out in this territory, and these may involve 'attacks' on specific minority practices on the one hand and demands for protection from religious discrimination by the communities on the other.

The debate over the recognition of Sharia law in the UK was recently thrown into the public spotlight when the Archbishop of Canterbury, Dr Rowan Williams said that the adoption of certain aspects of such law in the UK was unavoidable. He argued that adopting parts of Islamic Sharia law would help maintain social cohesion. For example, Muslims could choose to have marital disputes or financial matters dealt with in a Sharia court. He also said Muslims should not have to choose between 'the stark alternatives of cultural loyalty or state loyalty' (BBC News 7 Feb. 2008). Sharia law is Islam's legal system. It is derived from both the Koran, as the word of God, the example of the life of the prophet Muhammad, and fatwas – the rulings of Islamic scholars. But Sharia differs in one very important and significant way to the legal traditions of the Western world: it governs, or at least informs, every aspect of the life of a Muslim. Western law confines itself largely to matters relating to crime, contract, civil relationships and individual rights, whereas Sharia is more extensive. Sharia rulings have been developed to help Muslims understand how they should lead every aspect of their lives according to God's wishes. In two important areas British law has incorporated religious legal considerations. British food regulations allow meat to be slaughtered according to Jewish and Islamic practices, and this has become a touchstone issue for both communities. Secondly, the Treasury has approved Sharia-compliant financial products such as mortgages and investments. Islam forbids interest on the basis that it is money unjustly earned. These products are said by supporters to meet the needs of modern life in a way that fits the faith (BBC News 2008). Sharia law courts have been operating in the UK for some time. The Islamic Sharia Council opened in 1982 and has given advice on everything from inheritance settlements to whether or not Muslim women are allowed to wear wigs. But the vast majority of their cases are to do with divorce, and in particular with releasing women from bad or forced Islamic marriages. The divorce applications stem from the misuse of Islamic laws on marriage and divorce by husbands. Sheikh Sayeed, president of the council, said

> In every situation our motto is: reconciliation first. So we try to reconcile, but in cases where a marriage was enforced on a girl against her wishes, against her own opinion, we don't want to negotiate. What we do is, we try to make their guardians, their parents, understand the Islamic position, and also we tell them what is the position of British law on marriage.

Najma Ebrahim, a former coordinator with the Muslim Women's Helpline, which received 2000 calls a year, 70–80 per cent of which are from women with marital problems, says the council is providing a vital service (Bell 2008).

Limitations of national approaches

Each country across the globe has specific and differing migration histories, patterns of ethnic relations and forms of racism, for example we can contrast the UK as discussed above and post-Apartheid South Africa. National ideologies and ways of dealing and thinking about each of these matters do form an appropriate agenda for research and investigation, but globalisation, contemporary migrations, growing trans-national ethnicities and international politics and law provide a set of conditions which mean that it is impossible to explain contemporary events and outcomes without a wider focus. The development of and study of exclusively national models of migration, ethnic relations and racism has been described as one of the 'main barriers' to social science understanding (Castles 2000: 17) and traditional models and accounts are in many ways inadequate. Although ethnic disadvantage in such important spheres as housing and education is still mostly analysed and remedied at the national level, Karen Phalet and Antel Örkény's (2001) comparative account of Dutch and Hungarian ethnic relations illustrates the importance of identifying structural changes at the trans-national level, the articulation of global market forces within local networks and trans-national forms of political identification and action.

Conclusion

This chapter has explored the linkages between ethnicity, migration and racism. Separated typologies of ethnicity, post-war migration flows and regional racisms have been developed in this field of social science but often with unequal weight being given to each of these processes. This chapter has examined the implications of bringing these typologies together and the opportunities and pitfalls of analysis using such frameworks at regional and national levels. The terrible contemporary power of these processes is evident across the globe. The link between undocumented migration and contemporary patterns of slavery is well documented and examples from Australia, Japan and China were used to illustrate the evidence of human trafficking. The increasing levels of conflict and hostility between Israel and Palestine focussed on the Gaza Strip illustrate the transition from a complex cosmopolitan order into segregating, ethno-racially divided sets of communities with expulsions, exiles and evictions central to this process. If the prospects for the creation of peace and a Palestinian state free from racial domination seem poor, the prospects for the resurrection of a Tibetan state free from Chinese racial domination seem even worse. The impact of Chinese ideologies of national and racial superiority is most tellingly felt in Tibet where migration, settlement and occupation are used as weapons of racial domination, together with entrenched hostility to ethnic, cultural, linguistic and religious difference. The central importance of understanding the linkages between racism, migration and ethnicity is also necessary even where there have been many decades of initiatives aimed at addressing these issues. The problems the UK still faces 40 years after the first race relations legislation was passed include high levels of ethno-racial inequality and segregation, rising right-wing extremism and mass evidence of racial hostility and violence. The nature and extent of racist violence in the UK and the EU, together with global evidence of ethnic minorities under current threat of violence and genocide across the globe, are the subject for the next chapter.

End of chapter activity

Compare and contrast the linkages between ethnicity, racism and migration in Palestine and Tibet using the two resources below as a starting point:

Adri Nieuwhof (2008) A Palestinian action plan to combat Israeli racism, http://electronicintifada.net/v2/article9987.shtml

International Campaign for Tibet (2000) Jampa, the story of racism in Tibet, Washington/Amsterdam: ICT available at www.savetibet.org/

Further reading

United Nations (2002) *International Migration,* **New York: UN**. This report provides a contemporary analysis of global patterns of migration.

Sage, J. and Kasten, L. (eds) (2006) *Enslaved, true stories of modern day slavery,* **London: Palgrave**. The voices of the enslaved are heard here, giving biographical insight into the experiences of those people subject to the varying forms of contemporary slavery across the globe.

Goldberg, D. T. (2008) *The Threat of Race, reflections on racial neoliberalism,* **Oxford: Blackwell**. This is a contemporary classic in its field revealing the process of racial domination at the core of selected contemporary states and international regions.

Winant, H. (2000) *The World is a Ghetto,* **Oxford: Basic Books**. This sets out to provide an account of racism as a world-system and provides a highly useful set of historical and contemporary argument and material.

References

Anderson, B., et al. (2006) *Fair Enough? Central and East European migrants in low wage employment*, York: Joseph Rowntree Foundation.

Banton, M. (1985) *Promoting Racial Harmony*, Cambridge: Cambridge University Press.

BBC News (2008) 'Sharia law is unavoidable', 7 Feb.

Bell, D. (2008) 'The view from inside a Sharia court', BBC News, 11 Feb, http://news.bbc.co.uk/1/hi/uk/7238890.stm.

Benyon, R. (2006) 'Race and immigration: is it the end of the affair?', www.jcwi.org.uk/policy/uklaw/raceandimmigration_spring06.html.

Bevan, V. (1986) *The Development of British Immigration Law*, London: Croom Helm.

Bloch, A. and Schuster, L. (2002) 'Asylum and welfare: contemporary debates', *Critical Social Policy*, 22, pp. 393–413.

Citizens Advice Bureau (CAB) (2006) *Shaming destitution: NASS section 4 support for failed asylum seekers who are temporarily unable to leave the UK*, by R. Dunstan, London: CAB.

Castles, S. (2000) *Ethnicity and Globalization*, London: Sage

Commission for Racial Equality (CRE). 2007. *A Lot Done, A Lot To Do*, London: CRE.

Craig, G. (2007) '"Cunning, unprincipled, loathsome": the racist tail wags the welfare dog', *Journal of Social Policy*, 36, 4, pp. 605–623.

Daly, M. (2003) 'Governance and social policy', *Journal of Social Policy*, 32, pp. 113–128.

Duvall, B. and Jordan, F. (2002) 'Immigration, asylum and welfare: the European context', *Critical Social Policy*, 22, pp. 498–517.

Duvell, B. and Jordan, F. (2003) *Migration, the boundaries of equality and justice*, Cambridge: Polity.

Eriksen, T. H. (1993) *Ethnicity and Nationalism*, London: Pluto Press.

Fitzpatrick, P. (2005) 'Public finds, benefits and tax credits', *Welfare Rights Bulletin*, 185.

Fitzpatrick, P. (2007) 'Benefits for Bulgarian and Romanian nationals', *Welfare Rights Bulletin*, 196.

Gilbert, A. and Koser, K. (2003) *Information dissemination to potential asylum applicants in countires of origin and transit*, London: Home Office, Findings 220.

Gillborn, D. (2008) *Racism and Education, confidence or conspiracy*, London: Routledge.

Goldberg, D. T. (2008) *The Threat of Race, reflections on racial neoliberalism*, Oxford: Blackwell.

Hayter, T. (2004) *Open Borders: the case against immigration controls*, London: Pluto Press.

Hess, J. M. (2006) *Statelessness and the State: Tibetans, citizenship, and nationalist activism in a transnational world*, International Migration, 44, 1, pp. 79–103.

Humantrafficking (2006) *Supply and Demand*, www.humantrafficking.org/issues/6/.

International Campaign for Tibet (ICT) (2000) *Jampa, the story of racism in Tibet*, Washington/Amsterdam: ICT, https://nl.savetibet.org/documents/document.php?id=13.

Joint Committee on Human Rights (2007) *The Treatment of Asylum Seekers*, 10th report of Session 2006-07, HL Paper 81-I, HC 60-I.

Law, I. (2008) 'Racism, ethnicity, migration and social security' in J. Millar (ed.) *Understanding Social Security*, Bristol: Policy Press, 2nd edition.

Lewis, H. (2007) *Destitution in Leeds*, York: Joseph Rowntree Charitable Trust.

Lister, R. (2007) 'Social Justice: meanings and politics', *Benefits*, 15, 2, pp. 113–25.

Lorimer, D. (1978) *Colour, Class and the Victorians, English attitudes to the Negro in the mid-nineteenth century*, Leicester: Leicester University Press.

Miles, R. (1993) *Racism after 'Race Relations'*, London: Routledge.

Morris, L. (2007) New Labour's Community of Rights: welfare, immigration and asylum, *Journal of Social Policy*, 36, 1, pp. 39–57.

Nieuwhof, A. (2008) *A Palestinian Action Plan to Combat Israeli Racism*, http://electronicintifada.net/v2/article9987.shtml.

Office to Monitor and Combat Trafficking in Persons (2008) *Trafficking in Persons Report* 4 June, USA, www.state.gov/g/tip/rls/tiprpt/2008/.

Phalet, K. and Örkény, A. (eds) (2001) *Ethnic Minorities and Inter-Ethnic Relations in Context, a Dutch–Hungarian comparison*, Aldershot: Ashgate.

Poulter, S. (1986) *English Law and Ethnic Minority Customs*, London: Butterworths.

Poulter, S. (1992) 'The limits of legal, cultural and religious pluralism', in B. Hepple and E. Szyszczak (eds) *Discrimination, the limits of the law*, London: Mansell.

Refugee Council (2007) *Parliamentary Briefing on the UK Borders Bill*, www.refugeecouncil.org.uk/policy/briefings/2007/borders.htm.

Robinson, V. and Segrott, J. (2002) *Understanding the decision making of asylum seekers*, London: Home Office, Research Study 243.

Sage, J. and Kasten, L. (eds) (2006) *Enslaved, true stories of modern day slavery*, London: Palgrave.

Saggar, S. (1992) *Race and Public Policy*, Aldershot: Avebury.

Sales, R. (2007) *Understanding Immigration and Refugee Policy*, Bristol: Policy Press.

Shlaim, A. (2009) 'How Israel brought Gaza to the brink of humanitarian catastrophe', *Guardian*, 7 Jan.

Somerville, W. (2007) *Immigration under New Labour*, Bristol: Policy Press.

Spencer, S., Ruhs, M., Anderson, B. and Rogaly, B. (2007) *Migrants' Lives beyond the Workplace; the experiences of Central and East Europeans in the UK*, York: Joseph Rowntree Foundation.

United Nations (2002) *International Migration*, New York: UN.

Weiner, M. (ed.) (2004) *Race, Ethnicity and Migration in Modern Japan*, London: Routledge.

Williams, F. (1989) *Social Policy, a critical introduction*, Cambridge: Polity.

Winant, H. (2000) *The World is a Ghetto*, Oxford: Basic Books.

6   Racist violence and racism reduction

Key issues in this chapter:

- The interlocking environments which promote racist hostility and associated violence
- The nature and extent of racist violence in Europe
- The strategy and tactics of racism reduction

At the end of this chapter you should be able to:

- Build an explanation of racist violence that addresses macro, meso and micro factors
- Understand the varying motives of those carrying out racist violence
- Conceptualise and compare anti-semitism and anti-Muslimism
- Identify a range of possible interventions that may be useful in tackling racist violence

Introduction

Much of this book has been concerned with the experiences, subjugations and naked violence ethnic and racial minorities face within the territory of dominating nation states across the globe. This chapter looks more closely at three dimensions of this question. Firstly, persisting patterns of contemporary racist violence at the heart of Western Europe which belie modernist conceptions of progress, enlightenment and civilisation are examined. Why is racist violence so durable? How can we build an adequate explanation for these processes and what are the range of motives driving these acts of violence? As the last chapter indicated, this project of regionalising European racism is akin to the analytical process of 'provincialising' post-colonial Europe (Chakrabarty 2000), it is just one region of many. Secondly, what is the evidence of the nature and extent of racial hostility and associated violence across

Europe? Anti-Roma, anti-Jew and anti-Muslim hostility and violence is explored here in detail as they, along with anti-black racism, are the dominant forms in Europe. The shape of Europe's racial crisis in the face of rising racial conflict is also identified. Thirdly, what is to be done? And why are the responses of nation states so ineffective? This section explores global, European and UK strategies, frameworks and initiatives aimed to challenging and reducing levels of such aggression, intimidation and brutality.

Racial and ethnic hostility, discrimination and exclusion take many forms, but broadly three categories can be identified. Firstly, the most severe acts involving mass societal aggression such as the annihilation of native peoples in North America, South Africa and Australia, the Nazi Holocaust, plantation slavery or more recent massacres of Tutsi by Hutu in Rwanda and ethnic cleansing of Kosovar Albanians by Serbs. Secondly, ethnic exclusion and discrimination which involves denial of access to societal opportunities and rewards, for example employment, education, housing, health and justice. Many instances of such exclusion and discrimination have been documented in Europe by the European Fundamental Rights Agency (FRA) affecting most harshly Roma, Sinti, Gypsy and Traveller groups. Poor mental and physical health, lower levels of educational attainment, restricted access to work and lower income levels have been linked to poor housing conditions for many of these groups. Lack of social rights has also constrained available opportunities for political participation. These processes are examined more closely in the next chapter. Thirdly, use of derogatory, abusive verbal language or forms of representation which are felt to be offensive (e.g. anti-Muslim Danish cartoons), which together with racist jokes, use of Nazi insignia and unwitting stereotyping and perjorative phrases may all constitute lesser forms of ethnic and racist hostility.

More broadly in the UK and across the EU diverse forms of racist hostility provide a constant source of tension and conflict including, anti-gypsyism, Islamophobia, anti-black racism and anti-semitism. Despite significant developments in policy and procedures across many institutions, there is a 'racial crisis' where increased understanding and evidence of the nature and extent of racist violence has failed to lead to any fundamental change, for example as shown in the UK (see Key concepts box below). Sources of inter-ethnic and inter-cultural conflict in the UK are cultural, political and economic and include opposition to the recognition of difference and super-diversity (for example opposing the use of minority languages in schools), contested control of territory and land (particularly for Gypsy, Roma and Traveller people) and disputes over access to social housing, schools and other resources. Continuing hostility, hatred and grievance have been suffered by refugees, asylum seekers and other migrant groups in many national contexts. More widely, everyday cultural ignorance, miscommunication and misrecognition of difference lead to offensive behaviour, affronts to dignity and lack of respect which have all led to various forms of conflict (Law 2008; also see discussion on the triggers to conflict in Chapter 4).

Explanations and motives

How do we explain and account for patterns of racist violence? This section seeks to answer this question through, firstly, building a multi-level examination of causal factors, secondly, identifying key aspects of the contexts and environments in which we live that make violence more likely, and lastly, through identifying the various motives that drive individual's actions.

Explanations

Explanations for racist violence require accounts which are able to draw together micro-pyschological processes, individual and group experiences, competition and socialisation, together with structural power relations. Racism has a number of key elements.

Key concepts: Six core elements of racism

- the signification of race characteristics to identify a collectivity,
- the attribution of such a group with negative biological or cultural characteristics
- the designation of boundaries to specify inclusion and exclusion
- variation in form in that it may be a relatively coherent theory or a loose assembly of images and explanations
- its practical adequacy; in that it successfully 'makes sense' of the world for those who articulate it
- its pleasures; an unearned easy feeling of superiority and the facile cementing of group identity on the fragile basis of arbitrary antipathy

The everyday practical adequacy and emotional appeal of racism for many people indicate that such attitudes and behaviour may be highly resistant to interventions seeking to reduce this hostility. The racism of the 'East End' granny may seem perfectly logical to her in the face of perceived threats to the job and housing opportunites of her own kin from incoming migrants, however objectively wrong she might be. Her logic may then be impervious to attempts to counter these perceived myths by, for example, presenting an alternative 'truth' about the real facts of how the labour market or housing market is working. The violent acts or verbal abuse of ethnic minorities and migrants of her young grandchildren may then also seem perfectly logical in the context of such family values, and may indeed be expected, encouraged and congratulated.

Racism takes many forms and includes mass societal aggression and genocide, structures of exclusion and discrimination and derogatory and abusive forms of behaviour, representation and language. A recent review of contemporary evidence of racist violence across 15 EU member states examined explanations of race hate and proposed a framework for understanding this process (FRA 2005: 187–93):

1 meta explanations, those which synthesise evidence from a range of studies into an overarching account and which draw on dominant theoretical explanations (such as competition theory) for racist crime, and adopt these theories to explain violent racist offending;

2 meso (contextual) explanations, which can be read as local, situated, contextual readings of why racist violence occurs among certain groups and in certain settings; and

3 micro (social psychological) explanations, which are explanations for racist violence that rest with the individual.

International economic, political and social processes provide a set of factors which are broadly outside the control of local authorities and community groups, but these may be highly significant in determining local patterns of racist violence. International hostilities including 9/11, 7/7 and the 'War on Terror', the Israeli–Palestinian conflict, and other conflicts which may be driving the movement of asylum-seekers and refugees may all be relevant here in increasing local tensions and perceptions of insecurity, threat and risk (FRA 2005). International economic restructuring reflected in local patterns of economic decline and loss of jobs may heighten local economic insecurities and associated conflict. But there appears to be no direct correlation between patterns of unemployment and economic activity and patterns of racist violence:

> the explanatory value of theories that are embedded in the idea of competition falls somewhat short when we consider that racist violence emerges in times of economic prosperity and political stability, and when immigrant populations are not increasing or changing their profiles.
>
> (FRA 2005: 188)

The increasing international links between extreme right groups and the expansion of internet newsgroups and other forms of web-based networks as a vehicle to mobilise and disseminate racist ideology may also have immediate local effects. The importance of media reporting of international, national and local news and events as one key factor in shaping the racist attitudes of 11- to 21-year-olds in the UK has been confirmed in recent research (Lemos 2005). Young people in this study expressed their hostility around a number of key themes including:

■ security fears/terrorism: 'Afghans – because they hijack planes and kill people';
■ too many incomers, 'asylum seekers – there's too many of them';
■ preferential treatment, 'Pakistanis, Muslims, Indians, Iraqis – because they do nothing at all for our country and get free housing, food and they have their own country', 'Refugees … they get more than us'.

The historical cultural reservoir of nationally shaped racism is highly significant, providing a persisting repertoire of hostile images, perceptions of superiority and legitimation for brutality and violence against many different groups, particularly the 'old' racism of the British Empire, British racial superiority and colonial domination. The decline of Empire resonates with the narratives of being neglected by public authorities and material decline through which poor white local communities may express their feelings of anger and resentment. Also, the output of the extreme right may seek to invoke these 'backward-looking' historical connections in order to reinvigorate contemporary hostility. The significance of national political debate and government policies may be paramount in focussing and amplifying local tensions, and there is evidence of a direct connection here. Political advocacy and implementation of controls on immigration and the targeting of debate on specific groups has in many national contexts led to significant increases in racist violence, for example Germany, Sweden and the UK (Bowling and Phillips 2002: 116). The extent to which racist hostility is permitted in both public debate and through the failure of government responses may parallel the sanctioning and failure to condemn amongst local communities. Equally it may be argued that condemnation of racist hostility and cultural racism in political speeches and in the news media, together with effective agency responses to race hate, may all promote wider community condemnation of such behaviour. But this is not the whole story, and there are many other intervening factors which need to be considered in order to explain differing levels of racist violence across different neighbourhoods and local areas within the same national context.

Local patterns are highly difficult to explain. For example, in one city in Northern England, Leeds, the City Council first adopted a Racial Harassment Policy in 1986. Evidence from the early years of that policy showed a sporadic pattern of racist violence being reported across most inner and outer estates and areas, which did not lend itself to easy explanation in terms of competition, territorialism, newness of household movements or activities of extreme right groups. Twenty years later, current levels of reported incidents of race hate in Leeds at between 4000 and 5000 across the city continue to indicate the durability, geographical spread and significance of such violence. Reported incidents have hugely increased during this period, which confirms significant improvements in public reporting, staff awareness and agency recording practices. However, reported incidents are acknowledged to be a fraction of the total number, with real levels of race hate incidents likely to be upwards of 10,000 per year in Leeds (Hemmerman et al. 2007). There is increasing evidence of racist violence in both rural and prosperous settings and patterns of racial victimisation show that this behaviour is not confined to poor inner city estates. Local disputes, local identities and informal networks may all be relevant in accounting for different rates of racist victimisation between different areas. Factors which strengthen the bonds between families, including declining economic opportunities and isolation from social networks outside the local area, can strengthen hostility to external threats and dangers, and incomers. Strong communities may often be highly exclusionary. A key to understanding how this process works is to examine local norms, values and sanctions to conform operating across a range of networks including families, friends/peer groups and other informal forms of association. There is a strong track record of research on racist violence in the UK (Gadd *et al.* 2005, Ray and Smith 2004, Webster 1998, Bowling 1998, Hesse *et al.* 1992) and these studies have sought to examine the relevance of these different types of explanation in North

Staffordshire, Manchester, Keighley, Newham and Waltham Forest respectively. This track record of research verifies that it is vital to address all these three levels of explanation in order to provide an adequate sociological account, and these are now examined in turn. An example of a recent study given below provides an explanation of racist hostility, evidence of the impact on victims and evaluation of institutional responses. The articulation and mobilisation of white resentment is a central factor here (see also in discussion of 'white backlash' culture below).

Racist hostility and racist victimisation in a Northern England city

This study arose from a set of local agency concerns about increasing racist hostility and violence in an area of low-income social housing in Leeds, together with a strong sense that what is needed is, firstly, a better understanding of how racist hostility works and, secondly, more effective action to respond to this highly durable problem. Fieldwork with victims, residents and agency staff to examine these issues was carried out by Ian Law, Lou Hemmerman, Ala Sirriyeh and Jenny Simms from the Centre for Ethnicity and Racism Studies at the University of Leeds from January to June 2007.

- Racist hostility and violence in Leeds has proved to be highly durable despite increased levels of reporting and improvements in policies and practices of relevant agencies including the local authority and the police.

- Dealing with individuals, by either supporting victims of racist violence or taking action against perpetrators has left community-wide patterns of racist hostility largely unchanged.

- Victims of racist violence identified widespread hostility in the area combining overt aggressive racism particularly from children and young people, more covert everyday racist talk from older people and intimidatory extreme right activity, as well as some positive interaction with local people.

- The drivers of racist hostility include white resentment of black and minority ethnic families' ability to access social housing, jealousy of lifestyle and possessions, and perceptions of unfair preferential treatment. Strong local family/community networks enforce hostility, hound families out and maintain an atmosphere of fear and intimidation. Poverty, abandonment and disempowerment and associated shame, rage and anger were often channelled into racist hostility and violence.

- Asian groups were the most unwelcome and hated in this area and black African families were highly visible key targets of racist hostility.

- Victims identified the failure of agencies to respond effectively given the scale of widespread racist hostility and the weakness of enforcement processes.

- Poor levels of service to victims and poorly implemented race hate policy together with a strong desire for more effective work with local communities were stressed by local agencies.

Source: Hemmerman *et al.* 2007.

Examination of individual life stories, biographies, emotions and intimate relations may all highlight key patterns across the large group of people in society responsible for acts of race hate. David Gadd *et al.* (2005: 9) in examining a sample of 15 perpetrators' life stories identify that they reveal:

patterns of severe, occasionally extreme, material and emotional deprivation combined with, or compounded by, histories of other kinds of offending behaviour, criminalisation, domestic violence, mental illness, and the abuse of drugs and alcohol

(2005: 9)

This group of young offenders are described as the 'usual suspects', a normal cross-section of those frequently arrested by the police, and as being young, poor, severely damaged, vulnerable, socially marginal and prone to violent behaviour. Whether such an account would be applicable to all those responsible for the thousands of race hate incidents logged every year is highly questionable. Gadd and other researchers (Sibbitt 1997) have confirmed that racist attitudes held by perpetrators of violent race hate crime are very similar to the attitudes held by 'ordinary people of all ages' across the locality. The scale of racist violence, acts of racial discrimination and racist attitudes indicates that many ordinary people placed in specific contexts are likely to be responsible for race hate, in addition to the marginal group identified above.

Environments

There are a complex, wide-ranging set of causes and motivations for racist violence. Identifying potential factors which make racist hostility and violence more likely, more acceptable and more durable involves consideration of a complex set of interlocking environments.

- *Virtual environment*: internet sites and networks which may be influential in encouraging racist violence.
- *International environment:* conflicts and events including ethnic and racial conflicts, acts of terrorism, which heighten local perceptions of insecurity and fear and which are used to rationalise racist violence.
- *National environment:* political and media messages on migration, ethnicity and racism which shape racial hostility.
- *Economic environment: factors* including patterns of unemployment and low pay, economic decline, exclusion from new economic opportunities.
- *Educational environment:* factors that make racist violence more likely such as patterns of underachievement, exclusion, racial and ethnic segregation, lack of explicit focus in schools, failure to challenge racism through school curriculum and ethos.
- *Physical environment:* features of local area that make racist violence attractive to perpetrators such as geographical isolation, lack of natural surveillance, layout of estates, poor lighting, lack of leisure facilities.
- *Family environment:* factors where racist hostility is socialised and legitimated across generations and genders, with old/young, female/male attitudes and talk promoting racism in different ways.
- *Local environment:* social/community factors, such as the balance between racist violence 'preventors' and 'promoters', and the level and nature of social interaction across ethnic/racial lines.

- *Adult/youth environment:* active local cultures/sub-cultures, values and norms of peer groups which may encourage racist violence.
- *Ideologically driven groups:* e.g. far right groups, which encourage racist violence.
- *Criminal environment:* which may provide tools, knowledge, motivation, peer pressure which knowingly or unwittingly promote/incite racist violence.

Within these environments, groups and individuals make specific decisions to carry out racist violence and here there may be a range of different types of motives operating. Changing justifications for persisting racist attitudes and shifting target groups make racism highly dynamic. Motivations may change and develop as patterns of violence progress.

Motives

Race hate may be the product of a mix of motives which are hard to disentangle in real situations (Law 2007). This section seeks to operationalise Michael Mann's (2005) historical and global evidence on perpetrators' motives in relation to racial and ethnic violence and examine their application to local contexts. Mann's life-long sociological work has been to provide a global account of the sources and operation of social power (1986, 1993, and third volume in progress). He has applied this to explaining ethnic cleansing (2005). Seven common groups of motivating factors can be derived from Mann, which if applied to contemporary race hate would render a typology, or categorisation, of motives as follows:

Typology of race hate motives

Ideological:	'because it fits with our world view'
Bigots:	'because we hate them'
Emotions:	'because it's fun'
Criminal-materialist:	'because we want/get something'
Territorial-political:	'because it's 'our' place'
Social group norms:	'because we all think it's OK'
Bureaucractic/disciplined/military:	'because we're told to'

Sources: Mann 2005, Law 2007.

Ideological

This category covers people willing to risk or inflict death or serious harm in pursuit of their values, with the perpetrator often protesting that he is the victim acting in some form of self-defence. This has been termed value-rational action by Max Weber (1978: I, 25). A recent review of research on perpetrators' motives by Sarah Isal (2005) strongly challenges popular assumptions that see most race hate incidents as being carried out by 'mission offenders', and instead suggests a continuum of motives ranging from political extreme right activity to neighbour disputes. Gadd *et al.* (2005) confirm that, for their sample of perpetrators, ideological racism was rarely, if ever, the sole factor motivating their offending behaviour. In certain localities such 'mission offenders' may, however, be key players, as Roger Hewitt (2005: 55) describes in his study of some council estates in London which contain,

> a core of violent racist adolescents and their adult mentors, plus a small supporting cast of racial bigots located within a wider pool of people who were at odds with the local political order in which, to them, minority concerns were given precedence.

Here, Hewitt seeks to delineate differences between groups involved in race hate. Some of the 'adult mentors' may be ideologically driven individuals who may be responsible for inciting race hate by other, younger people. A distinction is drawn by Mann and Hewitt between this group and bigots.

Bigots

Rather than pursuing higher political or ideological goals, bigots are obstinate, intolerant adherents of more populist, mundane or casual prejudices drawn from their immediate social context and social encounters. In their recent study of 15 race hate perpetrators in North Staffordshire, Gadd *et al.* (2005) found that the overwhelming majority were not 'hardened race-haters'. They had similar views to the wider community in which they lived and many felt justified, if not compelled, to project their misfortunes in dangerous and intimidating ways onto minority groups. Here a white backlash may be identified with perceptions and widespread talk of unfairness.

> Widespread talk about unfairness creates a substantial obstacle to tackling racism. It has created a screen which filters out the possibility of some whites fully understanding the meaning of racial harassment, and generates an almost impermeable defensiveness.
>
> (Hewitt 1996: 57)

These views may also be evident in hostile local reactions to anti-racist and multi-cultural policies and practices developed by local schools and other agencies. Race hate rage may also be incited by national and local media reporting of migration, racism and ethnic diversity, e.g. 'get tough' migration policies, or local media reporting of racist attacks by Asians in Oldham which incited racist violence by white youths. This wider context may draw ordinary people into an escalating process of dispute, conflict and violence.

Emotional violence

As stated above, expressing racism may bring an unearned easy feeling of superiority. Pleasure, joy and triumphant emotions may for some drive the process of race hate rage, particularly when preceded by a sense of personal humiliation or emotional anxiety. The shame, envy and disgust experienced by living in vulnerable, insecure economic and social settings, together with both a sense of personal failure and a sense that others are receiving more favourable opportunities may all facilitate race hate (Ray and Smith 2004). Such violence may provide a temporary release from such anxieties. As Gadd *et al.* (2005:1) argue, migrant and minority ethnic households may provide 'an uncomfortable reminder of local white people's inability to secure decent lives for themselves and their families'.

The role of alcohol, drugs or other methods of reducing inhibitions in the expression of emotional racism has been identified by a number of studies as a significant contributory factor (Bowling and Phillips 2002: 117).

Criminal-materialist

Some race hatred may be motivated by direct gain or benefit from such actions, including stealing personal property or protecting ongoing criminal activities from outside scrutiny. The significance of informal local networks may be central in determining community capacities for informal justice, informal crime control and informal security. Defensive protection from outsiders and protecting criminal activity through oppressive enforcement of local rules of trustworthiness and non-cooperation with state authorities may provide a rationale for pre-emptive and pro-active strikes against incoming households who may be seen to be un-amenable to local control. Burglary and vandalism were used in the Leeds example (see box above) to target black families who were thought by white residents/gangs to be giving information to the police on criminal activities in the local area. Here race hate is highly instrumental, and may be used as an aggravating factor in criminal activity (also see the box below on the links between an Italian criminal network, the Camorra, local authorities, property developers and anti-Roma violence).

Territorial-political

Strong attachment/loyalty to streets, estates, localities or indeed national territory and their associated social and political identities may provide a further instrumental motive for families and groups of young people to 'defend' space from potential 'invaders'. For example a local council report relating to the areas researched in the Leeds study confirmed that:

> Empirical evidence has clearly identified that on certain estates on specific streets there effectively exist 'no-go areas' for black and minority ethnic families due to the level of intimidation and harassment families have received. All monitoring systems have identified this trend.
>
> (Hemmerman *et al.* 2007: 7)

Lack of engagement in any form of shared activities with a common goal (such as community, youth or sporting activities) and lack of personal relationships between groups (such as friendship, partnering or neighbouring networks) may exacerbate such forms of race hate, informal racial and ethnic segregation. National and local political leaderships may also play a key role in either shaping racial hostility or reducing political legitimacy for such conflict. Lack of success in managing conflicting concerns between established residents over competition, e.g. for housing, and migrants and minorities over safety and security may provide durable conditions for the perpetuation of racial hostility.

Social group norms

Here, an informal (peer group, gang, family network) or more formal grouping may expect conformity with race hate behaviour and threaten withdrawal of protection/support or other sanctions if this expectation is not met. Recent research by Geoff Dench, Kate Gavron and Michael Young (2006) has highlighted key linkages between white residents' hostility and resentment of new migrants in the East End of London and the strength of family and localist loyalties, identifying the 'East End granny' as being the social type which expresses highest levels of racial hostility, precisely because it 'makes sense' in their world of social meanings. Roger Hewitt (1996: 57) has identified that socialisation by families into racist behaviour was less important than peer group culture and behaviour: 'Young people have their own culture of racist talk and actions, and this culture should be tackled directly'. So, youth cultures/sub-cultures may reproduce forms of racist hostility which amplify or run counter to family/parental attitudes and actions.

Bureaucratic/disciplined/military power

Legitimate organisational authorities may require routine compliance with race hate, ethnic cleansing and genocide in modern societies where such action becomes habitual, mechanised and impersonal. Armies, police forces and para-militaries are the main agencies here and their role has often been decisive in the worst examples of mass racial and ethnic cleansing such as in the Nazi Holocaust and Rwanda (Mann 2005 and see Chapter 4).

Such typologies tend to be static, 'freezing' motives at the point of violent action (Mann 2005: 29), but they also play a useful conceptual role in disentangling some of the complex drivers and forms of racist violence. Such an account is also more likely to be able to point to the range of different interventions that may be needed to challenge such hostility and violence in particular local contexts. To understand race hate we need to be sensitive to the interplay of key explanatory factors, the different articulation given to contexts and motives in individual biographies and local communities and key pressure points and triggers to events and incidents.

Evidence

European trends and anti-Roma violence

Across Europe recorded racist crime, anti-semitic crime and right-wing extremist driven crime is on the increase (FRA 2008a). In the 11 member states that collect enough data to examine trends there was a general upward trend in recorded racist crime in the period 2000–2006 (Denmark, Germany, France, Ireland, Austria [very slight], Slovakia, Finland, the UK), and also between 2005 and 2006 (Germany, Ireland, Austria, Slovakia, Finland, Sweden, the UK). Anti-semitic crime was also increasing between 2001 and 2006 in countries which did record this data, including France, Sweden and the UK, and crime with an extremist right-wing motive also showed a general upward trend in France and Germany between 2000 and 2006.

Due to poor state practices in monitoring and documenting racist violence, non-governmental organisations continue to play a key role in bringing this evidence to light and they confirm three key trends in this field. Firstly, increasing attacks against Muslim people and Muslim targets; secondly, increasing racist violence and crime against newer vulnerable immigrant groups including irregular migrants, asylum-seekers and refugees; and thirdly, continuing violence and abuse of the Roma, including abuse by state officials, for example the police, particularly in Central and Southern Europe. An example of recent anti-Roma violence is examined below. This highlights a number of significant factors:

- The mass forced eviction of Roma from camps and their homes in this locality due to repeated fire bombing, beatings and attacks by a mob of 300–400 people;
- The strength of popular support for such violence;
- The failure of criminal justice agencies to respond effectively, only managing to round Roma families up into one large camp for their protection and then facilitating their further evacuation out of the Naples area;
- The complexity of inter-related motives including criminal-materialist and territorial-political.

Anti-Roma Violence in Naples, Italy

On the evening of 10 May 2008, a young Italian mother of a six-month-old baby living on the Principe di Napoli Street in the suburban district of Ponticelli in the municipality of Naples, found a young girl – later identified as a 16-year-old Roma living in one of the city's camps – in her apartment carrying her baby in her arms. She shouted at the girl and snatched her baby from her and the intruder tried to run away. On getting down the stairs, the woman's father who had heard her shouting for help engaged and caught the Roma girl and in a short time many of their neighbours converged on the scene. Only a timely intervention by the police saved the intruder from the crowd threatening to lynch her. Soon afterwards, she was charged with attempted kidnapping and unlawful intru-

Attacks on the Roma in Naples
Source: Reuters

sion into a private home and transferred to a nearby correctional centre for minors. According to the media, the Roma girl involved had left a community based in Monte Procida where she had been staying since 26 April after having been arrested for stealing.

There was an immediate backlash against the Roma in Ponticelli, and law enforcement agents started patrolling the area to discourage attacks against Roma camps. Three hours after the supposed kidnap attempt, about 20 Italian residents of Ponticelli attacked a Romanian labourer returning home from work; he was beaten and stabbed in one shoulder. Fearing possible attacks against them, the

→

Roma on their part organised themselves to keep watch over their shacks and alert the residents in case of an attack. On the afternoon of 12 May, three Italian boys set the entrance to a Roma camp in the district on fire after pouring petrol around it. Meanwhile small groups of Roma who lived in isolated shacks in the district started abandoning their homes and during the night between 12 and 13 May, unknown persons set a number of these isolated shacks on fire. In the days following the supposed kidnap attempt, numerous attacks were carried out against the Roma. On the afternoon of 13 May, a group of about 300 to 400 locals led by women launched an assault against one of the biggest Roma camps in the district, home to 48 Roma families. Using wooden and metal clubs, the attackers succeeded in pulling down the metal fence. Once inside the camp, they shouted insults and threats, threw stones against shacks and caravans, and overturned some cars. At about the same time an abandoned building which until two days before had been used by six Roma families was set on fire. In two separate incidents on the same day, two Roma boys were beaten. Two Roma women were harassed and driven out of a supermarket close to one of the big camps while they were shopping. On the same day, law enforcement agents decided to evacuate smaller camps and concentrate the former residents in a bigger camp with a police cordon around it, in order to protect them better. During the night of the 13 and 14 May, another camp in the district was evacuated and the 60 persons living in it were moved to a school on the opposite side of the city. Others left their shacks in small groups of two to three families to look for hospitality in camps in other districts of the city, or to join relatives outside the city. On 14 May, two other abandoned clusters of shacks were set ablaze with petrol and incendiary bottles. In a short time, the shacks were burnt down before a cheering crowd of locals, who also showed their disapproval of the fire services' attempts to put out the fire. As the few remaining Roma left the place under police escort, the crowd chanted: 'we have won'; 'away, away'; 'you should all go away'. A third attack against another abandoned Roma camp by a group of local youngsters on motorbikes was partially foiled by rainfall, while the police managed to stave off the attackers at a fourth site.

By the end of 15 May, all Roma residents had been forced to leave the Ponticelli area to go to camps and a school in other districts. On the same day, images of the burning camps and frightened faces of Roma children on pickups watching their former homes in flames made the headlines on television and in newspapers. Some local administrators claimed that organised crime (the Camorra) may have been behind the attacks. (The Camorra is the oldest, mafia-style criminal organisation in Italy, it originates from this region and has been responsible for high levels of homicide in the areas in which it operates.) Other NGO observers, who helped the Roma organise their transfers and maintained contacts with police and municipal authorities, agree that

Destruction of Romini dwellings, Casilino. Roma child looking at the devastation after a Roma camp has been demolished by the municipal authority's bulldozers
Source: © Stefano Montesi.

organised crime may well have been involved, but insisted that there had been an orchestrated effort by other political actors and developers who have economic interests in the area. In support of their claims, they point to the fact that the area where the camps were located fell under the Urban Rehabilitation Programme (PRU) approved by the municipal council with a pre-financing amount of €67 million and the condition that work would have to start on the programme before and no later than 4 August, otherwise the pre-financing would be withdrawn. They argued that the Prefecture of

Naples had already planned to evacuate the camps and to demolish the shacks so that construction work could start in the designated PRU area. This points to direct links between criminal, political and property business networks, with anti-Roma violence being used as a means to achieve wider material objectives. The Under-Secretary of State for the Interior, in a statement addressing the Parliament on 29 May, unreservedly condemned the violence and intolerance against the Roma and reaffirmed the government's will to act firmly to remove the causes at the root of these manifestations of intolerance. He also stated that according to a report of the investigative branch of the Naples police department (DIGOS) forwarded to the judicial authority there was no evidence at that time of 'Camorra' criminality in the organisation or management of the attackers, without ruling out the possibility that local criminal elements may have used the situation to secure their presence on the territory.

Source: FRA 2008b.

These events in Italy serve as a reflection of the wider problems faced by Roma communities all over Europe. Roma, Sinti and Traveller groups are the most vulnerable groups in Europe, suffering problems such as poor and segregated housing conditions, discrimination and forced evictions in more than half of the member states of the EU. Systematic discrimination against the Roma is examined more closely in the next chapter.

Anti-semitism

Anti-semitism is anti-Jewish thinking, as well as attitudes and acts of prejudice and/or hostility against Jews, targeting people because of their Jewish faith and culture (FRA 2004: 227). The ending of the Second World War has been seen as constituting a major break in the history of European anti-semitism, although anti-semitic attitudes remained pervasive in many European countries including Germany and Austria. Secondary post-war anti-semitism has been defined as any form of anti-semitism that is itself a reflection of the establishment of the taboo of expressing anti-semitism (FRA 2004). This draws upon older stereotypes about Jewish power and influence in the media and is seen as a reaction to both the perceived exploitation of feelings of war guilt and the taboo on expressing anti-semitism itself.

A further key dimension of post-war anti-semitism relates to the formation of the Israeli state. Discussion in the previous chapter highlighted the process of racial Palestinianisation and the key role played by Zionism, the international Jewish political movement which founded a homeland for the Jewish people, the state of Israel, in Palestine. But to what extent is anti-Zionism and criticism of Israeli policy leading to 'new' anti-semitism, particularly in Europe? As a recent global report on anti-semitism confirmed (Stephen Roth Institute 2008), Israel is perceived categorically as one of the sources and embodiment of evil worldwide with the state, its citizens and Jewish supporters being continually compared to Nazis, particularly in their treatment of Palestinians.

Criticism of Israel is not necessarily anti-semitic, and anti-Zionism is not always a form of racism. But the danger of normalising and amplifying hostility to Israel and then to all Jews may lead to understandable, even respectable mainstream forms of anti-semitism (Hirsh 2007). The development of left-wing anti-Zionism and anti-semitism, for example in the UK and the USA, has increased since the 1980s but there has been more focus on the open and violent rise in right-wing extremist anti-semitism and Holocaust denial or 'revisionism', together with the electoral success of right-wing populist parties, for example in Austria. Perpetrators of antisemitic acts come from a variety of backgrounds and are driven by a variety of motives. More simplistic public perceptions of who is responsible has expanded from the 'extreme right skinhead' to also include the 'disaffected young Muslim' and the 'member of the anti-globalisation Left' (FRA 2008c).

Anti-semitic violence in Europe and North America

Anti-semitic violence continued to rise across many parts of Europe and North America in 2007, as levels of violence motivated by anti-Jewish prejudice remain historically high.

United Kingdom: official data presented by the Community Security Trust identified 2007 as the worst year on record for violent assaults since monitoring began in 1984, 114 personal attacks in 2007.

Germany: the official Committee for the Defense of the Constitution figures showed a 37 per cent rise in 'right-extremist antisemitic crimes of violence', from 43 in 2006 to 59 in 2007.

Canada: B'nai Brith's League for Human Rights reported an 11.4 per cent rise in overall incidents from 2006 to 2007, with levels of violent incidents remaining much the same; 1042 incidents reported in 2007 nearly double the 584 mark of 2003.

Russia: The SOVA Center for Information and Analysis reported that violent incidents targeting Jews 'increased dramatically' in 2007, as 9 crimes affecting at least 13 individuals were reported.

Ukraine: non-governmental monitors have recorded an overall rise in incidents of anti-semitic violence in 2007, including both violent personal assaults and attacks on synagogues, memorials and Jewish institutions.

The Stephen Roth Institute for the Study of Contemporary Antisemitism and Racism shows a 11.8 per cent rise in reported anti-semitic incidents in Europe, North America, and the former Soviet Union, from 510 in 2006 to 578 in 2007; incidents involving weapons, arson or an intent to kill – 'major attacks' – increased nearly four-fold from 17 in 2006 to 51 in 2007. Between 2000 and 2005, levels of anti-semitic violence fluctuated significantly in direct relation to events in the Middle East, which provided a new impetus for those already predisposed to anti-semitism in Europe.

Since 2005, this pattern has to some extent changed, with month-by-month patterns of anti-semitic violence levelling off, with more uniform rates that show little correlation with events involving Israel and the Middle East. But the threat has not diminished as the new norm is for very high levels of anti-semitic violence throughout the year. The Fundamental Rights Agency (FRA) reports that only five EU countries – Austria, France, Germany, Sweden and the United Kingdom – collect data on anti-semitic crime in such a way that allows for a trend analysis over time. Of those that do, France, Sweden and the United Kingdom experienced a general upward trend in recorded anti-semitic crime between 2001–2006.

Anti-semitic violence targets Jewish individuals, including religious leaders, as well as places of worship, community centres, schools and communities. Since 2005, both official and non-governmental statistics show that physical attacks on individuals constitute a growing proportion of overall anti-semitic incidents. Attackers have targeted and identified victims based on distinctive clothing and jewellery, or facial features. A result is a constant pressure to conceal one's identity. But for many Jews,

$\rightarrow$

and in particular those of Orthodox faith, a concealment of identity is neither possible nor desirable. Enhanced security can be credited for a reduction in attacks on Jewish sites and property in France, Germany and the United Kingdom, where successive governments have made a strong commitment to protect the Jewish community. However, the need for such security is a powerful indicator of the revival of anti-semitism in recent years. Human Rights First is aware of at least 40 attacks on synagogues and over 60 attacks on cemeteries and Holocaust memorials in Europe and North America in 2007.

Source: Human Rights First 2008.

In explaining current trends in anti-semitism, events in the Middle East do not appear to be the underlying cause. There has been an improvement in data collection across the EU and other countries from a range of statutory and non-statutory bodies which has improved the evidence base. Also, underlying social and economic tensions and insecurities do seem to be significant in determining these trends as there is a correlation between both levels of crime in general and levels of anti-semitism, and between anti-semitism and Islamophobia. So, although the targeting of particular groups, such as Jews, may be linked to strongly articulated justifications and forms of legitimation there are deeper cultural and motivational factors which cause underlying racial hostility against a range of differing groups.

Anti-Muslimism

The debate over anti-Muslim racism and associated violence has dramatically increased since the terrorist attacks of 9/11, although this has more frequently been termed Islamophobia. As with many concepts used to specify distinct forms of racism, the definition and meaning of Islamophobia has been widely discussed. In many of these debates a starting point has been the Runnymede Trust (1997) definition which has eight elements:

1 Islam is seen as homogenous, static and unresponsive to change.
2 Islam is seen as separate and 'other'. It is not seen as having values in common with other cultures, is not affected by them and does not influence them.
3 Islam is seen as inferior to the West. It is seen as barbaric, irrational, primitive and sexist.
4 Islam is seen as violent, aggressive, threatening, supportive of terrorism and engaged in a 'clash of civilisations'.
5 Islam is seen as a political ideology and is used for political or military advantage.
6 Criticisms made of the West by Islam are rejected out of hand.
7 Hostility towards Islam is used to justify discriminatory practices towards Muslims and exclusion of Muslims from mainstream society.
8 Anti-Muslim hostility is seen as natural or normal.

One key dimension of the debate over the concept focuses on the confusion between fear of Islam and associated attacks on Islam on the one hand and fear of Muslims and attacks on Muslims on the other (and also attacks on non-Muslims who have also been victims of anti-Muslim abuse such as Sikhs). Islamophobia, as with anti-semitism, may therefore be seen as concepts which include anti-Muslim and anti-Jewish racism but go beyond this to encompass additional elements and positions. Criticism of Islam is not necessarily racist. But the danger of amplifying hostility to Islam and applying this to all Muslims has led to mainstream, 'respectable' forms of anti–Muslimism.

In examining anti-Muslim racist violence some of the problems in interpreting an incident as 'Islamophobic' illustrate the difficulties of applying this concept (FRA 2006). For example, in reports of incidents by people who are Muslim, or who are characterised as Muslim because of their appearance or country of origin, the absence of specific insults or evidence could make it difficult to label an event as Islamophobic, whereas an attack on a mosque or graffiti with anti-Muslim statements or drawings is clearly Islamophobic. Also, as highlighted above, incidents or crimes may be driven by a wide variety of motives other than Islamophobia. These can range from general anti-foreigner/anti-migrant or anti-refugee/anti-asylum seeker sentiments – which might be labelled as a 'hate crime' – coming from a desire to commit crime against any target.

Islamic communities and other vulnerable groups have become targets of increased hostility since 9/11, with conflict also arising over increasing claims for public recognition by Muslims in European societies (FRA 2002). Very soon after the terrorist attacks against the USA a cross-European study showed that relatively low levels of physical violence were identified in most EU countries, although verbal abuse, harassment and aggression were much more widespread. Muslims, especially Muslim women, asylum seekers and others, including those who 'look' of Muslim or Arab descent, were at times targeted for aggression. Mosques and Islamic cultural centres were also widely targeted for damage and retaliatory acts. Latent and/or pre-existent anti-Muslimism was also evident in both increased extreme right and neo-Nazi activity and in wider political and media discourse.

A recent comparison of anti-semitism and anti-Muslimism across Europe (Pew Global Attitudes Project 2008) showed that hostility to Muslims in Europe was considerably higher than hostility to Jews, but that the increase in anti-semitism had taken place much more rapidly. In contrast to the USA and Britain where unfavourable opinion of Jews has been stable for several years at between 7 and 9 per cent, hostile attitudes to Jews were rising all across continental Europe from Russia and Poland in the east to Spain and France in the west. In comparison, one in four people in the UK and the US were found to be hostile to Muslims, but this was lower than in the rest of Europe as, for example, over half of Spaniards and Germans expressed anti-Muslimism. Patterns of racial hostility indicated a number of key features, individuals who were anti-Muslim were also likely to be anti-Jew, with levels of hostility higher amongst the older generations and lower socio-economic groups and those with lower levels of education. Also high levels of hostility to both groups were found across all political ideologies as Figure 6.1 shows.

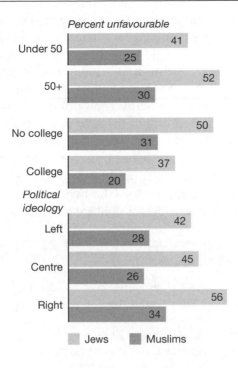

Percent unfavourable

Under 50 — 41 / 25

50+ — 52 / 30

No college — 50 / 31

College — 37 / 20

Political ideology

Left — 42 / 28

Centre — 45 / 26

Right — 56 / 34

Jews   Muslims

Figure 6.1 Bar graph showing anti-muslimism and anti-semitism combined data from France, Germany and Spain
Source: Report entitled 'Unfavourable view of Jews and Muslims on the increase in Europe' 9/17/08 from the Pew Global Attitudes Project, a project of the Pew Research Center, http://pewglobal.org/reports/display.php?ReportID=262

Europe's racial crisis

The everyday persistence of diverse racisms and exclusions which shape the life of a complex range of migrant and minority groups across Europe is clear. The European Union Fundamental Rights Agency (2008a), which has been documenting many of these trends, highlights ambivalent governance that both exacerbates and reproduces many of these surface/overt and structural racialisation processes, at the same time as producing an increasingly bewildering array of unevenly developed strategic and practice responses which frequently fail. This is particularly evident in responses to racist violence. There is a 'crisis' in strategies to tackle racist violence where legislation, techniques and approaches increasingly proliferate but fail to affect resurgent patterns of attack and murder. National reports, which are all available on the FRA website (http://fra.europa.eu/fra/index.php), are full of examples of poor legislation, poor criminal justice practice and poor data collection, alongside limited evidence of practical actions and commitments by some governments and agencies to tackle racist violence.

Franco Frattini, the EU justice commissioner, recently confirmed that five EU member states have major problems with endemic right-wing extremism and associated racist violence including Germany, France, Italy, Belgium and Denmark. These comments were made after a gang of 50 drunken youths shouting racist slogans attacked eight Indians in the east German town of Muegeln in Saxony and two African men were beaten by right-wing extremists in Mainz in western Germany, together with concerns over the role played by the National Democratic Party (NPD) in inciting these incidents (EUObserver 2007). (The NPD is a nationalist anti-immigrant group, directly associated with neo-Nazi and skin-head groups and which openly incites race hate on its website.) Amil, a leading anti-Nazi group in the Saxony region confirmed that there had been 137 neo-Nazi attacks on individuals in the first six months of 2007, and the Forsca research group confirmed that currently half of east German youth, aged 14 to 25, believed that neo-Nazism had many good points (I CARE 2007). There has been much debate over the banning of the NPD and this has been a legal fiasco ending in failure. This illustrates that Germany's response to such political racism and violence is in crisis, as it has been for many years, with confusion over what should be done, how it should be done and what works in tackling politically organised racial hatred. In the UK, there has also been increasing concern over the rising electoral support for political racism.

The extreme right and white backlash in the UK

The ascent to power of Margaret Thatcher in 1979 was widely seen as sounding a death-knell for far right extremism in Britain. By the end of 1980, John Tyndall, the leader of the National Front (NF) had left the party, which was plunged into organisational schism. In 1982, Tyndall embarked on a new political venture with the formation of the British National Party (BNP). The organisation exerted little influence in a political era dominated by Thatcherism. As far right parties began to make significant gains across Western and Northern Europe during the 1980s and 1990s, Britain became something of an anomaly, with the BNP remaining a marginal political actor. Even the BNP victory in Tower Hamlets in 1993 was regarded as something of a 'false dawn', with academic discussion focussing on the 'failure of British fascism'. However, since 2001 the BNP has made electoral advances which have served to question Britain's anomalous status. While remaining a peripheral political actor at the national level, the BNP has made significant local breakthroughs, most noticeably in Barking and Dagenham, Stoke-on-Trent, Epping Forest and Burnley.

Since 1999 the right-wing press and various politicians had re-ignited debates of 'unfairness' towards the indigenous 'white' population in a context of declining national sovereignty and the dual 'threats' of asylum and terrorism. Despite the lurch to the right of New Labour on diversity and multi-culturalism, the party has been compromised by its perceived inability to control England's borders and its past stigmatisation as a party of political correctness and 'loony' liberal policy. Into this political breech has stepped the BNP which, in areas such as Burnley and Barking and Dagenham, have been able to assume ownership of backlash sentiments. BNP voters attacked multi-culturalism and drew on discourses of 'unfairness' and 'equality' as a means by which they could 'justify' their actions. It is clear that the emergence of 'white backlash' in recent decades marks an important development and discursive shift in white racism.

While racist political mobilisations will be shaped by the local contexts in which they emerge, the spiralling political disaffection particularly towards Labour within socio-economically deprived boroughs, the politicisation of 'race', weak opposition parties, racialised geography, and a BNP party or branch able to present itself as a 'respectable' political actor are important factors accounting for their success in particular local areas.

Source: 'The Political Breakthrough of the BNP: the case of Burnley', *British Politics*, 4, 1 (Rhodes, J. 2009), Reprinted by permission from Macmillan Publishers Ltd: British Politics (4, 1), copyright (2009) published by Palgrave Macmillan.

Resurgent ideologically driven race hate is being documented in many European countries. Public political culture in the Netherlands has become more hostile and aggressive, and this, combined with a focus on Islamic extremism rather than right-wing extremism has allowed organised race hate groups to flourish. The Anne Frank Foundation documented a doubling of extreme right-wing acts of racist violence from 2006 to 2007, identifying a small core of 100 ideologically driven men in groups like Blood and Honour and Combat 18. Formation of anti-semitic, anti-Roma and homophobic paramilitary groups in public continues. In Hungary, Jobbik a far right party and over 1000 of its supporters inducted the founding members of its new paramilitary wing the Magya Guard in public out-side the Presidential Palace in Budapest in August 2007. In the Czech Republic, the extreme right National Corporativism movement, which mobilises amonst many skinheads, organised a demonstration in Svitavy in July 2007 to support the cause of a 23-year-old skinhead who was convicted of killing a Roman man.

For many European states racism is all about the activities of the extreme right. The central roles played by the black, the Jew and the Muslim in the construction of a racial Europe has recently been examined by David Goldberg (2008). He argues that the rule and law of 'post-colonial distinction' in Europe founds itself upon racial denial and masking of the causes of institutionalised racial violence and exclusion through the fictitious construction of panic-inducing post-colonial figures of vilification. So, for example, racialised policing, stop and search methods, are justified through panic about black criminals or Muslim terrorists. Racism is seen as operating only on the extreme fringes of society, not within mainstream European state institutions, with key forms of institutional racism, for example in policing, being ignored. The paradox here is that many of these global, international and national institutions are also increasingly developing a mass of creative, innovative and exciting interventions with the objective of reducing racism and racist violence in particular.

Racism reduction

Global approaches

In international politics some key working principles for building a racism reduc-tion agenda have been set out in a number of UN and UNESCO conventions and statements including the recognition of common humanity, the right to differ-ence and the claim that racism has no justification (Law 2007). Although these approaches have been criticised for primarily understanding racism as driven by individual prejudice and ignoring the intrinsic racialisation of liberal democra-cies (Lentin 2004: 310), this is not borne out by more recent activities. For example the World Conference Against Racism (WCAR) report (2001: 19) makes a specific recommendation on the link between prevention of racist violence and democratic governance:

We recognize that democracy, transparent, responsible, accountable and participatory governance responsive to the needs and aspirations of the people, and respect for human rights, fundamental freedoms and the rule of law are essential for the effective prevention and elimination of racism, racial discrimination, xenophobia and related intolerance. We reaffirm that any form of impunity for crimes motivated by racist and xenophobic attitudes plays a role in weakening the rule of law and democracy and tends to encourage the recurrence of such acts.

The WCAR programme of action is also pursued by the UN Special Rapporteur on contemporary forms of racism, racial discrimination, xenophobia and related intolerance, currently Doudou Diène. His assessment of strategic aims draws on the WCAR programme of action and identifies four key priorities:

- Monitoring and analysis of old and new forms of racism, racial discrimination and xenophobia.
- Political strategy: the expression of a firm political will to combat racism by governments.
- Legal strategy: the adoption and implementation of national legislation against racism, discrimination and xenophobia.
- Intellectual and ethical strategy: seeking to promote better understanding of the deep cultural roots of racism, and its ideological, cultural and psychological foundations, processes and mechanisms.

UNESCO adopted a new Integrated Strategy to Combat Racism, Discrimination, Xenophobia and Intolerance in 2003, drawing on studies on different aspects and forms of racism, xenophobia and discrimination around the world and consultations in different regions to discuss specific concerns and priorities. The revised strategy confirmed action priorities in the following areas:

- Development of scientific research and reflection on the phenomena of racism, discrimination and xenophobia.
- Revision and/or revitalisation of UNESCO's instruments dealing with racism and discrimination.
- Development of new educational approaches, elaboration of teaching materials and establishment of indicators.
- Mobilisation of opinion leaders and political decision makers against racism and discrimination.
- Preservation of diversity in multi-ethnic and multi-cultural societies.
- Combating racist propaganda in media especially in cyberspace.

The International Coalition of Cities against Racism was launched by UNESCO in 2004 to implement this strategy and share experiences and good practice across the world. This seeks to establish regional coalitions which have been set up in Europe, Africa, North America, the Caribbean and Latin America, and Asia and the Pacific so far. The European Coalition of Cities Against Racism (ECCAR) had its first meeting in Germany in May 2007. In consideration of good practice initiatives at a local level these initiatives indicate that action plans should take account of the relevance and significance of all these principles, and be cognisant of the pitfalls and dilemmas of simplistic approaches. In combating racist violence in local contexts, as ECCAR suggests, it is particularly important that relevant action is taken in a range of inter-related fields including local government responsibility, education, law and criminal justice, mass media and individual responsibility, and also in relation to racial segregation in housing.

Lessons on how to reduce racism can be drawn from global, European and national evidence. The lack of political will was identified as a key barrier in moving forward and here the key role played by NGOs in pressing for action has been confirmed (WCAR 2001). The participation by over 4000 NGOs and over 250 nation states in the World Conference Against Racism indicates both the significance of the international politics of anti-racism and the potential scope for cross-national and cross-organisation learning. This is also evident from assessment of EU approaches to tackling racist violence where improvements in data collection, enhanced penalties, youth projects and restorative justice initiatives, anti-racist campaigns and community-building initiatives were highlighted in a review of recent developments. In the UK, there is both extensive development of policy, practice and various forms of intervention to tackle racist violence as well as extensive evidence of mass racist violence. It has been argued that building a 'racism reduction' agenda involves developing community-based campaigning and preventative initiatives, improving reporting, intelligence gathering and surveillance, pursuing crime and conflict initiatives, improving agency practice, improving cross-sector learning/working, improving work with perpetrators and offenders and developing performance standards (Law 2007).

European approaches

Across Europe frameworks and initiatives for tackling racist violence have been developed by European institutions (e.g. the Council of Europe's European Commission on Racism and Intolerance, ECRI), European NGO networks (e.g. Coalition Europe, ENAR, European Network Against Racism, ICARE, Internet Centre Anti racism Europe), research centres, national institutions and national and local organisations. There is an increasingly rich set of evidence that can be drawn on to consider what has been tried, what has failed and what seems to have some impact in this field. ICARE (www.icare.to) provides links to 2000 organisations in 114 countries and is the information disseminator for the European NGO community working in the fields of anti-discrimination, human rights, anti-semitism, diversity and migration, with a focus on anti-racism. The purpose of ICARE is the empowerment of democratic, non-violent human rights and anti-racism work by offering information and reporting on events taking place, by facilitating communication, advocacy, campaigns and actions and by stimulating intersectional and international cooperation. One specific grouping that highlights work on race hate crime is Coalition Europe, which is developing a pan-European campaign in this field (www.coalitoneurope.org) and urges action in information and awareness raising, political and legal action and efforts to support and empower victims of racist violence. A recent meta-analysis of racist violence in 15 EU member states (FRA 2005) has highlighted 'good practice', giving examples which broadly address the areas of improvements in data collection, enhanced penalties and youth projects/restorative justice initiatives, including:

CEOOR, registering racist violence

A pilot project is ongoing in two medium-sized police zones in Belgium with a significant minority presence. The project will register racial discrimination and hate crimes (that is, hate crimes related to race/ethnicity, and religion), and includes acts of racist violence. The Centre for Equal Opportunities and Opposition to Racism (CEOOR) has developed a registration form for dissemination among police services and migrant organisations. These agencies are asked to complete a registration form every time they receive a complaint related to racist discrimination/violence.

Movie '*Provided that we talk to each other*'

The movie *Pourvu que l'on se parle* was produced in response to an upsurge in both anti-semitic and Islamophobic incidents in Belgium. Both Jews and Maghrebians are the victims of stereotypes, preconceptions and myths, and the movie *Pourvu que l'on se parle* demonstrates the commonalities between communities in a pedagogical and humorous fashion. It shows that the expectations and the hopes of majority and minority communities are very similar. As such it is an interesting response to racism and anti-semitism that has been used by teachers, educators and workers in socio-cultural training.

Police monitoring system

As a reaction to increased levels of violent racism in 2001 in Denmark that saw attacks on Muslims and the Jewish community, the authorities set out to reorganise the police monitoring system, which compiles a list of racially motivated crime, including racist violence. Local police offices were swiftly issued with instructions in 2001 in an effort to broaden and standardise the data collection mechanism. Although this can be held up as an example of 'good practice', it must be read alongside the fact that Danish legislation does not directly criminalise racist crime and violence.

The 'Alliance for Democracy and Tolerance – Against Extremism and Violence'

This is a broad alliance of programmes (XENOS, CIVITAS, ENTIMON), established in 2000, that encompasses many different initiatives and works with a range of actors from German civil society. Within the Alliance's ENTIMON programme is the initiative 'Together against Violence and Right-Wing Extremism', which supported 238 projects in 2003 and 153 in 2004, including conferences, courses, workshops, festivals, theatre projects and international encounters between young people. These also include local plans of action against violence, right-wing extremism and xenophobia which are directed towards young people in socially difficult environments. Political education measures form the focus of this part of the programme, which aims to foster the practice of tolerance, intercultural dialogue, the willingness to involve oneself in community tasks and democratic behaviour. Projects of national significance are supported (such as action events, Rock gegen Rechts (Rock against the Right), measures to support youth work in cooperation with the Bundeszentrale für politische Bildung (Federal Centre for Political Education; NFPDE0113) and other federal bodies, as well as projects to initiate civil commitment, especially on a community level. Evaluation confirms mixed success of this programme, with good levels of youth involvement but limited impact in both sustaining developments in intercultural learning and in reaching ideologically opposed young people who align themselves with the extreme right.

Programmes to assist young people to leave extreme right-wing organisations

A range of programmes exist in Germany; for example, since April 2001 the 'Federal Programme to Encourage Right-Wing Extremists to Leave this Movement' has been in operation. The programme was initiated by the Ministry of the Interior and run by the Federal Office for Internal Security. This preventatively orientated project has two aims: encouraging leading figures to leave this scene and attempting to prevent 'Mitläufer' (hangers-on) who are not firmly entrenched in the right-wing milieu from drifting into potentially violent environments. Within the framework of the programme, the BfV, in co-operation with the youth and employment offices, arranges jobs or training places, for example, for those willing to leave right-wing groups, or helps them in finding a place to live. In exceptional cases, financial help is also available in order to facilitate 'a return to democracy' for leading neo-Nazis (for example, by financing a new identity).

The Fundamental Rights Agency (FRA 2005: 2002) gives particular consideration to the success that criminal justice initiatives are having on victims of racist violence, identifying that, 'traditional criminal justice has made little headway towards successfully addressing racist crime and violence'.

Newer forms of restorative justice, which aim to resolve conflicts in informal settings with meetings between victim and offender, and sometimes involving wider meetings with families and communities, have developed in this field. Restorative justice is a process whereby victims and offenders are brought together to collectively resolve how to deal with the aftermath of the offence and its implications for the future. It is 'increasingly popular' in many criminal justice jurisdictions, notably in Austria, Belgium, Germany and the UK, but has been criticised for demoting racist violence to a form of 'secondary' justice, or 'soft option', leading to intimidation of the victim and failing to recognise the repeat history of violence.

Current practice may increase victims' feelings that racist violence is not being dealt with adequately and also very few reports result in sentencing of offenders, although in the UK there has been an increasing number of prosecutions for racially aggravated offences. Overall, the FRA concludes that although national reports are full of examples of poor legislation, poor criminal justice practice and poor data collection, there is also evidence of practical actions and increased commitment by governments and agencies to tackle racist violence.

UK approaches to tackling racist violence

There is a wealth of material available both in the UK and in other national contexts which documents policy, practice and various forms of intervention to tackle racist violence (Law 2007, Chahal 2007). The Stephen Lawrence case and the subsequent Inquiry was highly controversial and this led to renewed government attention to tackling racist violence.

Lessons from the Lawrence Inquiry

Stephen Lawrence was an 18-year-old sixth form student who was stabbed to death in Eltham, south London, on the night of 22 April 1993. His murder was motivated by racism and the Inquiry confirmed the extent of corruption and conscious and unconscious racism that pervaded the police force responsible for investigating the murder. 'Stephen's death exposed the painful extent of prejudice within the police and public authorities; indeed, within British society as a whole' (Jack Straw MP, Lord Chancellor and Secretary of State for Justice, 24 February 2009).

The *Stephen Lawrence Inquiry* in 1999 and the six subsequent progress reports on implementing the recommendations from this Inquiry set out a comprehensive national framework for pursuing good practice in response to racist violence (http://police.homeoffice.gov.uk/community-policing/race-diversity).

Ten years on from the Inquiry, there are some indications of positive change, most notably in the way the Crown Prosecution Service takes cases involving racist motivation more seriously. But there remain fundamental problems in relations between police and black and ethnic minority groups, including the persistent over-representation of these groups in 'stop and search' incidents indicating the continuance of racialised policing (Runnymede Trust 2009).

A recent UK report (CRE 2005) for the FRA highlighted good practice in three areas:

> *Targeted police initiatives on hate crimes*, such as those of the London Metropolitan Police Service and the Greater Manchester Police, which have been adopted more widely across the country. For example, a South West England targeted policing initiative has had an impact on racist crime there.

> *National Probation Service (NPS)*, Merseyside programme 'Promoting Human Dignity' and other NPS intervention programmes such as Newcastle and Greenwich which specifically target racially motivated offenders.

> *Multicultural educational programmes*, such as Kent County Council's Minority Communities Achievement Service that enables children to explore values such as sharing and equal respect and examines issues such as, fear, justice, being new, and ethnic diversity in school.

Policy and practice in this field is dynamic and there are significant signs of progress, together with persisting difficulties. Evidence from 250 agencies in 67 local areas across Britain showed increasing good practice including multi-agency working on policies, monitoring trends and considering individual cases, third-party reporting centres, common reporting forms, support for victims including provision of advice, counselling, personal alarms, 24-hour helplines and home security improvements as well as staff training (Lemos and Crane 2000). However, under-reporting and under-recording of racist incidents together with lack of appropriate response was still problematic and tensions between agencies and lack of resources hampered multi-agency work. Over 40,000 racial harassment reports had been received by these agencies with a relatively low level of action being taken as, across 27 local authorities, only 138 households had been rehoused by social landlords and only 124 possession proceedings had been taken which seek to evict those responsible for causing racial harassment. Other forms of legal intervention such as Anti-Social Behaviour Orders had only been used to deal with perpetrators in three areas, with concern over the time-consuming and uncertain process of applying for these orders. Across 35 areas, 2451 criminal prosecutions had been brought, with 10–15 per cent of cases reported to the police ending in prosecution. Police had criticised the Crown Prosecution Service for lack of attention to the racist element of cases. Victims and witnesses frequently feared reprisals if statements were made, use of professional witnesses was often seen as expensive and unproductive, and mediation as inappropriate. So, despite the development of innovative forms of intervention, many difficulties continue to produce poor outcomes for victims of racist violence.

The Commission for Racial Equality provided valuable advice on 'Defeating Organised Racial Hatred' in local contexts (2006). Initiatives highlighted include building anti-racist alliances through conferences and meetings, building cross-party opposition to political racism through statements, election compacts, community newspapers, leafleting, free council papers and media communications, working in partnership to combat far right messages and researching and publishing action guidance. So, strong leadership from local authorities and presenting cross-party unity can be an effective strategy in challenging and marginalising the far right and associated racist violence. Utilising effective communication strategies to counter racist myths is also key to reducing racist violence. Sustaining these messages and anti-racist activism throughout the year and not just at times of crisis has been found to be essential in this arena. It is also clear that little serious attention is being paid to these issues by many local authorities.

Community engagement and outreach work have been identified in many localities as effective in reducing tensions. The Southampton Community Outreach team have been engaged in work to reduce tension between local BME communities and asylum seekers. This involved inter-communal dialogue/community mediation, preparing and informing host communities about new-comers, building the capacity of individuals and groups to lead their own networks and organisations (Amas and Crosland 2006). Detached youth work (this is work which is not based in community centres but seeks to develop interactions out on the street with young people) has also been used to reduce racist violence (Home Office 2006).

Facilitating face-to-face individual interactions to promote understanding has also been reported as working successfully in some areas. Refugee Action believes that the best way to promote understanding is for people to meet a refugee and asylum seeker and hear their story, similar to initiatives involving Holocaust survivors in education. The work of the Refugee Awareness project in the North West, South West and West Midlands involves organising awareness-raising sessions in community centres, working with the local press, information provision, training volunteers and developing materials (Amas and Crosland 2006). Using community events to promote belonging and understanding has also been identified as useful here. The Living Under One Sun project engaged with Kosovan, Albanian, Turkish, West African and other groups to build interactions between children and families from different cultural backgrounds through cooking and sharing food and related activities (Hudson *et al.* 2007). Neighbourhood initiatives in churches, sports clubs, workplaces and schools to promote belonging for new Eastern European migrants has also been identified as being useful in achieving reduced anti-migrant hostility (Markova and Black 2007).

Promoting community leadership, neighbouring and activities to reduce misinformation have also been identified as having beneficial local effects in lowering inter-community hostility (DCLG 2007). The Home Office Guide Neighbourhoods programme has produced many good practice examples including the work of the Leicester North West Community Forum (Amas and Crosland 2006). This involved a range of initiatives including leadership training for 60 local residents as good neighbours including 25 refugees and asylum seekers and 'patch walks' bringing agencies and residents together in the area. The Walsall Wardens Scheme became involved in related work where local people were concerned about refugees and asylum seekers jumping the housing queue. Their work involved meeting new families, introducing newcomers to local families and community groups and improving communication with residents (Amas and Crosland 2006). Such work can also play an important wider role in reversing social and physical decline of poor estates which can breed resentment and hostility if left unchecked (Home Office 2006). Providing information to challenge myths about asylum seekers and refugees can aslo be productive. Refugee Action (www.refugee-action.org.uk) and the Information Centre About Asylum and Refugees (www.icar.org.uk) provide pocket guides and a range of related resources that can assist in public education to engage with popular myths and misinformation.

Many public services now collect data on racist incidents in order to assess levels of tension in particular areas and in order to target interventions. However, data is often collected and little effective use is made of this. Improving mapping of racist incidents and data analysis is therefore needed (Home Office 2006). The importance of identifying patterns and clustering in racist violence and the link with perceptions of street or neighbourhood territory and belonging has been highlighted by Webster (1993) and Hesse *et al.* (1992). Better evidence can improve the targeting of racist incident hotspots through increased surveillance, patrols, special operations and other initiatives which have been taken to reduce racist violence in specific localised areas (Home Office 2006).

In addition to identifying patterns of incidents, wider patterns of racist hostility also need to be identified for preventative work, for example through qualitative research. Such evidence can also inform risk assessment programmes. The London Borough of Merton has introduced racist violence risk assessment in housing lettings with specific attention given to the history of racist victimisation relating to both individuals and properties, and increased tenant support is given where risks are identified. Providing victim and witness information packs can also help to empower victims.

All these myriad interventions are not to be easily dismissed and there is tremendous opportunity to secure real improvements in the quality of life of migrants, minorities and racialised groups through pursuing a racism reduction agenda drawing on global and European priciples and frameworks, securing responsible governance and through empowering local communites and NGOs.

Conclusion

This chapter has explored the nature of Europe's racial crisis and has been concerned to locate and understand patterns of racist hostility and violence. Improving theory, greater understanding and better evidence of racist violence, on the one hand, accompanies deepening 'structural' racism and European racial stratification on the other. This is a central contradiction in the post-colonial era and is evident within the European politics of race. The establishment of the European Monitoring Centre for Racism and Xenophobia (EUMC) in Vienna in 1997/98, which subsequently became the FRA, and the implementation of systematic surveillance of patterns and trends in racism and xenophobia across the expanding number of EU member states represents a significant advance in understanding. But this has been accompanied by deepening structural racism and associated violence across this region. There is a crisis in strategies to tackle racist violence where legislation, techniques and approaches increasingly proliferate in the face of highly durable and resurgent patterns of attack and murder. This indicates that the 'fit' between causes of racist violence and the forms of intervention that have developed may be poor. Therefore, the prospect of more complex and comprehensive explanations of racist violence providing a secure foundation for equally comprehensive international, national and local anti-racist action may lead to this crisis being averted. Despite many dilemmas, capitulations and reversals in the twentieth century, anti-racism has remained a strong and potent social force and this is almost certain to continue.

End of chapter activity

This chapter has made particular use of the output of Europe's Fundamental Rights Agency which are an essential starting point for these debates. Using material on their website including national reports examine the nature and extent of racist violence in one European country you are unfamiliar with; who is targeted? Is violence getting worse? What is being done? Is this having any impact? Is racism in this national context different to other European countries? http://fra.europa.eu/fra/index.php

Web resources and further reading

In the UK there is a range of useful web-based sources of advice and guidance on tackling and understanding racist violence. Three independent non-governmental organisations provide national advice and information on racist violence. Firstly, the work of the Runnymede Trust (RT) in this area (Isal 2005, Khan 2002, www.runnymedetrust.org) is highly useful, in particular the most recent report on *Preventing Racist Violence* (Isal 2005). The Monitoring Group (TMG) is one of the leading campaign groups in this field and provides practical assistance to victims as well as advice at www.monitoring-group.co.uk. Current work by TMG includes a national study of racist violence and Chinese communities (Adamson *et al.* 2009). The Institute of Race Relations, a long-established group, similar to TMG and RT, is highly critical of state responses to racist violence; it provides practical information and a range of useful resources at www.irr.org.uk. A key website which is not open access, but which is used widely by a range of relevant agencies is provided by Lemos and Crane. They provide probably the most useful web-based source of advice on the overlapping fields of racist violence and community cohesion with their toolkits at www.raceactionnet.co.uk and www.cohesionactionnet.co.uk. These draw on a wide range of primary research and secondary material and give opportunities for practitioners to engage in discussion forums. The new Institute of Community Cohesion at Coventry University provides comprehensive good practice guidance in a web-based toolkit at www.coventry.ac.uk/icoco covering a wide range of areas. The Home Office crime reduction toolkit for racist violence (2006) and the community cohesion toolkit (2005) provide another set of highly accessible forms of advice and documentation of good practice at www.crimereduction.gov.uk/toolkits. A further toolkit highlighted by Chahal (2007) is aimed at providing youth workers with guidance in dealing with racist incidents, the 'I Ain't Racist But. Toolkit' can be accessed at www.lrec.org.uk. The Joseph Rowntree Foundation regularly publishes social research evidence relevant to this area and their series of research findings can be accessed at www.jrf.org.uk. The challenge of tackling political racism and the associated race hate promoted by extreme right groups is addressed in the information pack produced by the CRE as part of their Safe Communities Initiative (2006) available at www.cre.gov.uk.

References

Adamson, S., Chan, C. K., Cheung, T., Craig, G., Cole, B., Lau, C., Law, I. with Hussain, B. and Smith, L. (2009) *A State of Denial, racism against the UK Chinese population*, London: TMG.

Amas, N. and Crosland, B. (2006) *Understanding the Stranger: building bridges community handbook,* London: Calouste Gulbenkian Foundation.

Bowling, B. (1998) *Violent Racism,* Oxford: Clarendon Press.

Bowling, B. and Phillips, C. (2002) *Racism, Crime and Justice,* Harlow: Longman.

Chahal, K. (2007) *Racist Harassment and Housing Services,* London: Race Equality Foundation.

Chakrabarty, D. (2000) *Provincialising Europe, postcolonial thought and historical difference,* Princeton, NJ: Princeton University Press.

CRE (Commission for Racial Equality) (2005) *National Analytical Study on Racist Violence,* London: CRE.

CRE (Commission for Racial Equality) (2006) *Defeating Organised Racial Hatred,* London: CRE.

DCLG (Department of Communities and Local Government) (2007) *Improving Opportunities, Stregthening Society,* London, DCLG.

Dench, G., Gavron, K. and Young, M. (2006) *The New East End, kinship, race and conflict,* London: Profile Books.

FRA (Fundamental Rights Agency) (2002) *Anti-Islamic reactions in the EU after the acts of terror against the USA, Synthesis report,* Vienna: FRA, http://fra.europa.eu/fra/index.php?fuseaction=content.dsp_cat_content&catid=3fb38ad3e22bb&contentid=3fb4f8d82d72a.

FRA (Fundamental Rights Agency) (2004) *Manifestations of Antisemitism in the EU 2002–2003,* Vienna: FRA, http://fra.europa.eu/fra/index.php?fuseaction=content.dsp_cat_content&catid=3fb38ad3e22bb&contentid=4146a7b291fff

FRA (Fundamental Rights Agency) (2005), *Racist Violence in 15 EU member states,* Vienna: FRA, http://fra.europa.eu/fra/index.php?fuseaction=content.dsp_cat_content&catid=43c54ea09682f

FRA (Fundamental Rights Agency) (2006) *Muslims in the European Union, discrimination and Islamophobia,* Vienna: FRA, http://fra.europa.eu/fra/index.php?fuseaction=content.dsp_cat_content&catid=3fb38ad3e22bb&contentid=4582d9f4345ad

FRA (Fundamental Rights Agency) (2008a) *Annual Report,* Vienna: FRA, http://fra.europa.eu/fra/index.php?fuseaction=content.dsp_cat_content&catid=4860badc7f081

FRA (Fundamental Rights Agency) (2008b) *Incident Report, Violent Attacks against Roma in the Ponticelli District of Naples Italy,* Vienna: FRA, http://fra.europa.eu/fra/index.php?fuseaction=content.dsp_cat_content&catid=3fb38ad3e22bb&contentid=4898692b6b22f

FRA (Fundamental Rights Agency) (2008c) *Anti-Semitism, summary overview of the situation in the EU 2001–2007, updated version January 2008,* Vienna: FRA, http://fra.europa.eu/fra/index.php?fuseaction=content.dsp_cat_content&catid=449677441f3f3

Gadd, D., Dixon, B. and Jefferson, T. (2005) *Why do they do it? Racial Harassment in North Staffordshire,* Keele University/ESRC.

Goldberg, D. T. (2008) *The Threat of Race, reflections on racial neoliberalism,* Oxford: Blackwell.

Hemmerman, L., Law, I., Simms, J. and Sirriyeh, A. (2007) *Situating Racist Hostility and Understanding the Impact of Racist Victimisation in Leeds,* Leeds: CERS, University of Leeds.

Hesse, B., Rai, D., Bennett, C. and McGilchrist, P. (1992) *Beneath the Surface: Racial Harassment,* Aldershot: Ashgate.

Hewitt, R. (1996) *Routes of Racism, the social basis of racist action*, Stoke-on Trent: Trentham.

Hewitt, R. (2005) *White Backlash and the Politics of Multiculturalism*, Cambridge: Cambridge University Press.

Hirsch, D. (2007) *Anti-Zionism and antisemitism: cosmopolitan reflections*, Yale Initiative for the Interdisciplinary Study of Antisemitism, Working paper, New Haven, CT: Yale University.

Home Office (2005) *Community Cohesion, seven steps — a practitioner's toolkit*, London: Cohesion and Faiths Unit, Home Office.

Home Office (2006) *Racist Incidents Crime Reduction Toolkit*, London: Home Office.

Hudson, M., Phillips, J., Ray, K. and Barnes, H. (2007) *Social cohesion in diverse communities*, York: JRF.

Human Rights First (2008) *2008 Hate Crime Survey: Antisemitism*, www.humanrights-first.org/discrimination/reports.aspx?s=antisemitism&p=index.

ICARE (2007) 'Merkel under pressure to ban neo-Nazi party', *Internet Centre Anti-Racism Europe*, www.icare.to.

Isal, S. (2005) *Preventing Racist Violence*, London: Runnymede Trust.

Khan, O. (2002) *Perpetrators of Racist Violence*, London: Runnymede Trust.

Law, I. (2007) *The Racism Reduction Agenda*, Leeds: CERS, University of Leeds.

Law, I. (2008) *Defining the Sources of Intercultural Conflict*, Strasbourg: Council of Europe.

Lemos, G. (2005) *The Search for Tolerance: challenging and changing racist attitudes and behaviour amongst young people*, York: JRF.

Lemos, G. and Crane, P. (2000) *Action Being Taken to Tackle Racial Harassment*, York: JRF

Lentin, A., (2004) *Racism and Anti-Racism in Europe*, London: Pluto.

Mann, M. (1986) *The Sources of Social Power: Vol. 1, A History of Power from the Beginning to AD 1760*, Cambridge: Cambridge University Press.

Mann, M. (1993) *The Sources of Social Power: Vol. 2, The Rise of Classes and Nation States, 1760–1914*, Cambridge: Cambridge University Press.

Mann, M. (2005) *The Dark Side of Democracy, explaining ethnic cleansing*, Cambridge: Cambridge University Press.

Markova, E. and Black, R. (2007) *East European immigration and community cohesion*, York: JRF.

Pew Global Attitudes Project (2008) *Unfavourable view of Jews and Muslims on the increase in Europe*, http://pewglobal.org/reports/display.php?ReportID=262.

Ray, L. and Smith, D. (2004) 'Shame, rage and racist violence', *British Journal of Criminology*, 44, pp. 350–368

Rhodes, J. (2009) 'The political breakthrough of the BNP: the case of Burnley', *British Politics*, 4, 1, pp. 22–46.

Runnymede Trust (1997) *Islamophobia, a challenge for us all*, London: Runnymede Trust, www.runnymedetrust.org/uploads/publications/pdfs/islamophobia.pdf.

Runnymede Trust (2009) *The Stephen Lawrence Inquiry Ten Years On*, London: Runnymede Trust, www.runnymedetrust.org/uploads/publications/pdfs/ StephenLawrenceInquiry-2009.pdf

Sibbitt, R. (1997) *The Perpetrators of Racial Violence and Racial Harassment*, London: Home Office.

Stephen Roth Institute (2008) *Antisemitism Worldwide 2007*, www.tau.ac.il/Anti-Semitism/.

WCAR (2001) *Report of the World Conference Against Racism, Racial Discirmination, Xenphobia and Related Intolerance*, Durban: UN.

Weber, M. (1978) *Economy and Society, an outline of interpretive sociology*, Vol. 2, Berkeley: University of California Press.

Webster, C. (1993) 'Process and survey evaluation of an antiracist youth work project', in P. Francis and R. Mathews (eds) *Tackling Racial Attacks*, Leicester: University of Leicester.

Webster, C. (1998) 'Researching Racial Violence: A Scientific Realist Approach', in J. Vagg, and T. Newburn (eds.) *Emerging Themes in British Criminology: Selected papers from the 1995 British Criminology Conference*, Leicester: British Society of Criminology Website.

7

Exclusion and discrimination: Europe and the Roma

Key issues in this chapter:

- The nature and extent of processes of racial and ethnic exclusion, discrimination and marginalisation

- Racial and ethnic exclusion in Europe

- Social and political mobilisation of the Roma

At the end of this chapter you should be able to:

- Understand and apply the concepts of direct and indirect racial discrimination

- Assess racial and ethnic differentials in housing and education

- Evaluate the marginalisation of the Roma in a variety of material contexts

Introduction

This chapter examines the processes of racial and ethnic exclusion, discrimination and marginalisation which involves denial of access to societal opportunities and rewards, for example employment, education, housing, health, welfare and justice. After consideration of the conceptualisation of discrimination, overall patterns of racial and ethnic discrimination across Europe are examined together with detailed consideration of one key field: housing. This has been chosen here as it is a field which usefully illustrates multiple forms of everyday unequal treatment. Evidence from European societies on housing highlights the particular severity of living conditions experienced by the Roma. The estimated 10 million Roma are one of the most marginalised groups in Europe, and they provide a key focus for this chapter in illustrating the ways in which these processes work. The social and political construction of Roma identity, introduced in Chapter 2, seeks to establish commonalities in the experiences of a multitude of groups such as Gypsy and Tsigane and sub-groups such as Sinto, Kalderash and Boyash (Vermeesch 2006).

A Roma family
Source: AFP/Getty Images.

Defining the Roma

The term 'Roma' refers to persons describing themselves as Roma, Gypsies, Manouches, Kalderash, Machavaya, Lovari, Churari, Romanichal, Gitanoes, Kalo, Sinti, Rudari, Boyash, Ungaritza, Luri, Bashaldé, Romungro, Yenish, Xoraxai and other groups perceived as '*Gypsies*'. The term Traveller refers specifically to Irish Travellers who are not Roma and are native to Ireland. The terms 'Roma and Travellers' are not intended to minimise the diversity within these communities or to promote negative stereotypes.

Source: FRA 2006b: 16.

Chapter 6 highlighted contemporary patterns of anti-Roma violence, drawing on recent events in Italy. This chapter builds on this material and examines patterns of exclusion and discrimination which have affected Roma, Sinti, Gypsy and Traveller groups across Europe, using data on housing and segregation in Western Europe and education in Eastern Europe. The experiences of the Roma are also examined comparatively in relation to a range of other ethnic groups. We shall be looking at discrimination, disadvantage and segregation for ethnic minority and migrant groups in housing across Europe as this provides a useful example of the way in which these processes operate. Racism and related exclusionary practices contribute to an array of negative outcomes. People seen as 'different' are subjected to ill-treatment that ranges from being refused a property because of colour, to physical attacks aimed at keeping a household out of a particular neighbourhood.

So, this chapter will define and identify exactly how practices and processes of racial discrimination operate. Such practices become mechanisms that reinforce or create social exclusion and there are key linkages between this and other spheres of material conditions. The processes and patterns of discrimination are not random, but have a systematic and persistent character. This is clear from the fact that similar racist practices occur in the housing field in very different countries and these are explored here.

The analysis of racism and ethnicity in post-communist contexts has not so far been explored in this book, and this context was highlighted in Chapter 5 as a key arena for examining formations of racism, ethnicity and migration. Here, empirical evidence is used to examine similarities and differences between Western and Eastern Europe. This chapter examines patterns of racial exclusion and discrimination in Eastern Europe drawing on evidence from a range of countries including Romania, Slovakia, the Czech Republic and Hungary and focussing on the Roma and education. Inequalities facing the Roma in the UK were introduced in Chapter 4, and here more detailed consideration of patterns of both social exclusion and political mobilisation is provided.

Post-structuralist and postmodernist directions in contemporary sociological theory have nurtured an increasing focus on the complexity of interactions between different forms of discrimination. This builds on a well-established research focus on intersectionality in this field, initiated by Cooper at the beginning of the twentieth century, which was examined in Chapter 3. The critique of the conceptual inflation of racism, which warns against labelling institutional practices as racist since they may have exclusionary effects on other groups such as women, further supports the building of sociological complexity into the study of how discrimination works. This shift is also apparent in the development of international and national protections and remedies. Here, development of human rights approaches that emphasise particularly freedom from discrimination and respect for the dignity of individuals and their ways of life and personal development, seek to build a collective agenda that encompasses the needs and interests of all individuals and groups. The shift toward the creation of general equality commissions in the UK, the Commission for Equality and Human Rights, and, in Europe, the Fundamental Rights Agency, and the dismantling of institutions concerned with separate forms of discrimination such as race or disability further exemplifies this process. In future research, focus on the interactions between different structures of discrimination is likely to be key, together with critical evaluation of the construction and operation of equality and human rights organisations and their relations with oppressed and marginalised groups. In this chapter, a more limited approach is taken, seeking to establish how racial and ethnic discrimination works, together with a detailed focus on Roma experiences. The extensive task of developing a full account of intersectional discrimination is beyond the scope of this text, but firstly some of the general issues and problems involved in how we define and use the concept of discrimination are considered.

Understanding discrimination

Discrimination refers to the differential, and often unequal, treatment of people who have been either formally or informally grouped into a particular class of persons. There are many forms of discrimination that are specified according to the ways in which particular groups are identified, including race, ethnicity, gender, marital status, class, age, disability, nationality, religion, or language. The United Nations Charter (1954) declared in article 55 that the UN will promote human rights and freedoms for all, 'without distinction as to race, sex, language, and religion'. Later, in 1958, the Universal Declaration of Human Rights added a number of further grounds for possible discrimination, which were colour, political or other opinion, national or social origin, property, birth, or other status.

Social scientists need to consider all kinds of differential treatment, as this is a general feature of social life. As Banton (1994) notes, for example, the family, the ethnic group, and the state are all based on acts of discrimination. In families, different individuals have differing roles and obligations that require particular types of behaviour, for example husband and wife and parent and child. Members of ethnic groups may differentiate in their association with or exclusion of other people depending on the identification of their ethnic origins. States frequently discriminate between citizens and non-citizens in conferring rights and responsibilities. Although discrimination is often an individual action, it is also a social pattern of aggregate behaviour. So, structures of inequality may be reproduced over generations through repeated patterns of differential treatment. Here, individuals are denied opportunities and resources for reasons that are not related to their merits, capacities, or behaviour but primarily because of their membership of an identifiable group.

Discrimination takes many forms. Marger (2000) identifies a 'spectrum of discrimination' which includes wide variations in both its forms and severity. Broadly, three categories of discrimination are identified as comprising this spectrum. Firstly, the most severe acts of discrimination involve mass societal aggression together with violent racism and domestic violence which are two further examples of widespread discriminatory aggression. Secondly, discrimination involves denial of access to societal opportunities. Thirdly, use of derogatory, abusive verbal language that is felt to be offensive (e.g., 'Paki', or 'Nigger'), which, together with racist jokes, use of Nazi insignia, and unwitting stereotyping and pejorative phrases, may all constitute lesser forms of discrimination.

Dualistic notions of degradation and desire, love and hate, purity and disease, and inferiority and superiority may be involved in discursive strategies through which forms of discrimination are expressed. Explanations for discrimination require complex accounts that are able to embrace micro-psychological processes, individual and group experiences, competition and socialisation, together with structural power relations and aspects of globalisation. This type of multi-level approach was used and illustrated in the explanation of racist violence in Chapter 6.

Feminist perspectives on anti-discrimination law have challenged fundamental male assumptions which underlay the treatment and analysis of comparators. This means that in law evaluation of whether unfair treatment has occurred may be assessed in relation to how 'others' are normally treated. The vague notion of 'others' may in practice be white men. So rather than saying that discrimination law does not work because it is too weak, this critique would argue that it does not work because it is based on male norms. So this critique of liberal legalism, which is the notion that we are all equal before the law, involves revealing and challenging the invisible construction of white male norms, in law, public policy and sociology, which provide the benchmarks for assessing the scale of discrimination (Hepple and Szyszczak 1992). This critique is equally applicable to racial and ethnic discrimination. Further, other than using the position of the white majority as a test of differential treatment of minorities, making this assessment in comparison to indicators of human needs/rights provides an alternative method of sociological analysis.

What are other weaknesses inherent in the ideas of racial discrimination and the associated concept of racial equality? We need to be aware of the dangers and difficulties of utilising these concepts, and we need to develop a critical understanding of the fundamental assumptions on which these ideas rest. This section also considers some key problems involved in utilising the concepts of racial discrimination and racial equality, illustrated by evidence from the UK. In particular it considers the difficulties and ambiguities involved in operationalising notions of ethnic diversity, assessment of racial and ethnic hierarchies of inequality and the goal of racial equality which is illustrated using the example of housing.

Differentiation in racial stereotyping, socio-economic position, migration history, educational attainment, political participation and perceptions of social citizenship are significant across ethnic minority groups and they are becoming increasingly evident (Law 1996). Use of simplistic, inaccurate and misleading conceptions of their social location should be consistently rejected. A large scale study of minority ethnic groups in the UK (Modood et al. 1997) highlighted the divergence of socio-economic trajectories amongst these groups. Using data on earnings, unemployment and professional and managerial occupations as indicators of the extent of employment disadvantage it is evident that there is:

- severe and persistent disadvantage evident amongst Pakistani and Bangladeshi Muslims;
- relative disadvantage amongst Indians and Caribbeans;
- with Chinese and African Asians having problems only in gaining access to top jobs in large organisations.

This disadvantage is evaluated solely in relation to comparison with whites, therefore racial categories are crucial, here, in the identification of patterns of ethnic inequality. The adequacy of this form of evaluation needs questioning as it implies a broad policy concern with achieving ethnic minority representation in the labour market similar to that of the majority 'white' group. Here, then, difference is constructed as a policy problem. Clearly, a whole range of aspects of difference in, for example, educational and career aspirations, attitudes to self-employment or choice in the housing market exist across ethnic groups but to what extent are they appropriate for or amenable to policy intervention? The answer hinges on the meaning of the notion of equality and the ability to integrate issues of ethnic difference within this idea.

Similarly, remedying the fundamental comparative flaw in the concept of both racial discrimination, where the treatment of those subject to discrimination and exclusion is assessed against the treatment of the 'white' majority', requires a substantial transformation in policy assumptions and strategy. The assessment of equality of treatment and the degree of 'under-representation' against the 'white norm' is a prevalent assumption in discussion of racial and ethnic inequalities in, for example, housing allocations, educational achievement, benefit take-up or labour market position. Indeed the methodology of researching racial discrimination in many of these sectors and the practice of many equality and human rights agencies' investigations rest on such an assumption. How far is this appropriate? The problem of assessing the nature of racial or ethnic equality in provision of public services stems from the difficulties of reconciling differences in needs with notions of formal equality. For example, the assessment of the adequacy of levels of claiming welfare benefits amongst minority ethnic groups should be dependent not on the 'external' comparison with claiming levels amongst the white population but through an 'internal' comparison of levels of need with claiming. Similarly rather than comparing the difference in educational qualifications outcomes obtained between whites and minorities, a more useful comparison may be progression, attainment and educational value-added within ethnic groups. Furthermore, comparisons with the 'white norm' will tend to understate the scale of ethnic inequalities particularly where levels of deprivation and poverty are higher amongst minority ethnic groups. A general issue for policy makers, then, is the importance of greater sophistication and consultation in both national and local needs analysis in tracking ethnic diversity and constructing evaluations of both ethnic inequalities and policy targets (see also Harrison and Law 1997).

There is much conceptual confusion over the meaning of equality. Different notions of equality lead to different perceptions of problems and related policy objectives. Turner (1986) has identified four types of equality. Firstly, equality of human essence or ontological equality which is seen to emphasise fundamental equality between human beings with each person having an essential and universally free being. A problem for this position is the identification of any attribute which is held in common by the human species and hence this position requires a strong moral or religious argument which can override cultural relativity. Such arguments have been an important element in the challenge to scientific racism, although in emphasising formal individual equality this argument can also be used to challenge policies aiming to respond to difference, e.g. in needs or cultural requirements.

Secondly, equality of opportunity, the notion that access to education, employment, politics and other important social worlds should be open to all on a universalistic basis regardless of class, race, gender or other exclusionary criteria. In other words the supply side provision of opportunities should be open and equitable. This is itself ambiguous and contentious and a useful distinction can be drawn between equality of treatment, which implies a situation where no direct racial discrimination operates and individual fairness and rationalism are all that is required, and equality of access where no indirect racial discrimination operates and where institutional policies and procedures require careful review and amendment to ensure that there is no unintentional exclusion of particular individuals or groups.

Thirdly, equality of condition, where material conditions of life should be broadly equal across social groups; and hence the emphasis here is often with the implementation of programmes concerned with operationalising redistributive justice in order to encourage the demand for equally provided opportunities. Fourthly, equality of outcome; what is sought here is that social, economic and political opportunities are open to all, that compensatory action has redressed inequalities of condition and that together they have created representative or statistical equality across different parts of society.

In addition, Turner highlights three problems with these conceptions of equality: inherent mutual incompatibility, the massive social and political regulation required for policy implementation and conflicts between group equality and individual liberty. Some of these issues can be illustrated in relation to housing policy. The quality, condition and value of the housing stock across Britain varies enormously. To achieve racial or ethnic equality, in terms of housing outcomes, would require massive redistribution of wealth particularly in terms of property ownership, major structural changes in political control of housing policy and control of housing institutions and producers, and massive bureaucratic regulation of peoples' access to housing. Yet this broad, grand notion of racial equality is frequently operationalised as a yardstick to assess overall patterns through measurement and evaluation of indicators of housing outcomes such as tenure and physical and social housing conditions. Should the goal of policies be aiming to equalise the representation of ethnic groups across different forms of housing tenure and across the quality range of Britain or Europe's housing stock? Such an objective is likely to be both inappropriate and unfeasible. Major differences across ethnic groups in terms of aspects of housing demand, such as tenure preferences and locational choices, indicate that seeking to impose or achieve similar patterns of housing outcomes for minority ethnic groups as for whites would lead to a reduction in housing opportunities. An emphasis on consumer choice requires sensitivity to differences in patterns of housing decisions and choices across ethnic groups as well as attention to differences in cultural needs where identical housing solutions would be unhelpful.

Nevertheless, what is most remarkable in this field is the prevailing acceptance and acknowledgement of general racial inequalities of condition and outcome amongst many UK housing professionals and the recognition that group-based redistributive policies are justified. The impact of over 30 years of research and campaigning has been successful in this respect. The building of alliances between key agencies, individuals and the expanding black housing movement has been a crucially important factor facilitating this process. However problematic the vague notion of 'racial equality' is, it has provided an effective conceptual tool in the development of policy strategies. Indeed, its vagueness and generality have enabled it to evade the difficulties that more specific concepts, such as indirect discrimination, have encountered when deployed in individual cases and policy contexts.

The United Nations Third World Conference in Durban in 2001 affirmed the paramount importance of implementing the International Convention on the Elimination of Racial Discrimination. It also concluded that the major obstacles to overcoming racial discrimination were lack of political will, weak legislation and poor implementation of relevant strategies by nation states. In moving forward, the key role played by non-governmental organisations in campaigning for change and raising awareness of many forms of discrimination was acknowledged (Banton 2002, Law 2006).

Racial and ethnic discrimination and exclusion in Europe

General patterns of discrimination

This section draws on the most current, comprehensive assessment of cross-national evidence on racial and ethnic discrimination in Europe. It is important to understand this 'big picture' in order to be able to evaluate the nature and extent of such discrimination and to comprehend the depth and persistence of these practices. General trends in racism and discrimination in Belgium, Germany, Greece, Spain, France, Ireland, Italy, Luxembourg, Netherlands, Austria, Portugal and the UK show that a significant number of racial and ethnic minorities have subjectively experienced discriminatory practices in their everyday life (FRA 2006a; see box below). With many being particularly vulnerable to such exclusionary behaviour in the spheres of employment, housing, education and in interactions with the police. This high level of everyday, often casual, racial discrimination and the resulting perception across many groups and communities of systemic hostility will have a range of significant effects including alienation.

Ethnic minority experiences of racial discrimination in selected European countries

33 per cent	discrimination in employment including harassment at work, refused access to jobs and differential treatment in promotions
30 per cent	discrimination in access to housing, credit or loans
25 per cent	discriminatory treatment by the police in the last year and slightly less in educational establishments
24 per cent	harassment on the street, on public transport and by neighbours

→

20 per cent	denied access to either restaurants or discotheques and discriminatory treatment in restaurants or shops, even being denied entry to a shop
19 per cent	discrimination in interactions with providers of welfare benefits and with employment agencies with slightly lower rates in healthcare and social service institutions.
15 per cent	victim of racially motivated violence or other types of criminal offences

Source: FRA 2006a.

Across these differing national contexts targets and levels of discrimination vary widely. In Belgium, for example, Moroccan, Turkish, Congolese and Chinese people were key targets of discrimination with employment at 37 per cent being the sphere with the highest level of perceived discrimination. Lastly, and most worryingly, 86 per cent of those who had experienced discrimination did not report these incidents, which indicates a gulf of trust between minorities, migrants and public and private institutions in Europe. New evidence from 2009 onwards is being presented on racial and ethnic discrimination across Europe in a series of reports available at http://fra.europa.eu/fraWebsite/eu-midis/eumidis_output_en.htm.

There has been an accumulating mass of research evidence from the 1960s onwards which has sought to both establish an evidence base and win social and political recognition for the reality of mundane everyday racial discrimination in Europe and elsewhere across the globe. The response of many governments and their politicians and policy makers has been a flat denial. Reaching 'square one' on this issue, i.e. recognition of the reality of discrimination, has been a long and arduous task, let alone building a platform of successful interventions to tackle these fundamental problems. Here, the compatability between racial and ethnic exclusionary practices and institutional behaviours, environments and objectives may be one key link in explaining their durability and persistence, rather than the exceptional, unwitting or warped attitudes of isolated individuals. Nevertheless, there have been some landmark rulings and successes in achieving justice for victims of discrimination, as the following cases in Bulgaria illustrate.

Justice for Roma victims of racial discrimination in Bulgaria

Bulgarian courts have continued to implement Bulgaria's comprehensive anti-discrimination law with a number of key positive decisions being made.

In a judgment based on Bulgaria's comprehensive anti-discrimination law, the Plovdiv appeals court has ruled against a company operating a local discotheque for having denied its services to Roma youth. The court found the refusal of services to constitute direct discrimination. Bouncers stopped a group of Roma young people entering the club and rudely refused to let them as 'no Roma or Turks were allowed', non-Roma youngsters were allowed in.

In another case, Sofia City Court found an employer liable for race discrimination against a Roma job applicant. The decision is the first positive appeal decision under the anti-discrimination law. In February 2004, Anguel Assenov, 25, telephoned a company to inquire after a newspaper job ad for a

→

worker. He was told there were no requirements other than to be a man not older than 30. Mr Assenov asked whether he, as a Roma man, was eligible, and the employee who answered his call stated he need not even apply, as no Roma would be hired. The City Court declared an employer liable for discrimination committed by any of its employees regardless of their position, or decision-making powers. It held discrimination to be a serious breach of constitutional, international and domestic law, impinging on important pecuniary and non-pecuniary individual rights. The court declared the equality of all people and the prohibition of all discrimination to be universal human values fundamental to the rule of law and to contemporary democratic society.

The Sofia trial court has established important precedents in some of its rulings:

■ It has found the Prosecutor's Office liable for anti-Roma statements made in an official magistrate's decree, and has awarded the victim damages.

■ It has found the Minister of Education liable for racial segregation for tolerating the existence of an all-Roma school.

■ It has declared a trade unionist's anti-Roma public speech to constitute harassment and incitement to discrimination, and has ordered him to further abstain from it.

Source: ERRC (2006) www.errc.org/cikk.php?cikk=2602.

Exclusion and discrimination in housing: evidence from Western Europe

Across Europe ethnic minorities are living in comparatively poor housing conditions which contribute to entrenched patterns of social and economic inequality. This section examines patterns of racial and ethnic exclusion and discrimination in housing, drawing on national reports from 15 'old' EU member states in Western Europe in which references to all the studies and examples used in this section can be found (Harrison *et al.* 2006). The national reports are themselves all available at http://infoportal.fra.europa.eu/InfoPortal/infoportalFrontEndAccess.do. and provide a fascinating insight into the variation and diversity of racial segregation and discrimination across European countries from the shanty towns of Lisbon to the Roma camps in the industrial areas of Milan.

These groups are also subject to persistent, extensive and varied forms of ethnic, racist and national discrimination. This situation is complex and dynamic in terms of location, tenure and ethnicity. Within minority groups increasing socio-economic divisions are facilitating movement by some households out of inner city areas into suburban and rural locations, while other poorer households are increasingly concentrated in inner city areas. For example, polarisation within Somali and Chinese populations has been identified in Finland, with increasing divisions between those with low and high educational qualifications, job levels and housing conditions. Here also, ethnic minorities with higher socio-economic status were found to be less likely to be segregated in poor housing and social conditions. Across minority groups there are substantial differences in housing conditions or tenure patterns, and in the extent of discrimination and hostility.

Firstly, detailed assessment is made of the nature, types and extent of discrimination in housing contexts. Secondly, national examples are used to highlight issues of relative disadvantage, poor housing conditions, homelessness, tenure and marginalisation, together with movement and change over time. Thirdly, the impact of these housing conditions and locations on inter-related forms of disadvantage, inequality and exclusion is examined.

Racial discrimination: typology and evidence

To be able to identify and understand racial discrimination we need to know the mundane detail of how this operates and how particular practices cause deprivation and hardship. This section identifies, firstly, a typology of the different forms of discrimination we need to consider here, and secondly examples of the ways in which discrimination has operated. The different types of discrimination include:

- Direct discrimination, where disadvantaged treatment of a minority person or household occurs compared to normal treatment of indigenous citizens.
- Indirect discrimination, where regular or normal housing practices, requirements and conditions adversely impact on exclusion of minority households.
- Structural discrimination, where disadvantage in some aspect of material conditions for minority groups impacts on housing choices and opportunities. Structural mechanisms such as lack of information, lack of resources, and lower income levels may all operate as barriers in accessing housing and other resources.

Examples of direct racial discrimination in housing drawn from Malcom Harrison, Ian Law and Deborah Phillips (2006) are used below to highlight the variety of ways in which this works:

(i) Explicit discrimination

In Portugal, the local authority in Arcozelo, in Ponte de Lima, stated that no Roma families would gain access to its new-build social housing, while in another case Roma dwellings in Vila Verde were demolished. Also in this country there was discrimination against Roma families who were not allowed to buy newly built houses by some private building firms. In Greece, forced evictions of Roma are reported with great frequency, according to the *Greek Helsinki Monitor*. In Belgium, stereotyping by landlords of migrants as non-rent payers, having poor standards and being likely to over-populate the accommodation and associated discrimination is practised. Mainly in Brussels and Antwerp, complaints were made by Moroccan and Turkish people who were being discriminated against because of their colour by individual landlords, housing organisations and real-estate agencies. Similar evidence is given by *SOS Racisme* in France. In Austria, cases were reported of landlords stating that Africans were refused accommodation because they were seen as being often involved in police raids. Additionally, 'Natives only' and 'EU-citizens only' advertisements were reported in Austria, and 'For Germans only' and 'Only German speaking tenants with a regular income' in Berlin. In Italy, telephone discrimination was tested with estate agents responsible for letting apartments for rent. Nigerians, Albanians and Moroccans were the most discriminated against, at over 75 per cent of applicants. In Ireland 'no coloured need apply' advertisements for private rented housing have been reported, together with illegal evictions of foreigners by landlords. Meanwhile, discriminatory evictions of Travellers by local authorities are regularly documented. Discrimination against Roma, Somalis and Arabs in Finland was documented, with their being denied either renting or purchasing a dwelling because of an ethnic minority background. In Sweden, landlords, cooperative associations, housing brokers, stockbrokers and private agencies were all reported as discriminating actors, with landlords constituting half of all reported cases.

(ii) Deceptive discrimination

Here lies may be used. For instance, a flat is said to be already rented when it is actually vacant, or there is non-appearance by a person due to show a flat to ethnic minorities (these kinds of instances were also reported in Austria, Ireland and Spain).

(iii) Documentary discrimination

This may involve requiring ethnic minorities to produce documents (such as payslips) that are not required of other people, or non-acceptance of documents that prove a person's economic stability (as in Spain with access to rented housing). In Portugal a Portuguese guarantor was often required to obtain either rented accommodation or a bank loan to buy a house.

(iv) Price or housing condition discrimination

The practice of charging ethnic minorities higher prices for accommodation and/or of offering poorer quality properties to these groups is often identified. This clear exploitation of groups who had achieved adequate economic and labour stability to meet access criteria for accommodation was noted, for example, in Burgos in Spain. In Belgium, this process is identified as leading tenants into the hands of 'rack-renters' who let uninhabitable houses at high prices. This practice was referred to as 'discriminatory surcharges' in Germany. This is also documented in Ireland in relation to the Roma and private rented accommodation. In Vienna, Turkish households pay on average 24 per cent more rent per square metre than Austrians, often for poorer quality properties.

(v) Name/colour/accent discrimination

In Belgium, advocacy organisations identified the common practice of negative discrimination for rental accommodation in respect of people with a foreign name, as well as for those perceived as being of a different colour or as having a foreign accent.

(vi) Discrimination by local residents and pressure on institutions to discriminate

In an example from the Netherlands, a group of residents petitioned a housing corporation to refuse to rehouse a Moroccan man to a dwelling, and threatened him with violence and arson if he did move in. The failure of the corporation to deal with these threats was evidence of bowing to pressure to discriminate. In another Dutch case a landlord withdrew the offer of accommodation to a Roma family as local residents had objected. Refusal to challenge and deal effectively with racist hostility in local neighbourhoods is a driving force in this form of discrimination. In Dortmund, 3000 signed a petition opposing the development of a housing project proposed by the *Turkish Cultural Society* which also included a community centre and mosque.

(vii) Maximum quotas

Use of maximum quotas to limit and restrict the concentration of minority families on housing estates has been reported from more than one country (including for example Germany). The *Ishoj* case in Denmark is reported as a landmark decision which has prevented local municipalities from introducing quota systems there. (For a recent update on the key facts of this case see http://infoportal. fra.europa.eu/InfoPortal/caselawFrontEndAccess.do?id=35).

(viii) Discrimination in terms of quality of housing

Providing poor quality accommodation for ethnic minorities is one way of discriminating against them. For Finland, for instance, this is one of the most common complaints dealt with by the Ombudsman for Minorities, particularly in the allocation of social housing to Roma families.

Indirect racial discrimination also appears widespread across Europe, although this is sometimes more difficult to identify than direct forms of discrimination as it requires identifying or unpicking key institutional mechanisms that have an unjustifiably negative impact on specific ethnic, racial or national groups. Examples include:

(i) Refusal to provide land

Local authorities may through their control of land and available sites seek to use their powers to exclude provision for ethnic minorities. In Spain, a number of municipalities in Andalucia used grounds such as the lack of land or refusal to reserve land to restrict housing provision to Spanish people only.

(ii) Criteria for access to social housing

In the allocation of social housing in the Netherlands, the common use of length of residence, length of time on waiting list, or age, have been identified as discriminatory mechanisms to exclude ethnic minorities (because of both recent migration and a younger age structure). These practices lead to allocation of less popular, lower quality housing, and relative exclusion from higher quality rented property. In Denmark, racial discrimination in the administration of waiting lists by housing associations has been established, and the ability to speak Danish has been used as a discriminatory criterion in excluding other households from the whole sector of cooperative housing. In Milan, accruing points for Italian citizenship was found to be an unlawful indirectly discriminatory practice in the allocation of public low rent housing.

(iii) Income discrimination

The recent use of low incomes as a bar to living in certain districts (for instance by local government in Rotterdam) is seen as another form of indirect discrimination in access to housing, being disproportionately likely to exclude ethnic minority households.

(v) Housing stock discrimination

In several national contexts, the poor fit between the stock of social housing and the needs of larger minority families is a barrier to finding adequate accommodation.

Diversity and disadvantage in ethnic minority housing conditions

Indicators of housing conditions vary significantly across EU member states, which, together with wide differences in depth of data and evidence, makes comparative analysis problematic. There is also diversity across ethnic minority groups in tenure, household strategies and conditions. They generally suffer higher levels of homelessness, poorer quality housing conditions, poorer residential neighbourhoods (such as shanty towns), and comparatively greater vulnerability and insecurity in their housing status. Very serious housing problems include lack of access to basic facilities such as drinking water and toilets, significantly higher levels of overcrowding than for other households, and exploitation through higher comparative rents and purchase prices. Persistent difficulties are faced by Roma, Travellers, Gypsies and Sinti groups across the EU in securing adequate basic housing. There is also evidence of some improvement in patterns of housing conditions over time, but relative housing inequalities are highly durable. One evident feature is that several problems may occur simultaneously for low income households, with inadequate dwellings being accompanied by problems of high costs, overcrowding, limited choice, insecurity, or poor neighbourhood amenities. Relative disadvantage in housing conditions nonetheless stands out.

The diversity of ethnic minority experiences can be indicated by a closer examination of particular situations and examples. In Belgium, ethnic minority households often tend to be in poor quality, over-priced rented housing. Despite some improvements over time for specific minorities (including reduced levels of overcrowding amongst Turks), there have been increases in housing costs and a persistent gap in quality compared to mainstream Belgian households. In Germany, too, these groups occupy a disadvantaged position. They are more likely to be found living in flats and overcrowded conditions, with less access to amenities and paying comparatively higher rents. They have greater insecurity of rental contracts, live in poorer quality residential environments and are less likely to be home owners. In

France, persistent poorer housing conditions involves a combination of severe over-crowding, poor quality and old, deteriorating accommodation. Algerians, Moroccans, Tunisians and Turkish households experience the severest levels of over-crowding and least access to basic facilities such as a WC. In Finland, the housing conditions of the Roma are poor, with one-fifth living in inadequate conditions. In the Netherlands, ethnic minority groups are concentrated in urban areas, particu-larly the four big cities (the main groups being Surinamese, Moroccans, Turks and Antilleans or Arubans). These households are over-represented in flats, have higher levels of overcrowding than the native Dutch, and live in housing of lower quality. Ethnic minority households tend to live in more unattractive neighbourhoods, with less access to basic facilities including water, toilet and bathroom, and in insecure housing conditions such as sub-tenancies or fixed-term rent contracts. In Sweden, Africans and West Asians (particularly Iranians) are concentrated in lower quality rental housing, specifically tenement blocks in undesirable areas. In the UK, ethnic minority households are considerably over-represented amongst the homeless (although not as rough sleepers) and Gypsies and Travellers have faced conflicts over residential and transit sites. All ethnic minority groups have to varying extents been subject to racist hostility, as in many other countries. In Ireland, the Traveller community seems particularly vulnerable in the housing market: in 2000, one in four Traveller families was reported as living without access to water, toilets or refuse collection facilities (Harrison *et al.* 2006).

The severity of deprivation and disadvantage experienced by ethnic minorities in some countries is shocking and presents a very bleak picture indeed. In Spain, for example, the housing conditions of Moroccan migrants in Andalusia were found to be extremely poor: 75 per cent had no hot water, 57 per cent were in extremely damp housing, 49 per cent had no toilet, 45 per cent had no kitchen and 40 per cent had no running water. Meanwhile, the Roma are concentrated in shanty towns with 30 per cent of households living in sub-standard housing, exacerbated by poor facilities, overcrowding and poor local environments.

Even more striking, in Greece, housing conditions of the Roma are described as constituting a 'humanitarian emergency', with no access to sanitary facilities, refuse disposal, sewerage, water or electricity, and with discrimination in access to mortgages, price discrimination for rented housing, and direct and indirect dis-crimination by landlords. Furthermore, forced evictions and police raids on Roma camps have frequently been reported. Poor housing conditions are also identified for the Muslim minority in Thrace, while high levels of homelessness have been noted amongst immigrants and asylum seekers, with large numbers of nomadic Roma, asylum seekers and undocumented migrants living in squatting environ-ments of various types. In Thessalonica, 80 per cent of Albanian migrants were identified as homeless, with others living in poor quality housing having minimal facilities. Unacceptable living conditions in refugee reception centres have been recorded, with severe overcrowding and lack of basic sanitary facilities.

In Italy, the reported consensus amongst key actors is that migrants, refugees and asylum seekers face great difficulties in securing accommodation (and can encounter barriers such as discriminatory residential qualifications applied by providers of low-rent public housing). Homelessness and high levels of over-crowding are key features of 'migrant's' housing histories: 41 per cent of those with no fixed abode were 'foreigners'. This includes those using abandoned industrial warehouses, old apartment blocks identified for demolition, empty warehouses and camps. Nineteen such unauthorised settlements were identified around Milan, inhabited by Roma, Moroccans, Albanians and Romanians. Almost all parts of Italy have laws providing for Roma and Sinti camps, which are often in industrial areas, highly overcrowded, with poor access to essential utilities, and the target of racist eviction campaigns. Nationally, 27 per cent of squatters are authorised migrants with fixed jobs, with squatting resulting partly from barriers to accessing rented housing, including high rents, price discrimination and direct discrimination by landlords; 73 per cent of a national sample of 'authorised immigrants' were living in overcrowded conditions. In terms of quality of housing, one Italian study examined availability of facilities such as cooking, bathroom, drinking water and other utilities; over 15 per cent did not have either drinking water or heating systems in their accommodation.

Significant differences are sometimes identified in housing tenure patterns and conditions of minority groups. In the UK, for instance, Muslim communities (including Pakistanis and Bangladeshis) are more likely than some other minorities to be overcrowded and less likely to be home owners. They are also most likely to be living in poor housing conditions in terms of unfitness for habitation or serious disrepair. In Portugal, differing patterns are emerging in relation to different groups. African migrants have tended to build their own homes, with the proliferation of shanty dwellings and slums but with little increase in homelessness, unlike more recent East European migrants who tend to be homeless or in temporary forms of accommodation, such as disused containers with no amenities or hygiene. Recent studies point to improvement in the housing conditions of those re-housed, for example from the great shanty towns on the outskirts of Lisbon where overcrowding and lack of access to water and electricity are key characteristics. Similar to Spain, 31 per cent of Roma were found to be living in insecure, poor housing conditions, a figure that rose to 94 per cent in some localities.

Interlinked structures of racial and ethnic exclusion

The patterns of discrimination and the housing conditions ethnic minority groups experience has significant consequences, and linkages with other aspects of social and economic conditions. Poor mental and physical health, lower levels of educational attainment and lower income levels, together with many other dimensions of social exclusion, have identifiable links with poor housing conditions. In Sweden significant reductions in levels of employment and incomes result from living in racially and ethnically segregated metropolitan areas. Homelessness can carry major implications for other aspects of social exclusion. There is generally little reported information on ethnic minority street children and the experiences of unaccompanied minors in relation to housing. For adults, the lack of a fixed abode in Italy was noted as having severe consequences in denying access to public and private services including health, social services and credit, while also barring access to obtaining a driving licence. Difficulty in accessing credit and mortgage facilities was itself a key reported barrier to accessing housing. Consequently, those with a legal right to stay but who are forced to squat may then be unnecessarily excluded from these services. In Italy, Roma are particularly subject to these obstacles, which in addition to the isolated location of camps, present barriers for participation in work and civic society. Evidence from Spain highlights the lack of access to urban infrastructure such as shops and local services arising from the concentration of Roma in peripheral urban and village areas. Marginalisation of the Roma in terms of poor health, nutrition, education, social opportunities and social welfare has been identified for this group, for example in Finland and Greece. Geographical limitations and a widely spread population are also highlighted as being key barriers for the Sami (an indigenous ethnic minority) in Finland in terms of accessing social services, healthcare, jobs and education. However, these two groups are highly differentiated in that the Roma are much more likely to be subject to racism and discrimination than the Sami. Furthermore, Somalis in Finland are even more likely to be the subject of racist hostility than the Roma.

Gypsies and Travellers are one of the most at-risk health groups, with lowest life expectancy and highest child mortality rates and this is seen as directly linked to poor living conditions and life on unauthorised sites in the UK. The lack of sites and stopping places also has a disruptive impact on Traveller children's education, and creates difficulties in accessing healthcare and other public services. Evidence from Ireland also identifies the negative effects that living in unhealthy or dangerous sites can have both directly on quality of life and also in creating barriers and difficulties for Travellers in accessing healthcare, education, social welfare and other services. Although evidence is not always provided from each member state, such linkages are likely to hold good for other Traveller, Gypsy, Roma and Sinti people, as well as other migrant groups living in shanty towns, squatting and in other insecure, inadequate forms of accommodation.

For asylum seekers, it is argued in relation to Ireland that poor reception centres, substandard housing and social isolation reduce their capacity to become independent and fully participate in cultural, political, social and economic arenas. Furthermore, NGOs have suggested that direct allocation of housing provision for asylum seekers contributes to social exclusion from local communities, both physically and financially. In Austria, settlement practices for asylum seekers may not only exacerbate opportunities for their exploitation by 'speculators' on the illegal housing market, but also restrict opportunities for finding work, going to school and accessing social services. For refugees in Ireland, housing experiences and the rent allowance scheme are seen as creating a poverty trap which deters entry into the labour market (as this would involve sacrificing benefits).

The recognition of housing as a contributory factor in 'race'-related urban disturbances in the UK in 2001 encompasses an acknowledgement that housing is integral to wider patterns of disadvantage, poverty and social division (Kundani 2007). In Finland, correlations between poor housing, poverty, marginalisation, social exclusion and class are demonstrated. Meanwhile, in Sweden housing location has been identified as decisive for socialisation and interaction for children and adults, with poorer housing locations for migrants having significant detrimental effects.

Apart from real direct linkages between housing and other forms of disadvantage, perceived or mythical linkages may themselves indirectly lead to increased disadvantage and discrimination. Images and perceptions of ethnic minority groups' housing conditions and neighbourhoods, and their supposed links with crime, violence and drug trafficking, have also been seen as creating hostility and further forms of exclusion. For example, banks would be less likely to offer credit and loans, employers would be less likely to offer jobs, and local communities would be less likely to offer a peaceful, non-threatening environment. Portuguese evidence, both for those living in shanty towns and those re-housed from them, confirms this picture for some groups. Roma, people from Guinea, and Mozambicans have particularly identified the stigmatising effects of living in their neighbourhoods, whereas Angolan and Santomese communities did not hold this view. This indicates both the likelihood of different perceptions of various groups or neighbourhoods by outsiders, and different perceptions of exclusion across minority groups.

Not all ethnic minority households are in poor housing, and many overcome barriers to opportunity. They are not homogeneous or inactive victims who are supposedly unable to develop their own positive strategies, individually or more collectively. Yet despite this potential there are regularities and patterns of discrimination and disadvantage in housing domains, making it probable that, in a wide variety of contexts, ethnic minority households will be treated adversely by comparison with the majority households. There is certainly evidence of widespread direct and indirect discrimination. These are some of the key features likely to be found in many differing settings across Europe:

- Persistent difficulties faced by Roma, Travellers, Gypsies and Sinti.
- Changing patterns of ethnic minority housing needs, and diversity across these groups in tenure, household strategies and conditions.
- Poor quality housing conditions and residential neighbourhoods, and lack of access to basic facilities.
- Relatively high levels of homelessness, and significantly higher levels of overcrowding than for other households.
- Vulnerable and insecure housing status, discrimination, and exploitation through higher comparative rents or other costs.
- Some improvement in patterns of housing conditions over time.
- Poor mental and physical health, lower levels of educational attainment, restricted access to work and lower income levels linked to poor housing conditions or locations.
- Marginalisation of asylum seekers in housing conditions which restrict opportunities for finding work, going to school and accessing social services.
- Structural disadvantage, where aspects of other material conditions for ethnic minority groups affect housing choices and opportunities.

Exclusion and discrimination in education: the Roma

Roma and Traveller pupils continue to be subject to direct and systemic discrimination and exclusion in education resulting from a variety of interrelated factors including poor conditions of life, especially high unemployment, substandard housing conditions and poor access to health services. While some Member States have introduced elements of cultural or intercultural education strategies and initiatives addressing minorities and migrants, including the Roma and Travellers, it is clear that more systemic changes have to be introduced to remedy the present situation.

(FRA 2006b: 6)

The long history of discriminatory treatment of Roma and Travellers, both by states and in civil society, has placed these groups as the most vulnerable to racism in Europe. Marginalisation, discrimination and persecution have always been defining characteristics of the social life of the Roma since their entry into Europe in the fourteenth century. Exclusionary policies and open persecution were practised mostly in Western Europe. In Central and Eastern Europe, the Austrian monarchy and the Ottoman Empire aimed at eradicating nomadic lifestyles through assimilationist policies. During the Nazi period the Roma were specifically targeted and systematically persecuted resulting in mass extermination in concentration camps. After the war socialist governments in Central and Eastern Europe engaged in a concerted and culturally repressive effort to assimilate and settle the Roma populations. Although socialist policies improved conditions by increasing access to education and employment, they failed to provide equality of opportunity, offering jobs that were mostly unskilled, low-paying and physically demanding and education that marginalised them in the labour market, further weakening their access to decent housing, health and education and subjecting them to open racism and discrimination. In the 1990s anti-gypsyism (see Chapter 1) re-surfaced in European countries that were facing the prospect of increased numbers of Roma asylum seekers. At the same time, Central and Eastern European countries failed to tackle the reasons behind large numbers of Roma seeking to leave (FRA 2006b).

This section examines the nature and extent of patterns of racial discrimination and inequality these groups face in education. These issues were introduced in Chapter 4, which looked at Gypsy, Roma and Traveller (GRT) groups in the UK and found that these groups clearly have the lowest level of educational attainment of any ethnic group in the UK with, for example, minimal entry to higher education. Firstly, general trends are explored and then racial segregation and the forms of associated intentional school practices are identified.

Many Roma children receive no formal education at all, due to ongoing racial discrimination and processes of exclusion, and those that do attend may suffer racist humiliation and physical abuse by their teachers and peers. Also very few Roma will ever learn in school about Roma culture, history or language, or about the rich contributions Roma have made to the societies in which they live (ERRC 2008, OSI 2009). The Roma population in Europe is disproportionately young, due to a relatively high birth rate and a short life expectancy. Enrolment and attendance in primary education is low in most European countries and absenteeism is a persistent, common and serious problem affecting all Roma and Traveller pupils. Transition to secondary education is low and dropout rates increase with age, as a result of both moves into employment and low levels of educational attainment. Indirect discrimination in enrolment resulting from differential application of bureaucratic regulations requiring proof of residence status, or other documentation not readily available, and direct discrimination by open refusal of school authorities to enrol Roma and Traveller children have been well established (FRA 2006b). Placement of Roma and Traveller pupils in classes lower than their age group, largely due to erratic attendance, academic failure or temporary abandonment of school, has also been found; this prevents peer group integration, has a demoralising effect and can result in higher dropout rates.

Formal and informal practices of segregating Roma and Traveller pupils persist, despite strategies and policies that have been developed to combat them. Although systematic segregation no longer exists as educational policy, segregation is practised by schools and educational authorities in a number of different, mostly indirect ways, sometimes as the unintended effect of policies and practices and sometimes as a result of residential segregation. Segregation has taken place within a classroom by sitting Roma pupils in a different part of the room. Arrangements have also been made to instruct them in separate classrooms within the same school (following the same curriculum or a 'simple version'). Any form of prolonged segregation, even with the objective of improving educational attainment, has negative social and educational consequences. Performance problems that are wrongly attributed to assumed 'ethnic' or 'cultural' attributes reinforce negative stereotypes and 'label' pupils collectively rather than on the basis of an objective assessment of their individual performance. In those cases where such segregation involves placing such classes in different school buildings, it may have even more pronounced negative effects. Schools and educational authorities may segregate pupils on the basis of a perception of 'their different needs' and/or as a response to behavioural issues and learning difficulties. The latter could also lead to the frequent placement of Roma pupils in 'special schools' for mentally handicapped children, which is still a worrying phenomenon in countries such as Hungary, Romania, Slovakia and the Czech Republic. In some countries, more than half of the Roma child population is sent to schools for mentally handicapped children where they are denied the right to mainstream education and emerge stigmatised as 'stupid' and 'retarded'. As such, they live out their adult lives under-educated, unemployed or condemned to low-paying, menial jobs, unable to realise their fundamental rights and deprived of basic human dignity. Although some countries have tried revising the conditions for placement (e.g. in the Czech Republic, Slovakia and Slovenia) and efforts are made to avoid it, there may still be indirect incentives for unaware parents to actually prefer special education, in order to avoid the effort and discipline required by mainstream schools.

Racial segregation in primary schools in Croatia

A case was submitted to the European Court of Human Rights in 2004 by the European Roma Rights Centre (ERRC) involving 14 Roma children forced into segregated classes in Croatia. All of the children attended separate Roma-only classes in Croatian primary schools at that time. Their placement in segregated classes stemmed from a blatant practice of discrimination based on race/ethnicity, the pervasive anti-Roma sentiment of the majority community, and the unwillingness of the Croatian authorities to remedy these illegal acts. In addition, the children were subjected to a curriculum in the Roma-only classes that was significantly reduced in scope and volume as compared to the officially prescribed teaching plan, which resulted in lower quality education. Data provided by Croatian education officials confirmed this practice of segregation. In some communities, over 80 per cent of the Romani children were confined to segregated classes.

Source: ERRC 2008, http://www.errc.org/db/03/9F/m0000039F.pdf.

Wider patterns of anti-Roma hostility in relation to education are also evident. In Bulgaria, 86 per cent of respondents in a 2005 Gallup Poll said they would not want their children attending a school where more than half the children were Roma. This partly explains government failures to implement school desegregation programmes. In Hungary, general anti-Roma hostility was reported by about 37 per cent in 2003 and although decreasing it still affects a large section of Hungarian society. In Romania, research conducted by the National Council for Combating Discrimination in 2004 showed a significant level of discrimination in relation to employment, authorities and schools. In Serbia, discrimination has been identified as one of the key obstacles to equal access to education for Roma. In Macedonia, a UNICEF report on the Situation Analysis of Roma Women and Children states that 80 per cent of people polled apply negative stereotypes to the 'Gypsies' (OSI 2009).

In the Slovak Republic, de facto segregation of Roma children in special schools continues to attract criticism from international bodies. Approximately 80 per cent of Roma children are placed in specialised institutions, and only 3 per cent reach secondary schools. In Romania, Roma children are systematically placed in schools of 'distinctly lower standards than others, or are relegated to the back of the classroom or placed in separate classes.' Approximately 70 per cent of Roma students are educated in schools in which they are the only pupils and where they receive poor quality education. In Poland, separate classes for Roma in primary schools persist, notwithstanding the government's acknowledgement of the need to eradicate this practice. Roma children encounter discrimination in access to education in Russia as well, and are also victims of discrimination in education in some Western European countries. Certain countries have already taken concrete steps to integrate Roma children into regular mainstream classes. Thus, in Poland, the Roma children were sent to separate classes under the pretext that they did not speak Polish, although many were fluent. The Polish Minister of Education vowed that starting in the school year 2008–2009 separate Roma classes will not be formed. Likewise, integration of

Roma pupils into mainstream schools is also a priority for the European Union, which has established a strong link between the provision of sub-standard education to Roma (due to their segregation or over-representation in special schools) and their marginalisation and poverty (ERRC 2008).

Social exclusion of Gypsies, Roma and Travellers in the UK and political mobilisation in the UK and Europe

Gypsies, Roma and Travellers currently fare very badly in many dimensions of equality including longevity, health, education, political participation, influence and voice, identity, expression and self-respect, and legal security. Particular conflicts have arisen over housing and sites, media coverage and wider hostility where anti-Gypsy prejudice is often expressed with significantly less than is attached to expressions of prejudice against other groups. Also the criminalisation of this group has been accompanied by many high-profile cases and conflicts, including where they have been criminalised for being homeless (since those living on unauthorised encampments are very often legally homeless), criminalised for pursuing a nomadic way of life, and collective punishment for the crimes of specific individuals, whereby whole settlements are evicted because of the behaviour of certain of their members (TLRP 2007). Many Gypsy and Traveller families have been forced off the land they owned and found it increasingly difficult to find stopping places, which has brought them into greater conflict with other people and local institutions. Reduction in local authority sites and growth in the GRT population means that now over 30 per cent of this group live on unauthorised sites or, having nowhere to stop, they are sometimes forced to occupy public places, which overall has a huge detrimental impact on health, mortality, education and labour market position (TLRP 2008).

The most useful summary of the pattern of social exclusion facing this group has been produced by Cemlyn and Clark (2005). They confirm that there is a severe lack of adequate data on this group in relation to labour market position and poverty, and that successive governments and research studies have failed to identify the nature and extent of the economic context for this group and to go on to address these issues in the context of national anti-poverty and social inclusion strategies. However, the Social Exclusion Unit (2000), the Institute for Public Policy Research (Crawley 2004) and the work of the now defunct Commission for Racial Equality (2006) have begun to highlight this group in terms of racism and ethnic inequality. Cemlyn and Clark confirm that many Gypsy and Traveller children are 'poor in multiple and different ways'. Many are financially poor and there are many dimensions to the 'poverty' faced by such groups. Also despite the paucity of robust data on the income of Gypsy and Traveller families, both anecdotal information and other studies show that some families have few financial resources. Moreover, there has been a decline in previous economic outlets for Gypsies and Travellers, particularly in the crowded urban environments (Power 2004). And, local authority restrictions on working activities on official sites, such as pursuing trading activities or operating businesses, have undermined aspects of the Traveller economy (Kiddle 1999). Many find that simply being a Gypsy or Traveller, and lacking basic literacy skills, prevents them from accessing mainstream wage labour jobs or training. Because of this, access to social security benefits is important for some families. However, research has shown levels of discrimination and disadvantage in accessing the benefit system for those who are frequently nomadic, with some evidence of specific surveillance directed towards Gypsies and Travellers on the assumption that they commit benefit fraud, so that families can be denied benefit where there is little, if any, evidence of actual fraud (Cemlyn and Clark 2005: 153).

In many local authority areas, despite conflict with residents and media hostility, efforts have been made on a variety of fronts to improve communication, social inclusion and provision of services to both settled and non-settled Gypsy and Traveller families. A recent evaluation of multi-agency partnership working to achieve these objectives in Scotland concluded with the view that many families had been helped towards the services they needed and a good number were able to describe how this had helped health and well-being. But as yet these developments had not achieved a generalised impact across the Gypsy/Traveller Community as a whole (Macneil et al. 2005). Here, additional resourcing was seen as constituting positive discrimination and this was supported by many agencies given the clear failures of non-specific mainstream service delivery. So the UK experience can provide a wide range of examples of innovative practice across different local authority areas as new ways are found to improve patterns of provision, but substantial inequalities remain.

In a recent review of the proposed Education and Skills Bill, the Traveller Law Reform Project (TLRP 2008: section 2.3) argued that the existing barriers of bullying and racism against Gypsies and Travellers that are common in schools and colleges contribute to their low attendance record. The endemic problem has been the reluctance of local authorities to respond to the needs of GRT people, for example the London Gypsy and Traveller Unit states that there has been no strategy on how to provide adequate, useful vocational training for the 14–16 year-olds whom the Government recognised were not benefiting from school. They argue that there is a need to oblige all local authorities to have a Traveller Education Service resourced commensurate with the population identified in Gypsy and Traveller Accommodation Assessments, without which many children would completely drop out of the system. The experience of TLRP member groups in London is that where no Traveller Education Service exists, very poor practice is common in schools, especially concerning bullying and discrimination (TLRP 2008).

There has been increasing national mobilisation of Gypsy and Traveller organisations in the UK with a primary concern to campaign for law reform in a variety of fields including housing, planning and education, particularly calling for access to land for caravan sites, and access to schooling. The Gypsy and Traveller Law

Reform Coalition (G&TLRC) was an alliance of Gypsies, Irish Travellers, New Travellers and other travelling groups who came together to promote the Traveller Law Reform Bill and policies to increase and improve site provision. This coalition consisted of all the national Traveller groups including the Gypsy Council, the National Travellers' Action Group, the UK Association of Gypsy Women and the Irish Travellers Movement, the Advisory Committee for the Education of Romanies and Travellers (ACERT) and a range of other related organisations including Gypsy and Traveller support groups and units. This was disbanded (the reasons for this require further research) in 2006 and Friends, Families and Travellers, the Gypsy Council, the Irish Traveller Movement and the London Gypsy and Traveller Unit sought to establish a way of continuing the valuable work on law reform achieved by the Coalition. These four organisations agreed to set up the Traveller Law Reform Project (TLRP) (http://www.travellerslaw.org.uk/index.htm), which primarily aims to bring about positive changes in the law in relation to the rights and needs of all the Gypsy and Traveller communities. At national level, as with other minority groups, there is an all-party parliamentary group of MPs and others concerned to advocate these concerns. This works closely with members and representatives of these minority groups but speaks on their behalf. The APPG Gypsy and Traveller Law Reform is a parliamentary group committed to raising the social inclusion of Travellers and improving relations between the settled and Traveller community (Law *et al.* 2008).

The developing strength of such groups is a marked feature of both national and international politics and indicates the importance of recognising and evaluating both the political agency of this most marginalised group and the neo-liberal human rights agendas through which the increasing number of NGOs active in this field are advocating on behalf of Roma people (Trehan and Kóczé 2009). One key outcome from these activities has been the 'Decade of Roma Inclusion 2005–2015', an initiative supported by the Open Society Institute (OSI) and the World Bank which was launched in 2005. This is an international effort to combat discrimination and ensure that Roma have equal access to education, housing, employment and healthcare (for further details see the Decade website at www.romadecade.org). Nidhi Trehan and Angela Kóczé argue powerfully for the need to construct grassroots alternatives to the dominant, neo-liberal paradigms within which Romani peoples are materially and symbolically captured – paradigms informed both by 'older', dichotomised ('Occidental'/'Oriental') understandings of cultural difference and by 'newer' EU pressures brought to bear on Eastern Europeans to prove their Western credentials, which have led at times to their further separation from the Roma, or to the consolidation of a racialised social order in which they and other travelling peoples are ironically fixed in (last) place (Huggan and Law 2009). Building alliances can often be a fragile and difficult process and one of the oldest Roma-led groups which has sought to do this is the International Romani Union. A recent statement from the IRU sets out their goals below.

International Roma Union, action plan 2009-2019: objectives

1. Ensure positive discrimination in employment to raise the socio-economic status and improve life condition of Romani people by securing 1 million jobs for Romani people throughout Europe by 2019.

2. Enable Romani children reach their true potential in education by providing adequate support to 1 million Romani children and young people to enter, remain and finish education successfully.

3. Eliminate all forms of Romani people exploitation and traumatisation by the end of 2019; reducing by 15–20 per cent human trafficking – especially children and women, reducing by 20–25 per cent labour exploitation, reducing by 25–30 per cent trauma and sufferings inflicted on Romani children in institutionalised environments.

4. Increase by 20 per cent the access of Romani people to health and housing services provision by 2019.

5. Increase by 15–20 per cent the participation of Romani women in all aspects of socio-economic and political life.

6. Decrease by the end of 2019 the criminal and anti-social activities involving Romani people by 20–25 per cent.

7. Increase by 20–25 per cent the access to socio-economic and political rights of Romani refugee, migrants and displaced persons by 2019.

8. Enable a framework for the standardisation of Romani language and preservation of native dialects by 2019.

9. Promote and ensure well equipped and qualified human resources to work on specific areas of the Romani Nation Building Action Plan.

10. Accessing the above identified priorities and rights will become the foundation for both social integration and building the Romani nation by constructing social capital through viable and sustainable market, social and hierarchical relationships within European mainstream society.

Source: IRU (International Roma Union) (2009) *Romani Nation Building Action Plan*, London: IRU, author Floarea Maria (Florina) Zoltan and co-author Bajram Haliti.

Conclusion

The location of the Roma at the bottom of racial and ethnic hierarchies in Europe has provided a central focus for this chapter, together with examination of the mundane reality of everyday discrimination, exclusion and marginalisation. The concept of discrimination has been examined and forms of direct, indirect and structural discrimination have been examined in a variety of contexts. It is clear that despite a move away from the study of racial discrimination, for example in UK social science which had established a definitive track record of studies in the 1970s and 1980s, the strength and importance of these practices remains a highly durable and significant feature of the lives of minorities and migrants across Europe whether looking for a job, finding somewhere to live, trying to secure quality education or going shopping or to a nightclub.

It was found that ethnic minorities in Europe are generally living in comparatively poor housing conditions which contribute to entrenched patterns of social and economic inequality. They are also subject to persistent, extensive and varied forms of ethnic, racist and national discrimination. The situation is complex and dynamic in terms of location, tenure and ethnicity. Within some minority groups, households are moving out of inner city areas into suburban and rural locations, while other poorer households are increasingly concentrated in inner city areas. Across and between migrant and minority ethnic groups there are substantial differences in housing conditions, tenure patterns, and the extent of discrimination and hostility experienced. Nonetheless, housing disadvantage is widespread, and often severe.

Apartheid-like patterns of Roma/non-Roma segregation in schooling, particularly in Central and Eastern Europe, indicate the severity of contemporary racial divisions. The complete lack of schooling for many Roma children and massive dropout rates expose the failure of state institutions and are also indicative of high levels of widespread anti-Roma racism. In response to persistent exclusions and persecution many Roma/Gypsy/Traveller groups together with their allies have led a process of political mobilisation which has had some notable successes within the EU. The social and political terrain, of exposing and challenging discrimination, addressed in this chapter remains a key site for research and intervention.

End of chapter activity

A summary of the situation of Roma across a variety of social contexts in the enlarged European Union was produced by the European Commission in 2004 (see this report at http://ec.europa.eu/employment_social/fundamental_rights/pdf/pubst/roma04_en.pdf) Also a recent 2009 report on discrimination against the Roma is available at http://fra.europa.eu/fraWebsite/eu-midis/eumidis_output_en.htm.

Using materials from the FRA, ERRC and other sources assess the extent to which change in patterns of discrimination, inequality and political recognition of Roma rights is taking place.

Web resources and further reading

Harrison, M., Law, I. and Phillips, D. (2006) Migrants, Minorities and Housing, Vienna: FRA, http://fra.europa.eu/fra/index.php?fuseaction=content.dsp_cat_ content&catid=43c54ec8e9d0. This meta-analysis of trends across 15 'old' EU member states provides additional evidence on spatial segregation and debates over integration beyond the material presented here on discrimination in housing.

EDUMIGROM project output (www.edumigrom.eu/). This project is examining ethnic differences in education and diverging prospects for urban youth in an enlarged Europe through comparative investigation in ethnically diverse communities with second-generation migrants and Roma in nine countries of the European Union.

Vermeesch, P. (2006) *The Romani Movement, minority politics and ethnic mobilisation in contemporary Central Europe*, Oxford: Berghahn Books.

Trehan, N.and Kóczé, A. (2009) 'Racism, (neo-)colonialism, and social justice: the struggle for the soul of the Romani movement in post-socialist Europe' in G. Huggan and I. Law (eds), *Racism, Postcolonialism, Europe*, Liverpool: Liverpool University Press.

These two pieces provide a very useful critical examination of the processes of Roma mobilisation in Central and Eastern Europe.

References

Banton, M. (1994) *Discrimination*, Buckingham: Open University Press.

Banton, M. (2002) *The International Politics of Race*, Cambridge: Polity Press.

Cemlyn, S. and Clark, C. (2005) 'The Social exclusion of Gypsy and Traveller children' in G. Preston (ed.) *At Greatest Risk: The children most likely to be poor*, London: CPAG.

Commission for Racial Equality (CRE) (2006) *Common Ground – equality, good race relations and sites for Gypsies and Irish Travellers*, London: Community Fund.

Crawley, H. (2004) *Moving Forward: the provision of accommodation for Travellers and Gypsies*, London: IPPR.

ERRC (European Roma Rights Centre) (2006) *Justice for Victims of Racial Discrimination in Bulgaria*, www.errc.org/cikk.php?cikk=2602.

ERRC (European Roma Rights Centre) (2008) *Barriers to the Education of Roma in Europe: A position paper*, www.errc.org.

FRA (Fundamental Rights Agency) (2006a) *Migrants' experiences of racism and xenophobia in 12 EU member states*, Vienna: FRA.

FRA (Fundamental Rights Agency) (2006b) *Roma and Travellers in Public Education*, Vienna: FRA, http://fra.europa.eu/fra/material/pub/ROMA/roma_report.pdf.

Harrison, M. and Law, I. (1997) 'Needs and empowerment in minority ethnic housing: some issues of definition and local strategy' *Policy and Politics*, 25, 3, pp. 285–98

Harrison, M., Law, I. and Phillips, D. (2006) *Migrants, Minorities and Housing*, Vienna: FRA, http://fra.europa.eu/fra/index.php?fuseaction=content.dsp_cat_content&catid=43c54 ec8e9d01.

Hepple, B. and Szyszczak, E. M. (eds.) (1992) *Discrimination: the limits of law*, London: Mansell.

Huggan, G. and Law, I. (eds) (2009), *Racism, Postcolonialism, Europe*, Liverpool: Liverpool University Press.

IRU (International Roma Union) (2009) *Romani Nation Building Action Plan*, London: IRU.

Kiddle, C. (1999) *Traveller children: a voice for themselves*, London: Jessica Kingsley Publishers.

Kundani, A. (2007) *The End of Tolerance*, London: Pluto Press.

Law, I. (1996) *Racism, Ethnicity, and Social Policy*, Hemel Hempstead: Harvester Wheatsheaf/Prentice-Hall.

Law, I. (2006) 'Discrimination', in G. Ritzer (ed.) *The Blackwell Encyclopedia of Sociology*, Oxford: Blackwell.

Law, I., Hunter, S., Osler, A., Swann, S., Tzanelli, R. and Williams, F. (2008) *Ethnic Relations in the UK*, EDUMIGROM Working Paper 2, Leeds: University of Leeds.

Macneil, M., Stradling, R. and Clark, A. (2005) *Promoting the Health and Wellbeing of Gypsy/Travellers in Highland*, Scotland: Highland Council.

Marger, M. N. (2000) *Race and Ethnic Relations*. Stamford, CT: Wadsworth.

Modood, T., Berthoud, R., Lakey, J., Nazroo, J., Smith, P., Virdee, S. and Beishon, S. (1997) *Ethnic Minorities in Britain, diversity and disadvantage*, London: PSI.

OSI (Open Society Institute) (2009) *Equal Access to Quality Education for Roma*, Budapest: OSI.

Power, C. (2004) *Room to Roam, England's Irish Travellers*, London: Community Fund.

Social Exclusion Unit (SEU) (2000) *Minority Ethnic Issues in Social Exclusion and Neighbourhood Renewal*, London: Cabinet Office.

TLRP (Travellers' Law Reform Project) (2007) *Response to Discrimination Law Review: a framework for fairness: proposals for a single equality bill for Great Britain – a Consultation paper*, www.travellerslaw.org.uk/pdfs/single_equality_response.pdf.

TLRP (Travellers' Law Reform Project) (2008) *The Education and Skills Bill and Related Matters*, www.travellerslaw.org.uk/pdfs/education_and_skills_bill.pdf.

Trehan, N. and Kóczé, A. (2009) 'Racism, (neo-)colonialism, and social justice: the struggle for the soul of the Romani movement in post-socialist Europe', in G. Huggan and I. Law (eds) *Racism, Postcolonialism, Europe*, Liverpool: Liverpool University Press.

Turner, B. (1986) *Equality*, London: Tavistock.

Vermeesch, P. (2006) *The Romani Movement, minority politics and ethnic mobilisation in contemporary Central Europe*, Oxford: Berghahn Books.

8

Representing racism, ethnicity and migration in news media

Key issues in this chapter:

- Methodological approaches to evaluating racism in news output

- Race and the role of the media in different national and regional contexts

- Anti-racism and the media

At the end of this chapter you should be able to:

- Conceptualise and evaluate racism in the media using a variety of methods

- Assess the role of media professionals in relation to reporting race

- Understand the operation of racism in Russia and the role that media has played

- Assess the ways in which race has been represented in media output in both the US and Europe

- Evaluate the extent to which representations of race in the media are changing

Introduction

The purpose of this chapter is to assess, firstly, the methods and approaches that may be used to examine racism in news media output, and secondly, the extent to which representation of race, ethnic minorities, and migrants has changed over the last 20 years. As the International Federation of Journalists (2005) identified recently, there are two conflicting roles that media professionals play in this context. Firstly, they may often be seen as responsible for shaping racism and intolerance, promoting ethnic, racial and religious hatred and inciting associated violence. Secondly, they have also contributed to the fight against racism, covering the struggle against Apartheid and the Palestinian Intifada, exposing racism, discrimination and human rights abuses and advocating for equality and justice. So we might expect to find both these forms of journalism evident in news organisations and their output, and it is important to identify and address both these broad standpoints when investigating patterns of representation. But which of these frames of reference dominates news coverage? how and why has change occurred? and what still needs to be done by institutions and organisations in this field?

Race has been a newsworthy topic of particular interest in Britain, Western Europe and the US for over 250 years. The news media have, over this time, been a key site for the representation of ideas about racialised groups, providing a mass of speculation, commentary and information. This cultural archive provides an immense store of knowledge, values and images that have assisted in the maintenance and reproduction of racist and anti-racist ideas, which fuse in both historical and contemporary forms of racial ambivalence. Fascination with the allure of race and racism and their contradictions, degradations and pleasures seem to ensure that their representation in the media, and particularly treatment and coverage in news and factual programming, remains a controversial and recurring issue of debate today. This chapter, and the research on which it draws, develops from a similar analytical concern, that of seeking to identify and address the ways in which privileging and silencing of key themes operates in race news. The chapter examines three key issues. Firstly, the conceptualisation and methodological evaluation of racism in news output. Then, looking more closely at key themes and messages, the shaping of hostility, hate and racism by journalists is explored, and thirdly the ways in which the opposite set of messages have been promoted and represented. This chapter draws on exemplars from Russia, America and Europe.

Studies of the news in the 1980s and 1990s across the UK, USA, Canada, Netherlands, Germany, France, Italy and Australia have all produced findings that show the complex ways in which ideas about race have been reproduced through reporting about minority ethnic groups and migration (Jakubowicz 1994, van Dijk 1991, Campbell 1995, Valdiva 1995, Iyengar and Reeves 1997, Meyers 1997). A common finding has been the confinement of coverage to a set of limited topics (van Dijk 1993):

- Immigration and associated debates over numbers, illegal entry, fraudulent activities, forms of confinement and control, and the threat to society, culture and nation.
- Crime with special attention given to racialised crime such as mugging, rioting, drugs offences, prostitution and violent offences.
- Cultural difference, which is often inflated, negatively interpreted and linked to social problems, including inner city decline and unemployment.
- Ethnic relations, including inter-ethnic tension, violence and discrimination.

Racism and anti-racism are powerful twin social forces that will continue to shape news communications through the twenty-first century. They operate in many different ways across differing national and international contexts, and there is still much work to be done to map this complicated terrain. Trans-nationally, global news communications are a rapidly changing environment where representations of race are subject to dynamic movement, with old images and messages continually being rehearsed and re-shaped in conjunction with the production of new images and messages of both inclusion and exclusion. Globally, the news media play a key role in both challenging established identities and related world-views and in initiating and transmitting ideas and images which influence and shape new world-views (Gabriel 1998: 187). Yet the forces of migration, ethnicity and racism also remain powerful, continuing to inspire conflict and war, seemingly untouched by the new power of global communications.

Back to fundamentals: conceptualising media racism

How can we systematically identify racism in media contexts? The complex chameleon-like character of racism, which is subject to variation and change across contexts and times, poses considerable problems for intellectual analysis. The stuff of racism and who becomes its target varies widely within and across different nation states. But everywhere racism involves the signification of race to define a collectivity and its linkage to negative attributes. Specification is therefore required of these two key elements to identify racism in the media; the signification of race and the evaluation of negative attribution. It is crucial to stress that races are entirely mythical and imagined creations.

Our first task is to identify exactly when and where race is being referred to in a text. For example, does the use of a photograph of a person's face in a news story always carry a racial meaning? We might agree where, for example, a young, male, black offender's mugshot is used to illustrate a story of gang-rape. But we may also argue that showing white people in particular roles, e.g. as experts in news stories, may equally hail particular white subjectivities and convey a racial meaning. So, when is race being signified and when is it not? Further, how are we to arbitrate in disputes over racial meaning? The concept of signification draws on the analysis of signs which has developed from the work of Ferdinand de Saussure and Roland Barthes (see Hall 1997 for a thorough introduction to these ideas). A sign is the association of the signifier (a picture, word or thing) with the signified (an idea, concept, mental picture or meaning). In this case the signified, race, refers to a distinct group of persons who are seen to share common physical or physiognomic characteristics. Signifiers of race may include words (e.g. black, white, Caucasian, Negroid, ethnic, immigrant, Gypsy) or pictures (persons of common skin colour) and are open to complexity and variation in meaning and interpretation. The invisibility or normality of constructions and representations of whiteness combined with discursive strategies of racial denial pose particular problems for media analysis (Gabriel 1998). But the key point that the meaning of racial representations 'can never be fixed' (Hall 1997: 270) is illustrated by the varied and conflicting means employed to identify and measure such meaning.

Our second task is the measurement of negative attribution of race. This is often treated in a vague and ambiguous manner, and negative attribution may have a range of different meanings depending on how this is assessed. These include the following;

Different methods of measuring negative attribution of racial groups

- ■ measurement of negative attribution of minorities against a dominant white norm;
- ■ assessment of racial and cultural representation in comparison to 'real' life;
- ■ evaluation of the privileging and silencing of different cultural voices in relation to Eurocentric norms; and
- ■ perception of negative attribution of racialised groups by themselves.

(Source: Law 2002, 2009)

Whitecentrism

Firstly, whitecentrism – the comparison of treatment against a 'white norm' – is often used, for example, in the assessment of the portrayal of minority ethnic groups in television programmes. Cummerbatch et al. (1996) analysed a sample of fictional television programmes and found that in one particular aspect of portrayal there was no negative attribution, as 6 per cent of minority ethnic characters were criminals compared to 8 per cent of white characters. This may be a useful method for the construction of arguments around issues of inequity and unfairness in programmes and films, but this approach relies on a problematic notion of equal representation which defines difference negatively and by implication places a 'burden of representation' on programme makers. It implies that portrayal of minority ethnic groups should conform with the pattern of portrayal of whites and therefore places 'white' norms at the centre of the analysis and privileges these as given and unquestioned.

In the UK, work by the Glasgow Media Group (1997a, 1997b, Philo 1999) has also sought to operationalise whitecentric analysis through study of the proportional representation of minority ethnic individuals as presenters and hosts on British television and in television advertising. Analysis of television programmes in June and August 1996 showed that a large section of entertainment and factual programming was exclusively 'white', for example weather forecasts, documentaries, current affairs and quiz, game and chat shows. Analysis of advertising on ITV and Channel 4 in June and August 1996 was used to investigate the presence of non-whites and the roles they occupied. Overall, it was found that there was no general under-representation in advertising using demographic comparison, with 5.3 per cent of non-whites in Main Leads.

In the US, Robert Entman and Andrew Rojecki use this method to produce an index of media treatment of race (www.raceandmedia.com). They provide comparison of black and white roles in film, appearance in television advertisements and entertainment shows, and representation in news stories. They are careful to distance themselves from any argument that attempts to assess quantitative representation in relation to reality, e.g. where reporting of black perpetrators of crime in local television and press news items may appear to be over-representation in comparison to crime statistics. However, they also seek to move beyond quantitative whitecentric analysis to unravel the more fundamental ways in which white American norms and values influence and determine media output (for further analysis see section below on race in the US media).

This concern to interrogate the significance and role of whiteness in media representations through a deeper analysis of meaning is a more recent feature of contemporary debates. The call to investigate whiteness and white supremacist stereotypes has been made by Cornel West (1990), Ruth Frankenberg (1993), Richard Dyer (1997) and John Gabriel (1998) amongst others. Gabriel (1998: 187) refers to the 'eruption of whiteness' resulting from processes of globalisation, and the reassertion of whiteness which is active in 'maintaining traditions, representing cultures and anchoring identities' in the face of rapid economic and cultural change. Interestingly, the media's role is seen here as one of the pivotal mechanisms in challenging the historically stable centrality of white dominant norms and hence the media is cast as radically subversive in its powerful disruption of white cultural identity. Gabriel's work is particularly valuable in articulating both contemporary uses/forms of whiteness and also corresponding strategies of resistance and intervention. He identifies white pride politics (explicitly racist celebration of whiteness), normative whiteness (implicitly racialised political discourses – liberal universalism and national identity – and cultural forms – sport, music, film), and lastly, progressive whiteness (a politics which condemns both white pride and normative whiteness and perpetuates 'white' dominance, characterised in Greg Dyke's description of the BBC as 'hideously white').

This analytical approach opens up valuable terrain for discursive interrogation of media representation, which moves well beyond the rather mechanistic strategies of assessing whitecentrism set out above.

Mimetic accuracy

Secondly, and more significantly, evaluation of negative attribution and negative representation may be made in relation to the 'real' through examination of mimetic, or imitative, accuracy. Ella Shohat and Robert Stam (1994) highlight the values and weaknesses of this approach. They emphasise the value of a 'progressive realism', which can be used effectively to 'unmask and combat hegemonic representations'. The many examples of passionate protest over distorted representation, based on these claims for progressive realism, range from that of Pakistanis in Bradford over their portrayal as the emerging 'Muslim underclass' in a sensationalist BBC *Panorama* documentary and wider criticism from Muslim groups over Islamophobia in the British media, to Native American criticism of complacent ignorance in their portrayal as Red Indians in Hollywood films. In questioning the effectiveness of this stereotypes-and-distortions approach, Shohat and Stam refer to the 'obsession with realism' which assumes that the 'real' and the 'truth' about a community are easily accessible, unproblematic and pre-existing.

Eurocentrism

Thirdly, following on from this critique Shohat and Stam reject 'naive referential verism' and instead favour an analysis which focuses upon the 'orchestration of discourses and perspectives' based on a commitment to polycentric multi-culturalism. This is seen as involving a move from analysing images to analysing 'voice'; where the critics' task is to pinpoint the 'cultural voices at play and those drowned out'. This involves a conceptual shift from the analysis of racism to an analysis of colonialist Eurocentrism where the basis of assessment is how far European social, economic and cultural norms are used to negatively attribute the norms of others.

Racialised voices

Fourthly, assessment of negative attribution of race may be made through an analysis of audience perceptions of the members of that signified race. Karen Ross (1997: 244) reports both the 'aching desire for black images to be created, reported, discussed and interpreted in ways which recognise their humanity, not simply their blackness' (Daniels 1990) and the 'unbearable scrutiny' to which black audiences subject the few black characters on television. The key distinction, which Ross highlights, is the gulf in knowledge between 'white' media practitioners and 'black' audiences of the detail of everyday life in minority ethnic households and communities. This does privilege the role of black and minority ethnic groups as critics, who have a right to be heard. The problems of counterposing these two racial categories is acknowledged by Ross, who is sensitive to both the homogenisation of blackness and the strategic need to retain and establish the commonalities in the perceptions of ethnic and 'racial' groups.

Audience research by Mullan (1996) for the ITC (Independent Television Commission) showed that the main sample of white viewers felt that news and current affairs programmes were fair (71 per cent), whereas 59 per cent of African-Caribbeans and 37 per cent of Asians saw these programmes as biased against them through perpetuation of stereotypes, lack of explanatory context and choice of issues for inclusion and exclusion. Minority ethnic perceptions of news content fitted closely with the definition of institutional racism used in the Stephen Lawrence Inquiry, these included perceptions of racial and ethnic bias against them, an inappropriate service for people from differing cultural and ethnic groups, and prejudice, ignorance, thoughtlessness and racist stereotyping which disadvantages minority ethnic people.

There are therefore a range of competing approaches available for assessing representation and racism and the dangers of labelling news as racist, neutral or anti-racist without adequate and careful analysis can be a common problem for both social scientists and news professionals.

Race and media in Russia

Racism, ethnic hostility and discrimination in Russia are systemic. Pogroms, deportation and displacement of entire communities, particularly Jews and members of other ethnic minorities, are a key feature of the history of both the Russian Empire and the Soviet Union. Although modern forms of anti-Muslimism are related particularly to post-Soviet political independence movements, particularly in Chechnya, Islam, as other non-Orthodox religions and spiritual practices, were persecuted and repressed in the Soviet Union. The thousands of black African students who came to the former Soviet Union for education have also been a key target for harassment, attack and abuse. In 2006 the UN sent its Special Rapporteur on Racism, Doudou Diène, to investigate accelerating racism in Russia (UN 2006). This mission was prompted by:

- an increasing number of racially motivated attacks, particularly against people of non-Slav appearance originating from the Caucasus, Africa, Asia or the Arab world and associated neo-Nazi activity;
- the rise of anti-semitism as well as other forms of religious intolerance, in particular against Muslims;
- the existence and the increasing importance of political parties with racist and xenophobic platforms;
- the social, economic and political marginalisation of ethnic minorities and other discriminated groups in the Russian Federation (UN 2006: 3).

The rise of mono-ethnic interpretations of Russian political nationalism since the collapse of the Soviet Union, and the underlying economic and social crisis are seen as central here in promoting a culture of ethnic hatred and racism. This rising hostility was reflected in the reports from opinion polls which respectively indicated that 53 per cent of respondents supported the slogan 'Russia for the Russians' and that 42 per cent would support a decision to 'deport representatives of certain ethnic groups' from their region. A disturbing high-profile case which illustrated these trends was the murder of Khursheda Sultonova, a 9-year-old Tajik girl, in St. Petersburg in February 2004 by a group of teenagers armed with baseball bats, chains and knives whilst shouting the slogan 'Russia for the Russians'.

The role of the Russian media in the dissemination of racist news messages, political opinions and comment has been severely criticised. The growing influence of parties with racist platforms in Russia, advocating anti-immigration, anti-asylum and hostility towards a range of groups, includes parties with representation in Parliament, such as Rodina or the Liberal Democratic Party of Russia. Racist messages are openly disseminated by both mainstream and 'specialised' media, for example in the association of Roma and Tajiks with drug trafficking and organised crime, Caucasians – in particular Chechens – with extremism and terrorism, or immigrants in general with unemployment of Russians and criminality. More than 100 newspapers regularly use hate speech and instigate racial hatred against foreigners, at least seven publishing houses with links to extremist movements support the publication of revisionist literature, and over 800 websites of extremist orientation give open space to leaders of neo-Nazi or extreme right organisations (UN 2006: 43).

Moscow, Russia, neo-Nazi demonstrators salute and chant 'Sieg Heil' ('Hail Victory!')
during a rally held to celebrate Hitler's birthday.
Source: Justin Jin/Panos Pictures

An excellent example of empirical study of hate speech in Russia (Lokshina 2006) draws on monitoring of a range of national and regional newspapers and some websites, providing a systematic overview which shows that 51 per cent of news items involved support for hate speech by journalists, 28 per cent were neutral and 21 per cent included condemnation by authors, with a wide range of different forms of racial and ethnic hostility being displayed. This piece is rare in identifying the big picture of media messages and highlights the positive tendencies in media communications that need to be considered alongside expressions of hostility and superiority. We continually need to be alert to this global context of racial ambivalence. Recently the European Commission on Racism and Intolerance (ECRI 2006) has confirmed the increasing occurrence of race hate speech in the Russian media together with a lack of adequate sanctions on journalists and editors for making shockingly racist statements. But it also identifies that some media have tried to draw attention to the growing problem of racism and intolerance and to expose the difficulties that visible minorities have in their everyday life in Russia.

Race and media in the US

This section builds on consideration of racial Americanisation explored in Chapter 1. The global news coverage of the inauguration of Barack Obama in January 2009 exemplified the contemporary newsworthiness of race, and the debate over whether he is and will be 'too black' or 'not black enough' has been one dimension of his successful presidential campaign. (Also see Chapter 9 on post-race thinking in the US and this event.) One example is that of a broadcast on the extreme right-wing radio talk show hosted by Melanie Morgan and Brian Sussman on KSFO radio in San Francisco which referred to Barack Obama as an, 'as you call, 'Halfrican'. Sussman responded, 'Halfrican … his father was from Kenya, his mother's white'. He added that, 'in my opinion – 'cause my opinion is your average white guy', Obama 'is not allowed to wear the African-American badge because his family are not the descendants of slaves, OK? He can't identify with the discrimination and the slavery and all of that that's gone into these black families for generations.' (For further examples of 'hate merchants' on US media see www.mediamatters.org). As Obama himself said, 'the press has scoured every exit poll for the latest evidence of racial polarisation' (18 March 2008, Philadelphia). This fascination and obsession with race has been examined in a number of studies (e.g. Campbell 1995).

In an extensive study of race and media, including news coverage, Entman and Rojecki (2000: 44) confirm that 'complex ambivalence' characterises white racial attitudes, and that various media, including television, film and advertising, play a 'depleting role' reducing social understanding, which shifts prevailing ambivalence towards racial animosity. Harmful 'voids' or silences in the media, such as the pervasive nature of white affirmative preferences in the social division of welfare, parallel the presentation of an irresponsible black social world through stereotypes of laziness, welfare cheating, murderous violence and sexual excess. The relative invisibility of violence against African-American women in news coverage was combined with the presentation of a repeated range of stereotypical images; savage, violent, sexually excessive black fathers, drug abusing criminal mothers and inadequate victims. In a wider review of American news it was found that African-Americans were generally portrayed as 'rap stars, drug addicts or welfare mothers', Latinos were portrayed as 'aliens and foreigners', Asian Americans as 'inscrutable, manipulative' invaders of US business and Native Americans as 'Indian drunks' (CIIJ 1994). These stereotypes were seen as exemplifying whitecentric newsroom decisions and homocentric news values (a pre-occupation with nations and people like oneself and with defining those who are unlike as alien or threatening) (Aldrich 1999).

Race and rape in US news

The Reverend Jesse Jackson, in comments made on a television panel, pointedly criticised the frequent linkages between black men and sexual controversy in American news (Dennis and Pease 1997). Cases such as the sexual harassment allegations against Justice Clarence Thomas, child sexual abuse charges against Michael Jackson and the rape conviction of boxer Mike Tyson were used to illustrate the sensational depth and high news values given to such stories. Two studies of media coverage of violence against women in the USA illustrate further serious issues in production, representation and consumption of race-related news. The first study focuses on local news on television and in the press in Atlanta, Georgia (Meyers 1997). As Marian Meyers argues, local news tends to give more space to common, ordinary non-celebrity violence against women, in comparison to national network news where coverage tends to be limited to sensational or celebrity cases, such as the trial of Mike Tyson discussed below. This local study found that violence against African-American women was less likely to receive news coverage than violence against white wealthy women, and further that those African-American women who were represented in news items were more likely to be blamed as victims than white women (Meyers 1997: 66). This relative invisibility of African-American women is indicative of a wider 'myth of invisibility' where there is less coverage of minority ethnic issues and communities in news generally which is seen as resulting particularly from the whitecentrism of newsroom decisions (Johnson and Sears 1971, Pease 1989, Campbell 1995). In addition, Meyers argues that news coverage of violence against African-American women also reinforces stereotypes about them and about African-American men and their propensity for involvement in violence, drug abuse and prostitution. Drawing on specific cases, she highlights the representation of fathers as prone to violence and sexual excess and mothers as inadequate, drug dealing and criminal. The focus on African-American female survivors of violence as drug and alcohol users and their involvement in prostitution are seen as contributing to their representation as being responsible for the violence against them (Meyers 1997: 119–20). Although firmly situated within the stereotypes-and-distortions tradition of media content analysis with all its constraints and problems, Meyers shows that, despite the unevenesss of coverage, such cases of violence increasingly feature on the news. They do, however, fail to depart from the 'grammar of race' (Hall 1981). But the extent to which a case of race-related rape is seen by news producers as more unusual, interesting or controversial and hence worthy of coverage because of its racial content is challenged by this research. The evidence of relative invisibility indicates the opposite position, with less attention being given to coverage of violence against African-American women.

The case of Mike Tyson and Desiree Washington was, in contrast, one of the most 'prominent, perhaps notorious, news stories' in 1992, in the USA (Lule 1997). This provided an opportunity to examine in detail extensive news representation of race and rape. In 1992 former heavyweight boxing champion Mike Tyson was accused and subsequently sentenced to six years' imprisonment for the rape of Desiree Washington, a contestant in a Miss Black America beauty pageant. Jack Lule (1997) has carried out an analysis of five major newspapers' reporting of this case over a nine-month period (July 1991–April 1992) which consisted of more than 500 stories. Lule (1997: 382) argues that the reporting was 'flawed by its reliance upon racist imagery'. Tyson was cast in two ways in the reports: the black savage, inhuman, violent, sex-obsessed beast; or as the victim of social circumstance, including racism, who finally faltered. But Lule acknowledges two further key features of news coverage: there was no explicitly bigoted racist rhetoric employed and, secondly, the complexity of issues of gender and class which intertwined with representations of race. As with the case of Judge Clarence Thomas who was accused of sexual harassment by a former black junior colleague, Anita Hill (see Hall 1992), identities became fragmented. In this case, a vocal section of the black community was reported as siding with Tyson, the black male, against the 'bitch who set me up', a black female. Nevertheless, Lule affirms his view that news reporting reproduced 'modern racist symbolic types'. He refers here to modern racism as encompassing a position which takes the view that racial discrimination no longer exists and that problems facing the black community can be attributed to individual faults. Interestingly, Lule accepts that members of the press are not overtly racist and are concerned to challenge the 'covert expression of racist stereotypes' and the language of news. In examining news language, Roger Fowler (1991: 17) argues that stereotypes are 'socially-constructed mental pigeon-holes into which events and individuals can be sorted', and that they are a key creative feature of news which embody 'homocentric' news values (a pre-occupation with nations and people like oneself and with defining those who are unlike as alien or threatening). Criticism of Lule's analysis, following Hall's discussion of the Thomas/Hill case, could be made in that he contributes to reducing the complexity of issues, positions and identities at stake in news reports to the two major stereotypes he identifies, squeezing content evaluation into two badly fitting categories. In replying to this criticism in a wider context, Fowler (1991: 232) emphasises the power of news discourse in that it 'constructs' readers/viewers/listeners as they must switch on to 'paradigms and stereotypes' presented to them, even if they are operating critically, in order to understand the meaning and signification embodied in those news items. The extent to which such construction of news is biased, predisposed or prejudiced in relation to issues of race and ethnicity is then of key importance.

Migration

Coverage of migration has been probably the most consistently criticised sphere of news presentation relating to minority ethnic groups; for example Greg Philo and L. Beatie (1999: 181) state that television news has presented a predominantly negative perspective on the migration process. In the USA, the most common news stereotype about migration is that immigration policy is 'out of control' with an overwhelming focus on the uncontrolled movement of illegal immigrants from Mexico. This is seen as a result of 'sloppy journalism [which] turns a complex and encouraging reality into a simplistic and ominous fiction' (Miller 1997: 27). Robert Samuelson, a *Newsweek* journalist, wrote that 'The United States cannot be a sponge for Mexico's poor', (24 July, 2000). He argued that 'our interest' (the American public) lies in less immigration, particularly because 'many Mexicans have little desire to join the American mainstream' and also because this 'would hurt those already here' through depression of wages, increased anti-Hispanic racism and the overwhelming of schools and social services. For Samuelson, the economic benefits of immigration are seen to be 'transcended' by the concern for national unity. This position echoes some of the campaign radio and television adverts used by right-wing candidate Pat Buchanan in the 2000 presidential campaign. Here, the overwhelming of English language by the numerous languages spoken by migrant groups was portrayed as undermining American society and causing serious disruption, for example, in schools.

In reporting on the key issues for the American electorate, *Newsweek* (6 November 2000: 37) explicitly focussed on the failure of George Bush and Al Gore to address the immigration question during the 2000 Presidential Election campaign and asked them to address a 'central issue: how many immigrants are too many?' In calling for a return to the 'numbers game' *Newsweek* effectively demands that both Democrats and Republicans should 'play the race card'. This article portrays immigration as 'politically explosive', warning that 'whoever is elected won't be able to duck it for long'. The abandoning of the race card was a distinct feature of Bush's presidential campaign; ignoring immigration policy, steering clear of racially coded appeals and presenting himself as a supporter of 'affirmative access' (if not fully fledged affirmative action) and tougher hate-crime legislation in the televised presidential debates. Cohn writing in *New Republic* (13 Nov 2000) 'Why the Republicans abandoned the race card', analysed the increasing failure of the Republican political line that Democrats had caved in to black militancy through increasing federal spending on welfare, hence taxing middle class white suburbanites to subsidise inner city blacks. Increased Democratic emphasis on welfare reform, crime reduction and balanced budgets made this line less potent, hence the new Republican show of embracing anti-racism and diversity is seen as a roundabout way to appeal to moderate whites, particularly women. The 2000 US election therefore strongly paralleled the 1997 UK election of Tony Blair with a strategic view that turning away from the 'old' rhetoric about race and immigration was vital to electoral success. This has been further confirmed in the 2008 presidential election where overcoming 'problems that are neither black or white or Latino or Asian, but rather problems that confront us all' (Obama, 18 March 2008) resonated through Obama's campaign.

Exposing racism in US news

Entman and Rojecki (2000) find little hard evidence of the attention given by news media to exposing racism, whereas there is much useful reflection on the ways in which coverage can or should be improved. Is there a lack of such items because news media are complicit in the process of denying racism and racial discrimination? Or is this because this aspect of news coverage is seen as not central to Entman and Rojecki's chosen thematic analysis, hence it has not been adequately researched so far? Or is this because there is actually little US news coverage which exposes racism and highlights the benefits of ethnic diversity for other reasons?

In their analysis of the coverage of poverty they do note the important equation of poverty with suffering, by repeated reference in news items to racial discrimination, racism and police brutality (Entman and Rojecki 2000: 252). However, it is suggested that the connection between these two issues, poverty and racism, was rarely explained and also that it was frequently suggested that discrimination was common in previous decades and was 'over and done with long ago'. This material evaluating poverty and its linkages with threats (crime, violence and drugs) or suffering (racism, unemployment and homelessness) draws on news coverage from 1990 and 1993/94. As such, US news is depicted as abetting denial of racism and discrimination. But is this the whole story? Are most news depictions of instances of racism in American society framed so as to deny their contemporary significance and importance? This question is examined here through the use of a limited and selective set of recent examples.

On 5 September 2000, the *Chicago Tribune* and WGN (World's Greatest Newspaper) television news in Chicago reported on the case of a long-running racial discrimination suit against R.R. Donnelly and Sons, a printing plant in Dwight, Illinois. This case was front page news in the Business Section, Bias complaint put in new light. The central picture is of one of the key figures in the class-action lawsuit, Alan Roundtree, who is shown in church (he is an interim minister) smiling and holding the hand of an elderly seated African-American woman as if being congratulated for his role in this story. The headline reads,

> Testimony from current and future R. R. Donnelly employees is bringing to life charges of racism contained in a discrimination suit against the printing giant. Allegations include white workers dressing as Klansmen and wearing blackface.
>
> (Chicago Tribune, 5 Sept. 2000)

Rita Harrison, another black worker, told of a flier that circulated in her Donnelly place of work in Indiana spelling out the rules of an imaginary 'hunting season' targeting black people. Racist graffiti, racial discrimination in hiring, promotion and redundancy (e.g. when 31 per cent of white workers and only 1 per cent of 575 black workers were re-located) and regular racist abuse are presented forcefully and sympathetically in this article. Rather than the journalists' news coverage being in denial of racism, it gives voice to the lead attorney for the black workers who said about the company:

> They're in denial. [Donnelly] has a culture that is racist and its workers have endured treatment that is really outrageous.

The article arose through coverage of new testimony being filed which documents the black workers' experiences. The piece does acknowledge the vagaries of news coverage, noting that the case initially drew headlines three years ago when it was filed and had subsequently been forgotten by the media. Overall, the coverage of this case indicates a variety of features. Firstly, there is concern to present a serious account of a major case of employer discrimination. Secondly, the evidence, voice and images of black workers are foregrounded, sub-lines highlighted that in the face of everyday 'racial put-downs' you 'just put your armor on'. Thirdly, denials from company management are presented as such with no supporting comment. This example does illustrate that there are items which do not 'fit' the picture presented above. Clearly, discrimination cases such as this can be read by some as black people 'whining' and blaming employers for their own faults, but that does not imply that such news coverage abets denial of racism generally.

On 6 November 2000, *Newsweek* reported on violent racist attacks against Korean- and Asian-Americans, 'The New Victims of Hate, Bias crimes hit America's fastest growing ethnic group'. The picture used to illustrate this story shows a smartly dressed young Korean-American, John Lee, who suffered a fractured skull after being beaten outside his dormitory at State University of New York, Binghamton and he was told 'you damned Chink, that's what you get'. The caption reads: 'Scared. "I could have died out there, the system let me down".' This story uses John Lee's case to illustrate publication of a report from a coalition of Asian-American civil rights groups about increasing reporting of violent attacks. The article criticises the stereotype of Asian-Americans as ultra-successful and the associated denial of racism aimed at this group, by the FBI, the police and also other black and Latino students. The comments of the President of the Asian Student Union at SUNY are highlighted in the article,

> People think if you're Asian you're automatically interning for Merrill Lynch and you're never touched by racism. (Rizalene Zabala, student activist)

This article gives voice to Asian-Americans, criticises institutional racism and exposes little-reported violent racism, there is no evidence here of denial.

A further argument that Entman and Rojecki make is the failure of US news coverage to report the persistence of racial advantage that accrues to whites, for example the invisibility of white preference in university entrance for the children of college benefactors and alumni. This may indeed be so and is particularly evident in the debates over affirmative action, which were discussed in more detail in Chapter 5. In this context, it is interesting to note Ellis Cose's article in *Newsweek* (18 Sept. 2000), which chooses to focus on the advantages of whiteness, 'What's White Anyway'. This is not to discount the argument but to suggest that such news items must also be fitted into our understanding of the 'big picture' of news coverage. The article focuses on the historical need to claim whiteness in order to access citizenship in the US. It traces the decline and erosion of the 'specialness of whiteness', here Cose may fall foul of Entman and Rojecki's claim that this contributes to a denial of durable white privilege. In addition, in rather general terms, the item argues that race science has been thrust aside and that we are faced with the problem of how to reduce racial categories to the 'irrelevance they deserve'. Such speculation is at odds with the title of the *Newsweek* special in which this article appeared, 'Redefining Race in America' (18 Sept. 2000) – are we being asked to redefine or reject totally race-thinking? The thrust of the Special edition is acknowledgement of the increasing number of people who have mixed ethnic and cultural backgrounds. Here a key social shift in the US was argued to involve a move away from race towards ethnic diversity. This could be seen to encompass a lessening of both attention on, and the continued existence of, racism and racial discrimination. Linguistic cues refer to 'America the blended', the 'Age of Color' and a 'multiplicity of ethnic forces'. A reader's letter printed in the 9 October edition of *Newsweek* confirms Entman and Rojecki's point:

> Your special report on race was so eager to describe how race had changed that it neglected to tell how it hasn't. Black people in the US continue to fare worse than whites in accumulated wealth, life expectancy, unemployment, imprisonment rates and other significant social indicators.
>
> (Joel Olson, Phoenix, Arizona).

In fairness, a passing reference in the main item, 'The New Face of Race', does make this precise point but it is swept aside in discussion of the 'tricky cross-currents' of colour. There is also attention here to renewal of anti-Hispanic racism arising in response to immigration from Mexico which contradicts assertions of journalistic denial.

The *Newsweek* special edition on 'Redefining Race in America' was in a long tradition of such special race reports over the last 30 years including editions which have focussed on civil rights programmes, the role of black men, affirmative action, the Los Angeles riots and O.J. Simpson. Entman and Rojecki (2000) were highly critical of the edition on affirmative action (3 April 1995) entitled 'Race and Rage' which they argue heightened racial animosity through framing the issue as one of irreconcilable difference of interest between black beneficiaries and white 'losers'. However, they also acknowledge that coverage addressed the complexity of affirmative action programmes, gave useful case studies of programmes and gave space to William Julius Wilson and a black *Newsweek* Editor, Ellis Cose, who argued in favour of such action. Five years on, with a realisation that attacking affirmative action had not generated white votes in the 1996 Presidential Election and that a majority of the American public continued to support affirmative action, affirmative action, as with immigration, had receded as a key political battleground. Instead both the political and *Newsweek* message changed to one of emphasising ethnic diversity.

> Every day, in every corner of America, we are redrawing the colour lines and redefining what race really means. It's not just a matter of black and white anymore: the nuances of brown, yellow and red mean more – and less – than ever.
>
> (*Newsweek*, 18 Sept. 2000)

So, white–black divisions are now referred to as 'ancient' history, yet new divisions are still being presented in racial terms; red, yellow and brown. These precise terms were picked up on and used by Bush in one of the televised Presidential debates in October 2000 and are likely to be continually repeated in the news and by the public. Hispanic immigration, increasing intermarriage across ethnic groups, the reduction of white Californians to a numerical minority in their state, a total of three states and the capital city having a non-white majority, the coming emergence of Latinos as the nation's largest majority by 2010 and of course the 'new' popularity of stars such as Jennifer Lopez and Ricky Martin are seen as changing the face of America. However, we do also see a brief nod to the 'old' divisions in this piece which recognises the 'suffering from poverty, imprisonment and racial profiling' disproportionately borne by African-

Americans. But this is brushed aside in the new world where now it is 'suddenly cool to be mixed'. Here, the talking up of ethnic and cultural hybridity is also implicitly presented in racial terms. *Newsweek*'s 'America 2000: a Map of the Mix' (18 Sept. 2000) presents a picture of the population of each state as either white, black, Hispanic, Asian and Pacific Islander or American Indian/Eskimo/Aleutian Islander, we have no 'mixed' category here. A further item which discusses the 'flood' of Hispanic immigrants into South and MidWest America is entitled 'Brown Against Brown'. Why is it that racial terms are emphasised in this way? We are told that 'scores of towns have *browned* virtually overnight' (emphasis added). The article provides anti-racist reporting, exposing hostility from 'white old-timers', who made comments such as 'the s.o.b.s live like riffraff', criticising rising crime, chickens in the yard and 'yakking' in Spanish, as well as hostility from long-established Mexican-Americans (Chicanos) to the newcomers. One recent migrant, Perez, is reported as saying Chicanos may be my race (*raza*) but not my people (*gente*), resenting their hostility and displaying the taken-for-granted nature of race-thinking which is equally reflected in news reports.

Pessimistic lessons also need to be learnt from the American experience in relation to racial inequality and employment in news organisations ('Minority hiring goals released', *Politico: the forum for Latino politics*, 26 Oct. 1998). Twenty years ago the American Society of Newspaper Editors (ASNE) set a goal for newsrooms across the country to reflect the racial and ethnic makeup of the communities they cover by the year 2000. According to the ASNE 1998 Newsroom Census, 11.46 per cent of newspaper journalists are from ethnic minorities compared to 26 per cent in the USA population, whereas in 1978 these minorities accounted for less than 4 per cent of newsroom employees. So, despite some significant change, there is still a huge gap in the representation of minorities here. The ASNE has now set 2025 as the year when this goal should be reached despite criticism of the distance of this goal by the National Association of Black Journalists. In examining the scale of change in minority airtime in American broadcasting, a study from the Southern Illinois University of the Big Three evening newscasts showed that minority journalists covered 15 per cent of stories in 1998, compared to 7 per cent in 1991 ('Minorities gain air time', *Politico*, 19 Feb. 1999). Also this study reported that minority journalists made up 20 per cent of the 163-member network news staff. In the USA, therefore, despite major affirmative action programmes which have shaped a 'river' of individuals' careers (Bowen and Bok 1998, Leicht 1999) and assisted in producing a large pool of talented minority journalists it will take at least 50 years for newspapers to achieve minimum parity in the representation of minorities. On this evidence a post-racial America is still some way off (also see fuller discussion of post-race thinking in the next chapter). Further work does need to be done, across different national contexts, to assess the linkages between changing patterns of minority staffing and changing patterns of news coverage of minority issues.

Race and media in Europe

European trends

The identification of strong negative messages and mechanisms in news coverage across Europe has also been established (FRA 2002). Country reports on media coverage confirmed that once a negative discourse on migrants or ethnic minorities was established it tended to remain prevalent. This became a 'fixed repertoire', where event coverage involved a repetitive chain of statements, actions and conclusions (for example in the coverage on protests against immigrant settlements in Italian metropolitan areas, resolved with public order interventions and segregation). It was found that journalists provided a reading of the events which shaped hostility and was markedly different to the perceptions of inhabitants of neighbourhoods that had become the focus of reporting (because of conflicts, protests, or decay) and that they did not recognise themselves or their positions in the way their problems or lives were shown in the media. For example in Italy and Greece news coverage was found to be fuelling hysteria or alarm about (the settlement of) immigrants, an alarm which was then appeased by police operations. An anti-immigrant consensus was constructed in the Italian press coverage on such cases, by combining several forms of stereotypical and negative portrayal supported by representations of 'public opinion', or directly through the mobilisation by political authorities. In Spain, coverage of clashes in areas of immigrant settlement created a distorted image of the events, focussing on the illegal position of immigrants (who were not quoted), used generalising associations between the immigrant community and conflict, and suggested the existence of unified mobilisation by the Spanish 'neighbours' against them (FRA 2002: 36). Another general feature of news found in almost all countries was that migrants' or minorities' voices were rarely heard and were not treated as regular news sources, for example in Spain, Finland and Sweden. News about these groups particularly concentrated on issues of crime, violence and criminality and here Roma and Sinti groups were a key target. Anti-racist or humanitarian positions of organisations defending refugees and migrants were not always taken seriously and were sometimes the object of vilification, for example in the conservative/tabloid press in Italy and Austria.

Changing patterns of representation in the UK

Most studies of race in the news are highly selective and miss the 'big picture' of the complete set of themes and range of stories presented, focussing instead on the more obvious and glaring negative examples. A benchmark empirical study in the UK, presented fully in *Race in the News* (Law 2002) aimed to address this gap in knowledge and called for an inquiry into institutional racism in news organisations.

Daily coverage of race news on television, radio and in the broadsheet and tabloid press was analysed over a six-month period (November 1996 to May 1997) and this showed a significant shift in coverage between the 1980s and the 1990s, moving from overt hostility to anti-racism towards the presentation of an 'anti-racist show'. It was argued that, this 'great anti-racist show' may, in some news organisations, be operating as an outward, empty attempt of mere display, masking continuing normative and progressive whiteness in news organisations, racial and ethnic inequalities of power and employment and a collective failure to provide appropriate quality news services for black and minority ethnic communities and consumers. Such a 'show' may well, therefore, be playing against a backdrop of institutional racism. Nevertheless, in the case study of British news, just under three-quarters of news items studied presented a broadly anti-racist message, including items which sought to expose and criticise racist attitudes, statements, actions and policies, which addressed the concerns of immigrant and minority ethnic groups and showed their contribution to British society, and which embraced an inclusive view of multi-cultural British identity. There are a complex of factors which account for this process including changing cultural, political and government discourse over race issues, changes in minority ethnic employment profile in some news organisations, increasing recognition of anti-racism and multi-culturalism in regulatory environments and competitive rivalry in news production.

The Stephen Lawrence story dominated the news agendas in the late 1990s and was described as the 'biggest sea change in media coverage of race', by Michael Mansfield QC (*Media Guardian*, 19 April 1999). He notes the indifference of news organisations and current affairs programmes to the case early on (1993/94) compared to the extensive news, documentary and drama coverage more recently. Also, in relation to race crime more generally he recognises significant improvements in both local and national coverage. What this sea change will bring next in terms of trends in race news is uncertain. At best, we can expect courage, innovation and creativity in identifying institutional racism and forms of racial, ethnic and cultural exclusion. In Britain the overall picture of institutional racism that emerged from news coverage highlighted the immigration service, criminal justice organisations, football clubs, health authorities and trusts, the armed forces and private employers such as Ford as key problem areas. There is no silence here about the range and diversity of institutional racism and racism is not simply reduced to the problem of racist individuals as some critics have suggested (Gordon and Rosenberg 1989). The improved news coverage of anti-racist campaigning activity is a key change since the 1980s which reflects an increased openness to minority voices. British news and documentary-making contains a powerful thread of output that does excel in carrying these messages and debates forward. The renewal of confidence in anti-racist voices together with strong anti-racist political leadership may further strengthen and deepen this process across the news media.

In the absence of adequate representation of minority ethnic groups in major news organisations, particularly at senior levels, readers, listeners and viewers from those groups will probably continue to remain concerned about racial and ethnic bias in the production of news and dissatisfied with the quality and appropriateness of news services for them. Despite these patterns of inequality news output has undergone a significant transformation in its coverage of minority ethnic affairs and migration. Nevertheless, the persistence of a significant core of hostile racist news messages and the failure of legal and regulatory action to provide an effective response to these problems warrants more comprehensive action. Many social institutions in the UK, including the armed forces, have been subject to thorough investigation of institutional racism; news organisations have not.

Technological and regulatory changes are increasingly producing an environment that facilitates rapid changes in news organisations and their output. Media industry fragmentation, flexible working practices and changing relationships between news producers and their multi-cultural audiences are producing great opportunities for improving the provision of appropriate and professional news services. In this context, it is realistic to place a burden of expectation on major news organisations that coverage should continue to show a trend of improvement.

In January 2006, it was highly unexpected to see a new call for the news media to tackle institutional racism coming from Sir Ian Blair, the Metropolitan Police Commissioner. This echoes the author's call for such an investigation based on evidence from a decade earlier (Law 2002). The Commissioner's prolonged attack on newspapers for their differential racialised treatment of murder victims compared their treatment with that of the police: 'We do devote the same level of resources to murders in relation to their difficulty, the difference is how they are reported. I actually believe the media is guilty of institutional racism in the way they report deaths' (*Guardian* 27 Jan. 2006). Newspaper editors were very quick to dismiss his claims and Trevor Phillips from the CRE argued that: 'A blanket condemnation of the media belongs to yesterday and not today. The media could still do more to be even handed in its reporting'. However, it is very interesting to note that only a few months later, in April 2006, the CRE published two reports which did just that. *Careers in Print Media: what people from ethnic minorities think*, and *Why ethnic minority workers leave London's print journalism sector* both identified the racialisation of news organisations. The second report showed that workplace norms in print journalism were shot through with everyday racism in terms of attitudes, language and treatment of ethnic minority journalists. The first CRE report showed that ethnic minorities were aware and conscious of high levels of racism and discrimination in this sector.

There is no doubting the fundamental shift and focus in representation or race in the news that has taken place in the last 5–10 years with the obsessive focus on and debate surrounding Muslim issues. This was clearly shown prior to 9/11 by John Richardson in his book, *Mis-representing Islam, the racism and rhetoric of British broadsheet newspapers* (2004). His research found that broadsheet newspapers argued predominantly that Muslims are homogenous, separate, inferior, the enemy and that they can be regarded as Islamophobic, predominantly re-framing Muslim cultural difference as cultural deviance and increasingly as a cultural threat, whether a military or terrorist threat, or a threat to the democratic stability of other countries or a threat to women. Underlying this is a central dominant idea that Muslims are essentially barbarians in need of civilisation. Richardson's careful analysis of journalism identified prior to 9/11 a set of key frames of meaning available for journalists to draw on in interpreting more recent events.

A continuing linkage between blackness, violence, masculinity and dangerousness and the ensuing high-profile misrepresentation of young black men in the news media has been excaberated by both government and media response to a series of shooting, stabbings and related violent incidents in the UK (Sveinsson 2008, Law 2002). National controversy over black male youth has focussed on the problems of gangs and gang-related violent crime, under-performance in education and the labour market, school exclusions, over-representation in the criminal justice system, absentee fathers and low aspirations. In response, Gus John (2008) argues that there are a large number of young black men who have high conformist aspirations and who succeed. These paradoxical trends may in fact be complementary with increasing internal social and economic division occurring amongst this group.

Media coverage of Gypsies and Travellers has historically been markedly hostile and, as noted above, the most recently arrived Roma in the UK have been subject to highly visible media hostility and vilification (Craske 2000). This group probably receives the most unfavourable media coverage of any minority group, with headlines like 'Stamp on the Camps' being used by the *Sun* newspaper in calling for government and police action on Gypsy and Traveller sites (BBC News, 11 March 2005).

Media hostility towards Bangladeshi migrants has been clearly evident since their arrival in the UK, but patterns of media coverage have changed over the last 30 years; for example the BBC was recently accused of pro-Muslim bias by Sikh and Hindu leaders because of the large number of programmes showing Islam in a positive light, a total of 41 programmes since 2001 (*Independent*, 8 Sept. 2008).

In relation to press coverage of asylum seekers' persistent themes of reducing migrant rights, the burden on the welfare state and the dishonesty of migrants have been regularly presented with active shaping of editorial hostility. A 2004 study by ICAR (Information Centre about Asylum and Refugees) showed how this directly contributes to increased community tension and harassment of asylum seekers, but it did also show how the local press were more positive in some areas. This is confirmed by Finney (2004) in her work on press portrayal of asylum seeker dispersal. She shows how the *South Wales Echo* took a very different perspective to national discourse and examines how positive and humanitarian-focused coverage contested and challenged negative portrayal (Law 2009).

Conclusion

The task set out in this chapter was to address issues of the conceptualisation and measurement of racism and debates over how to assess racism in the media and to examine evidence from a range of different contexts. This may seem too intellectual for some, a task to be dismissed as irrelevant when racism is so glaringly obvious. Yet to engage and seek to challenge and undermine racism requires attention to the complex chameleon-like character of racism, which is subject to variation and change in form and content across contexts and times. Given this complexity, it is useful to identify those elements that are universal. The two key elements identified were the signification of race characteristics to identify a collectivity and the attribution of such a group with negative biological or cultural characteristics. To measure racism in the media specification is therefore required of these two elements, the extent and nature of the signification of race and an evaluation of forms and mechanisms of negative attribution. In examining the conceptual tools, available from earlier studies, to measure negative racial attribution in the media, four methods were found to predominate. These involved either measurement of the negative attribution of minorities in relation to whiteness, assessment of racial and cultural representation in comparison to 'real' life, evaluation of the privileging and silencing of different cultural voices in relation to Eurocentric norms, and privileging the perceptions of negative attribution held by racialised groups themselves. The power of interrogating hegemonic whiteness and its symbolic sense of moral and aesthetic superiority was found to be a much stronger form of critique than that of 'standardising whiteness', i.e. comparing the representation of minorities against a white norm. The power of claims for 'progressive realism' was seen in the ways in which this had inspired many examples of passionate protest over distorted media representation by minority groups. The critical task of pinpointing the different 'cultural voices at play and those drowned out' in media texts was seen to be valuable in foregrounding questions of the omissions and silences in patterns of representation. The value of privileging the voices of minorities themselves in assessment of media output was seen as particularly important because of the gulf in knowledge of the detail of everyday life in minority ethnic households and communities between white media practitioners and minority audiences. Lastly, data on minority perceptions of news output in the UK has shown that many from African-Caribbean and Asian communities felt that these organisations failed to provide an adequate news service for them. Minority ethnic perceptions of news content fitted closely with the definition of institutional racism used in the Stephen Lawrence Inquiry, these included perceptions of racial and ethnic bias against them, an inappropriate service for people from differing cultural and ethnic groups, and prejudice, ignorance, thoughtlessness and racist stereotyping which disadvantages minority ethnic people.

In this field there is a tendency to focus on 'bashing the bias' in news output and failing to recognise the ways in which news media can contribute in the widest sense to an anti-racist, inclusive, humanitarian project. There has been some evidence of declining media, political and social hostility to both settled minority ethnic groups and new migrant groups which provide the conditions for the creation of a climate of greater trust in which more open discussion and debate of sensitive issues affecting minority ethnic groups in the news can fruitfully take place. These more progressive social spaces are continually subject to the swift remembering, reinvention and restatement of hostile messages, as seen in Russia, America and Europe in the first decade of this century. The strength of white backlash culture (Gabriel 1998) and racially and ethnically constructed forms of political nationalism must never be under-estimated, and the strength of repeated linkages between violence, crime, race and migration remain the most worrying aspects of contemporary news coverage. Recent evidence on race and sport in UK and US media also confirms the re-invigoration of racialisation and whitecentrism in coverage of Black and Asian athletes (Law and Hylton 2009).

Global systems of communication appear to have reawakened nationalist, political myths and old fears of the Other, rather than contributing to enlightened public understanding (Brinks *et al.* 2006). The focus on political myths and conspiracy theories, and the use of communications media to promote these, is one of many tendencies in this arena. This does not undermine the radical case that exposing and challenging journalistic and media practices which buttress xenophobia, hatred and nationalist myths is a vital and urgent contemporary task. In the US, the historical construction of Jewish conspiracy theories amongst the American far right and the contemporary construction of countries of the world as either good or evil (a dualist Manichaean tendency) in American foreign policy, together with the myths of American virtue and its cultural and moral superiority in world affairs illustrates the scale of these problems. In the UK, 'malign media intervention' by the BBC in constructing the Islamic threat and in presenting American orthodoxy as 'balanced' reporting could be seen as paralleling anti-semitism, for example coverage by the liberal press in 1899/1900 Vienna and the construction of the Jewish threat. The increasing electoral support for the extreme right in the UK, although small and historically short-lived, is seen as being tied particularly to increasing media interest and improving sophistication in exploiting both traditional and newer opportunities in this field. Anti-semitic internet sites and rising expressions of holocaust denial are also indicative of this latter trend. Evidence from both the UK and Sweden shows the continuing exploitation of a more traditional form of communication, the letters page in local newspapers, to express racial hostility. The use of various media to promote New Right and neo-Nazi ideas in Germany and Austria is also worrying. The re-framing of Rudolph Hess as a hero for the extreme right, the relationship between German and Austrian nationalism and the Holocaust and newer hostility to asylum seekers and foreigners illustrate some of the connections between politicians, media and audiences. In Russia, there is the use of television programmes to provide a platform for extremist, anti-semitic groups and the widespread use of books, internet sites and pamphlets to peddle conspiracy theories, Orthodox nationalism and apocalyptic and anti-Jewish myths. Also, recent religiously driven nationalist campaigning through the media to rehabilitate Rasputin as a symbol of 'martyred Russia' provides a strong warning message for those engaged in current debates over global media communications.

End of chapter activity

Using the *Diversity Toolkit for Factual Programmes in Public Television* (FRA 2008), http://fra.europa.eu/fra/index.php?fuseaction=content.dsp_cat_content& contentid=478de35bcdb41&catid=3eddba5601ad4&search=1&frmsearch= diversity%20toolkit&lang=EN, as a guide to critical issues and questions and cross-European resources, what does 'managing diversity' in the media mean? How have different public service broadcasters across Europe addressed this issue? And what fundamental problems remain?

Further reading

Downing, J. and Husband, C. (2005) *Representing 'Race'*, **London: Sage.** A very useful text which addresses conceptual debates and draws on evidence from USA, Europe, Australia and the UK.

The following sources provide further material in patterns of race and media representation in America, Europe, the UK and Russia addressed in this chapter.

Entman, R. M. and Rojecki, A. (2000) *The Black Image in the White Mind, media and race in America,* **Chicago: University of Chicago Press**

FRA (Fundamental Rights Agency) (2006) *Racism and Cultural Diversity in the Mass Media,* **Vienna: FRA.** http://fra.europa.eu/fra/index.php?fuseaction=content.dsp_cat_content&catid=3fb38ad3e22bb&contentid=3fb3f9cfb3592

Law, I. (2002) *Race in the News,* **Basingstoke: Palgrave.**

A variety of recent research reports on ethnic minority groups and communications in the UK are also available from Ofcom at www.ofcom.org.uk/.

Lokshina, T. (2006) '"Hate Speech" in the media: monitoring prejudice in Russia' in J. H. Brinks, S. Rock and E. Timms, *Nationalist Myths and Modern Media, contested identities in the age of globalisation,* **London: Tauris Academic Studies.**

References

Aldrich, L. S. (1999) *Covering the Community: a diversity handbook for media*, London: Sage.

Bowen, W. G. and Bok, D. (1998) *The Shape of the River*, Princeton, NJ: Princeton University Press.

Campbell, C. (1995) *Race, Myth and News*, London: Sage.

Brinks, J. H., Rock, S. and Timms, E. (eds) (2006) *Nationalist Myths and Modern Media, contested identities in the age of globalisation*, London: Tauris Academic Studies.

Centre for Integration and Improvement of Journalism (CIIJ) (1994) *News Watch: a critical look at coverage of people of colour*, San Francisco: San Francisco State University.

Commission for Racial Equality (2006a) *Careers in Print Media: what people from ethnic minorities think*, London: CRE.

Commission for Racial Equality (2006b) *Why Ethnic Minority Workers Leave London's Print Media*, London: CRE.

Craske, O. (2000) 'Breathing uneasy sighs of relief', *Central European Review*, 2, 27, July, www.pecina.cz/files/www.ce-review.org/00/27/craske27.html (accessed 6 Aug. 2008).

Cummerbatch, G. and Woods, S. with Stephenson, C., Boyle, M., Smith, A. and Gauntlett, S. (1996) *Ethnic Minorities on Television*, London: ITC.

Daniels, T. (1990) 'Beyond negative and positive images', in J. Willis and T. Wollen (eds.) *The Neglected Audience*, London: British Film Institute.

Dennis, E. and Pease, E. (eds) (1997) *The Media in Black and White*, New Brunswick: Transaction.

Dyer, R. (1997) *White*, London: Routledge.

ECRI (European Commission against Racism and Intolerance) (2006) *Third Report on the Russian Federation*, Strasbourg: ECRI. www.coe.int/t/e/human_rights/ecri/1-ecri/2-country-by-country_approach/russian_federation/Russian%20Federation%20third%20report%20-%20cri06-21.pdf.

Entman, R. M. and Rojecki, A. (2000) *The Black Image in the White Mind, media and race in America*, Chicago: University of Chicago Press.

Finney, N. (2004) *Asylum Seeker Dispersal: public attitudes and press portrayals around the UK*, PhD thesis, University of Wales, Swansea.

Fowler, R. (1991) *Language in the News*, London: Routledge.

FRA (Fundamental Rights Agency) (2002) *Racism and cultural diversity in the mass media*, Vienna: FRA http://fra.europa.eu/fra/index.php?fuseaction=content.dsp_cat_content&catid=3fb38ad3e22bb&contentid=3fb3f9cfb3592.

Frankenberg, R. (1993) *The Social Construction of Whiteness: white women, race matters*, London: Routledge.

Gabriel, J. (1998) *Whitewash, Racialised Politics and the Media*, London: Routledge.

Glasgow Media Group (1997a) *'Race' and the Public Face of Television*, Glasgow: GMG.

Glasgow Media Group (1997b) *Ethnic Minorities in Television Advertising*, Glasgow: GMG.

Gordon, P. and Rosenberg, D. (1989) *Daily Racism*, London: Runnymede Trust.

Hall, S. (1981) 'The whites of their eyes: racist ideologies and the media', in G. Bridges and R. Brunt (eds) *Silver Linings: some strategies for the eighties*, London: Lawrence and Wishart.

Hall, S. (1992) 'The question of cultural identity', in S. Hall, D. Held and T. McGrew, *Modernity and its Futures*, London: Sage/OU.

Hall, S. (ed.) (1997) *Representation: cultural representations and signifying practices*, London: Sage/OU.

ICAR (2004) *Media image, community impact*, London: ICAR.

International Federation of Journalists (2006) 'IFJ calls for Ethical Journalism Campaign to counter collapse in media standards', 17 Nov., www.ifj.org/en/articles/ifj-calls-for-ethical-journalism-campaign-to-counter-collapse-in-media-standards.

Iyengar, S. and Reeves, R. (eds) (1997) *Do the Media Govern? Politicians, voters and reporters in America*, London: Sage.

Jakubowicz, A. (ed.) (1994) *Racism, Ethnicity and the Media*, Sydney: Allen and Unwin.

John, G. (2008) Quoted in 'The silent majority', *Media Guardian*, 25 Aug.

Johnson, P. B. and Sears, D. O. (1971) 'Black invisibility, the press and the Los Angeles riot', *American Journal of Sociology*, 76, 1, pp. 698–721.

Law, I. (2002) *Race in the News*, Basingstoke: Palgrave.

Law, I. (2009) 'Changing representations of race in the news', in M. Pritchard (ed.) *The Contexts for Communication, media, representation and society*, Chester: Chester Academic Press.

Law, I. and Hylton, K. (2009) '"Race", sport and the media', in K. Hylton, *'Race' and Sport, critical race theory*, London: Routledge.

Leicht, K. T. (ed.) (1999) *The Future of Affirmative Action, research in social stratification and mobility*, Vol. 17, Stamford, CT: JAI Press.

Lokshina, T. (2006) '"Hate Speech" in the media: monitoring prejudice in Russia', in J. H. Brinks, S. Rock and E. Timms (eds), *Nationalist Myths and Modern Media, contested identities in the age of globalisation*, London: Tauris Academic Studies.

Lule, J. (1997) 'The rape of Mike Tyson: race, the press and symbolic types', in D. Berkowitz (ed.), *Social Meanings of News*, London: Sage.

Mac an Ghaill, M. (1999) *Contemporary Racism and Ethnicities, social and cultural transformations*, Buckingham: Open University Press.

Meyers, M. (1997) *News Coverage of Violence against Women*, London: Sage.

Miller, J. (1997) 'Immigration, the press and the new racism', in E. E. Dennis and E. C. Pease (eds) *The Media in Black and White*, New Brunswick, NJ: Transaction.

Mullan, B. (1996) *Not a Pretty Picture, ethnic minority views of television*, Aldershot: Avebury.

Pease, E. C. (1989) 'Kerner plus 20: minority news coverage in the Columbus Dispatch', *Newspaper Research Journal*, 10, 3, pp. 17–38.

Philo, G. (ed.) (1999) *Message Received*, Harlow: Longman.

Philo, G. and Beattie, L. (1999) 'Race, migration and media', in G. Philo (ed.) *Message Received*, Harlow: Longman.

Richardson, J. (2004) *Mis-representing Islam, the racism and rhetoric of British broadsheet newspapers*, Amsterdam: John Benjamins Publishing Company.

Ross, K. (1997) 'Viewing (p)leasure, viewer pain: black audiences and British television', *Leisure Studies*, 16, pp. 233–248.

Shohat, E. and Stam, R. (1994) *Unthinking Eurocentrism, multiculturalism and the media*, London: Routledge.

Sveinsson, K. (2008) *A Tale of Two Englands, race and violent crime in the media*, London: Runnymede Trust.

Valdiva, A. (ed.) (1995) *Feminism, Multiculturalism and the Media*, London: Sage.

van Dijk, T. (1991) *Racism in the Press*, London: Routledge.

van Dijk, T. (1993) *Elite Discourse and Racism*, London, Sage.

van Ginneken, J., (1998) *Understanding Global News*, London: Sage.

West, C. (1990) 'The new politics of cultural difference', in R. Ferguson, M. Gever, T. T. Minh-ha and C. West (eds) *Out There*, Cambridge, MA: MIT Press.

United Nations (2006) *Mission to the Russian Federation*, New York: UN, www.unhcr.org/refworld/docid/46723d7e2.html.

9

Prospects for a post-racial, post-ethnic world

Key issues

- Post-racial thinking

- Racism and ethnic conflict across the globe

- Contemporary patterns of conflict, hostility and discrimination

- Group claims for recognition, rights and difference

Learning points

- Advocates and critiques of post-racial thinking

- Assessing patterns of minority domination

- Understanding racial crisis at planetary, national and local levels

- Evaluating future scenarios for racism and ethnicity

Introduction

How should we understand the meaning of racism and ethnicity in a post-civil rights, post-apartheid, post-colonial, post-national, post-racial world? This chapter examines the prospects for moving beyond racial and ethnic divisions and conflict. Firstly, the meaning of the 'post-racial' is explored. This has been the subject of widespread recent popular debate following the election of a black American President and it has also been an increasing feature of intellectual debate in this sociological field. Varying positions and interpretations of this debate are examined. But racism and ethnicity are not in decline, and many sociologists have been wrong in predicting their demise, including Max Weber, as discussed in Chapter 3.

> Weber may be criticised along with almost every other social thinker from the time of the French Revolution to the outbreak of World War 1 for failing to give sufficient weight to racial, ethnic and national conflicts.

> (Stone 2003: 29).

The experiences of minority groups around the world also shows that this decline is not in evidence. The second section of this chapter explores the minorities most under threat of violence, exploitation and marginalisation, using examples from Somalia, Burma/Myanmar, China and Japan. The international recognition of minority rights and minority political mobilisation is also considered. Lastly, the nature and extent of the 'global racial crisis' is analysed, together with some of the key themes emerging from earlier chapters and their future implications.

Post-thinking

There is increasing debate within international politics and social science over the extent to which we are moving into a new post-racial world. The election of a black American President, increasing complexities in the mobilisation of identities, accelerating migration and the creation of super-diverse societies have all been seen as changing planetary racial and ethnic dynamics. St Louis (2002) provided an early examination of the prospects for a post-race sociology and politics examining two key protagonists at opposite sides of this debate, David Goldberg (2002, 2008 and see discussion in Chapter 5) and Paul Gilroy (2000, 2004). Here, on the one hand, Goldberg argues that race remains a 'primary ascriptive marker' of individuals and groups which can be used to validate discrimination, marginalisation and violence. Gilroy, on the other hand, argues that race has no biological basis and this absurd idea should be forensically rejected, that social science should operate without 'easy recourse to racialised forms of description and explanation', and that anti-racism should give way to an expansive and inclusive humanism (St Louis 2002), and the creation of intellectual and other types of spaces to think and articulate positions outside of existing racial categories. Yet both positions are not incompatible and both propose a critical recognition of the fundamental role of race and racism in the contemporary world.

The duality of race and its articulation in systems and strategies of domination and liberation was introduced in Chapter 1. Race ideas have taken many different forms in different places and have been mobilised both to implement imperial conquest and domination and to voice narratives of emancipation and liberation. The development of a range of archives of race thinking and notions of racial origins and ancestry to name and label perceived divisions between groups of people was identified. Early pre-capitalist sources, or archives of knowledge, and contexts for race thinking include differing forms of white, black, yellow, Islamic, Semitic and gypsy racial categorisations, both in the East, for example China and Japan, and in the West. Key linkages between colonialism, genocide, mercantile capitalism and plantation slavery were established, including the intertwining of race with imperial expansion, the rise of nation states and the formation of racialised modernity, and genocidal strategies in Africa and Australia. The progressive power of race to mobilise groups in the context of struggles of resistance, emancipation and liberation include opposition to slavery, African nationalism, Pan-Africanism and Negritude. The contribution of Edward Blyden, W.E.B. Du Bois and Frantz Fanon has been an essential part of these debates. The historical grounding in the global formation of race indicates the complexity of race thinking and its power to inspire both mass violence and mass resistance. Moving beyond race therefore necessarily involves a rejection of emancipatory narratives of, for example, black identity and many forms of anti-racism, together with a shift to wider narratives of human rights.

A generative cluster of philosophical ideas, theories and practices drawing on the work of scholars such as Homi Bhabha, Judith Butler, Jacques Derrida and Paul Gilroy has been identified as signs of the emergence of a post-race paradigm (Nayak 2006). Here there is a primary focus on a 'language of hybridity and transnationalism as a means for understanding the changing nature of post-colonial racialised existence', a language that inadvertently 'obscures the roots of racism' and that radically under-estimates both the durability of these roots and the tenacity of their hold on contemporary, everyday social life (Lentin 2004: 315, Huggan and Law 2009). For the sociologist Alana Lentin, among others, this has led to a confusion of post-colonial racism with 'post-racism', and to a curious reluctance on the part of many, particularly post-structuralism-influenced, critics to give due attention to the material conditions surrounding racisms of both the present and the past. These conditions are better dealt with, according to Lentin, in the work of earlier anti-colonial thinkers, from Frantz Fanon's personally experienced 'fact of blackness' to Aimé Cesaire's still unrivalled analysis of the racial machinery of colonial/imperial regimes (Lentin 2004: 316–17; see Chapter 1). In more empirical work, an examination of the perceptions and experiences of young children growing up in mixed-race and inter-ethnic families by Ali (2003) has argued for the necessity of post-race (as opposed to post-racism) thinking, the recognition of hybridity and the claiming of mixed identities.

Post-thinking implies an aftermath, a coming after or a supplanting of previous relations and ideologies. When did the post-racial begin? The challenge to German fascism, the gradual termination of European colonialism and the discrediting of scientific and hierarchical forms of racist justification have all had far-reaching effects on the nature of racism. As Miles has commented, 'the hegemonic power of racism only began to be dissolved within Europe in the 1930's' (Miles 1993: 214). Indeed, the success of anti-racism has led to a resurgence of coded, non-hierarchical racist discourse, which have variously been called 'new', cultural or differentialist. A key feature of such discourses is that they frequently involve strategies of denial, e.g. 'I am not racist, but...'. Analysing the discursive strategies in such racist arguments is of particular value in understanding their operation and effects. Suffice to say that these denials often operate as a strategy of defence through positive self-representation, thereby facilitating counter-attacks against anti-racism. Denial of one's own racism and its link to our capacity for aggression, whether expressed as violence or indifference, is a more widespread reaction and it is a powerful emotional defence against the acknowledgement of distressing or painful self-knowledge (Pajaczkowska and Young 1992).

'Post-colonialism' is a portmanteau term which – much debated itself – usually involves some recognition that the impulse to decolonisation necessarily carries traces of the very processes of colonialism and imperialism it wishes to disavow (Gikandi 1996). Post-colonial racism can be a racism of *reaction*, based on the perceived threat to traditional social and cultural identities; or a racism of (false) *respect*, based on mainstream liberals' desire to hold at arm's length 'different' cultures they are anxious not to offend. Most of all, post-colonial racism, at least within the contemporary European context, is a racism of *surveillance*, based on what Étienne Balibar calls the strategic transformation of a 'project of inclusion into a program of exclusion', whereby 'foreigners' become 'aliens', 'protection' disguises 'preference', and 'cultural difference' slides into 'racial stigmatisation' – all in the interests of representing the European *people*, which is a very different entity to the European *population* as a whole (Balibar 2003: 122). At the heart of this process, claims Balibar controversially, is a structure of European 'apartheid' revolving around both the official treatment and the unofficial perception of migrant workers from Africa, Asia and other, economically disadvantaged parts of Europe (Balibar 2003; see also Dainotto 2007). These workers, who '"reproduce" their lives on one side of the border [but] "produce" on the other side, are 'neither insiders nor outsiders'; instead, they are

> insiders officially considered [as] outsiders, [whose uncertain status] produces a steady increase in the amount and violence of 'security' controls, which spread everywhere in the society and ramify the borderline throughout the 'European' territory, combining modern techniques of identification and recording with good old 'racial profiling'.
>
> (Balibar 2003: 123)

The discriminatory treatment of such workers, Balibar suggests, indicates that the ideal of a *democratic* Europe does not necessarily imply a *desegregated* Europe, certainly not in terms of the ascription of citizenship and other basic political rights. On the contrary, uneven access to citizenship and nationality has been built into the development of the so-called 'New Europe', and these structures of discrimination, a feature of all of the established European states, are one of the most conspicuous inheritances of the colonial past (Balibar 2003: 121; see also Brah 1996). A country may be both post-racial, where the inequities of racism have been challenged and erased in some quarters, and racialised, with related divisions and ideologies being core to some key dimensions of social, political and economic relations. Notions of post-race, post-racial and post-racism are valuable in suggesting processes of critique and disengagement with race-thinking and racial power relations. The problem with this oppositional stance, as with the term post-colonialism, is that it 'becomes a vague condition of people anywhere and everywhere' (Loomba 2005: 20).

The advocacy of post-national cosmopolitanism as liberation from the binding and wearisome attachments of locality, ethnicity and nationality has also been the subject of recent debate (Habermas 1998, May *et al.* 2004). The dark side of both democracy and globalisation examined below in relation to the current position of minorities around the world does, however, constrain the prospects for this position. Advocacy of complex, hybrid identities, global polis and citizenship, and the transcendence of the nation state are some of the key elements of a post-national politics. Here there is a tendency to under-estimate the opportunities for participation in multi-national cosmopolitan politics, and the value of belonging for many people. The solidarities on which people depend, whether family, community, clan or group, can be too easily dismissed, especially as these solidarities may form the central basis for struggles of the less privileged (Calhoun 2004).

The simultaneous and ambivalent way in which these processes operate, with, for example, cosmopolitan aspirations and narratives working alongside entrenched racialised immiseration, has been explored in a recent examination of post-colonial London (Keith 2005). Here the ways in which the 'perennial rein-vention of racist intolerance' and the 'forces of ethnicised and racialised closure', or 'everyday racism' (Essed 1991), operate alongside what may be called 'everyday multiculturalism', forms of intercultural dialogue and 'moments of communica-tion' are examined. Drawing on research in two areas of inner-city London, Keith identifies these conflicting discourses as being located separately in different areas of the city. The Isle of Dogs is framed by local actors as a site of racial conflict and Deptford is framed as a site of harmony/neighbourhood communality. But for Keith (2005: 153–65) the simplicity of these positions is exposed by research with young people which shows that social life is complex and these two narratives are more integrally connected in informal social networks, localities and groups with a variety of forms of communication, consumption and use of space both cross-ing racial and spatial boundaries, and enforcing racial danger.

Beyond academic debate, a wider set of public discussions and reflections are taking place with a recent global focus on the election of America's first black President:

> On election night, it seemed as if some, if not all, of our problems had been solved. Even as the president-elect cautioned that the hardest part was still before us, hadn't we already begun to hear that his candidacy had transpired in a post-racial society? And wasn't it possible that the principles that this historic event affirmed – democracy, inclusiveness, multiculturalism – might inspire the rest of the world to practice greater tolerance and compassion? Yet that same night, a group of white kids chanting 'Obama' beat up a young African-American man in New York, while in Springfield, Massachusetts, a church with a predominantly African-American congregation was burned. The next morning, we opened the papers and were reminded that sectarian wars were still raging in trouble spots around the world.
>
> (Prose 2008)

US President Barack Obama is greeted by Turkey's President Abdullah Gul during a welcoming ceremony at Cankaya Palace in Ankara, 6 April 2009
Source: © Jim Young/Reuters/Corbis

Is racism over? The advocacy of the need to recognise a material move beyond racial divisions, particularly in the USA, has been a key target for critical race theory, a specific body of American legal scholarship that emerged from the 1970s onwards in response to the successes and failures of the Civil Rights movement (Matsuda *et al*. 1993, Bell 2008, Marable 2000, Hatch 2008). Building on the work of Anna Cooper, discussed in Chapter 3, there has also been a focus here on examining intersectionality, and the inter-linking of gender, sexuality and nationalism in the reproduction of systems of racial domination (Collins 2005). In the post-civil rights era, discussion of racial progress is seen as concealing entrenched racial injustice. This is termed 'colour-blind racism', where it is assumed that racial inequalities are the outcome of natural, economic or cultural differences between groups and the use of the race idea is rejected as necessary for the end of racism (Hatch 2008). The struggle for racial equality is not complete and this body of work is concerned to illuminate the continuing power of racism and racialisation beneath the rhetorics of liberal democracy, individualism, meritocracy and progress.

There are a number of societies which have attempted to abolish racism, including Cuba, which passed such legislation after the Cuban revolution in 1959. Slavery was abolished late in Cuba, in 1886, and Afro-Cuban men and women continued to live as apparently free labourers in extremely poor housing, with no schools, until that revolution, and also with no access for black people to particular hotels, beaches, schools and jobs. The Cuban revolutionary government's decrees which emphasised 'total and absolute equality', as Fidel Castro has recently confirmed (Castro 2007), has failed to eradicate racial discrimination and inequality despite 50 years of uninterrupted political commitment to this goal.

Fidel Castro's comments on racism in Cuba

'Blacks ... still have the hardest, most physically wearing and often worst-paid jobs.'

'When you go to our prisons, you discover that many come from the marginalised barrios, they're the children of families who live in one room, in those forgotten barrios.'

'[Cuban TV shows that] criminals were mostly black and mestizo kids ... What good does that do associating the crime that's most irritating to society with a particular ethnic group?'

'What remains is ... subjective discrimination among people with some education, some culture, people who have lived for many years within the Revolution and have seen the enormous achievements [by blacks and mestizos]. But that discrimination is reflected in society.'

'[Very few blacks among the higher ranks of government] because we're still reaping the harvest of the fact that a lower proportion of blacks and mestizos were able to enter university.'

'The first thing I ask about [when visiting educational and other institutions] is ethnic composition.'

Source: Castro with Ignacio, 2007: 227–233.

Cuba is a very mixed, multi-cultural and cosmopolitan country which is, at the same time, riven by persistent racial inequalities and racial discrimination which is clear in examining the composition of both political, military and government elites and those in prison, prostitution and poverty.

Ethnic conflict in Central Africa, anti-Roma racism in Europe and oppression of indigenous peoples and other minorities across many regions, together with rising levels of conflict, violence and indiscriminate killing, do not indicate that we are moving towards a post-ethnic, post-racial world. The racist riots against Roma in Spain and Italy and the criminalisation of Roma from Romania in Italy and Finland in 2008 are indicative of the gravity of the current anti-Gypsy movement in Europe (ERIO 2009).The racialisation of regions, nations and sub-national/local contexts is pervasive but this is often denied or underplayed. Racial and ethnic divisions are highly significant but they are also flexible and fragmenting. The idea of race itself is increasingly criticised yet it persists in genetics and genomics (see Chapter 2). UN peacekeeping, the use of international and national law to challenge racial discrimination and levels of knowledge and understanding of racism, ethnicity and migration have all increased. Global racially based social structures undeniably exist and persist but their legitimacy is increasingly questioned. The nature and extent of some of these paradoxes, and in particular Europe's racial crisis, was introduced in Chapters 2, 6 and 7. Winant (2006: 999) engages with the perils of predication and suggests a coming 'global racial crisis' as he argues that we are likely to see better theory and greater understanding of racial identity and related 'human waste' on the one hand, and deepening 'structural' racism and planetary racial stratification on the other, this for him illustrates a central contradiction. Later in this chapter some of the questions that arise from such a proposition are explored, including is the notion of a racial crisis adequate? What form do these crises take? How are group claims for recognition and rights being dealt with by nation states? And what are the prospects for moving beyond race and ethnicity in contemporary society?

In the context of insecure national states and global inequalities, population mobility and international migration will lead to greater cultural diversification of national populations. New technologies and changing patterns of consumption are driving the construction of larger regional and global cultures. These globalising, cosmopolitan forces are also stimulating new forms of ethnic defensiveness and hostility to migrants, e.g. in the USA, and towards long-established minorities as evident in the development of anti-semitic movements and in anti-minority hate speech in Russia. The strength of racial and ethnic loyalties and their practical adequacy for many people in making sense of their position in the world in pre-modern, modern and contemporary times indicates the likelihood that such conflict will continue, despite international declarations and interventions, creative national policies and inter-ethnic mixing. But who are the minorities under most threat of death, genocide and devastation now? What role does ethnicity play in causing these conflicts and to what extent does increasing ethnic diversity contribute to the increasing threat of murderous conflict. This is examined here together with the meaning of and politics of minority rights in order to assess the extent to which these agendas provide a meaningful and adequate platform for the construction of viable local, national and regional societies.

Varying categories of racialised regions around the world were introduced in Chapter 5 and these were identified as interactive and overlapping landscapes with each having racial and ethnic distinctiveness in terms of history, conditions and articulation. Within Europe, French racism is different to British racism or Hungarian racism, particularly in the way that race and nationalism are articulated. European racism is different to other regional racisms, for example in Russia, China or East Asia, in the way it is articulated, its targets and its effects. In the next section we look more widely at racial and ethnic conflict around the world and in particular those areas where racial and ethnic minorities are under grave and serious threat of mass violence to highlight the contemporary power of patterns of minority domination, and in particular those situations where conditions are deteriorating.

Minorities

The proliferation of conflict, the oppression of minorities, indiscriminate killing and creation of mass refugee flows are some of the key trends which shape both the contemporary and our future world. Conflict in the Horn and Central Africa, the Middle East and Western Asia since 2007 is on the increase. The dynamics of ethnic and religious divisions and associated conflict and killing in these regions has often spread within and across borders to affect larger populations, and in many cases including Ethiopia, the Central African Republic and Chad the determining factor appears to be the 'export of the ethnic dynamics of conflict to kin population across borders' (Lattimer 2008: 45). Conflict rather than democracy has spread within and beyond the borders of Afghanistan, Israel/Palestine, Pakistan and the case examined below, Somalia.

Groups under threat

The level of ethnic and cultural diversity in a society does not have any significant effect on the likelihood of racial and ethnic conflict and associated violence and genocide (Lattimer 2008). This thesis draws on quantitative longitudinal analysis of a range of causal hypotheses (Harff 2003) and provides an empirical challenge, particularly to national political discourse which seeks to either control or reduce migration, or reject the creation of multi-ethnic and multi-cultural societies in the name of reducing racial and ethnic conflict. Whereas factors such as the habituation to illegal violence among the armed forces or police, prevailing impunity for human rights violations, official tolerance or encouragement of hate speech against particular groups and, in extreme cases, prior experience of mass killing are all much more likely to increase the likelihood of violence and atrocities being committed. The Minorities Rights Group (2008) has recently calculated the top 20 regions where minorities are most under threat around the world, with a particular focus on the poorest and most marginalised groups. Minorities are defined as nondominant ethnic, religious and linguistic communities, which may not necessarily be numerical minorities, and include indigenous and tribal peoples, migrant communities and refugees.

Top 20 countries where minorities and particular ethnic and religious groups are under threat of systematic violent repression

1. **Somalia**	Darood, Hawiye, Issaq and other clans; Ogadenis; Bantu; Gabooye (Midgan) and other 'caste' groups
2. **Iraq**	Shia, Sunnis, Kurds, Turkomans, Christians, Mandeans, Yezidis, Faili Kurds, Shabak, Baha'is, Palestinians
3. **Sudan**	Fur, Zaghawa, Massalit and others in Darfur; Dinka, Nuer and others in the South; Nuba, Beja
4. **Afghanistan**	Hazara, Pashtun, Tajiks, Uzbeks, Turkomans, Baluchis
5. **Burma/Myanmar**	Kachin, Karenni, Karen, Mons, Rakhine, Rohingyas, Shan, Chin (Zomis), Wa
6. **Dem. Rep. of Congo**	Hema and Lendu, Hunde, Hutu, Luba, Lunda, Tutsi/Banyamulenge, Twa/Mbuti
7. **Pakistan**	Amaddiya, Baluchis, Hindus, Mohhajirs, Pashtun, Sindhis, other religious minorities
8. **Nigeria**	Ibo, Ijaw, Ogoni, Yoruba, Hausa (Muslims) and Christians in the North
9. **Ethiopia**	Anuak, Afars, Oromo, Somalis, smaller minorities

→

10. **Chad**	'Black African' groups, Arabs, Southerners
11. **Sri Lanka**	Tamils, Muslims
12. **Iran**	Arabs, Azeris, Baha'is, Baluchis, Kurds, Turkomans
13. **Central Afr. Republic**	Kaba (Sara), Mboum, Mbororo, Aka
14. **Lebanon**	Druze, Maronite Christians, Palestinians, Shia, Sunnis
15. **Cote d'Ivoire**	Northern Mande (Dioula), Senoufo, Bete, newly settled groups
16. **Uganda**	Acholi, Karamojong
17. **Angola**	Bakongo, Cabindans, Ovimbundu, pastoralists, San and Kwisi
18. **Philippines**	Indigenous peoples, Moros (Muslims), Chinese
19. **Burundi**	Hutu, Tutsi, Twa
20. **Haiti**	Political/social targets

Source: Lattimer 2008: 50–51.

The multiplicity of groups under threat and the complexity of these contexts indicates the importance of both recognising the global significance of the forces of ethnicity, racism and migration and developing a wider understanding of these issues across a range of regional situations. It is not possible to deal with all these contexts here, instead two examples from the top five in this list are chosen for closer scrutiny from different regions of the world; Somalia in the Horn of Africa and Burma (the Union of Myanmar) in Southeast Asia.

Somalia: clans, conflict and crises

The Somali social order has built upon racial, status, language, class and clan stratification (Bestman 1999). Centuries of ethnocide and injustice in Somalia committed by larger clans against weaker clans and other minorities continues. Inter-clan violence in Somalia is similar in character to inter-ethnic or sectarian conflict in other parts of the world as ordinary people are targeted purely because of their clan identity which together with indiscriminate shelling, for example in Mogadishu, and mass refugee flows has created a humanitarian catastrophe with over a million people dying from war, violence and disease (World Bank 2005, Lattimer 2008, BBC News 2009b). A third of the population need food aid, over 1 million people have been displaced, there has been no effective government since 1991 and world attention has been focussed on the surge in Somali piracy. Despite the existence of minority groups, Somali society is relatively homogenous linguistically (Somali) and religiously (Islam). Clans and sub-clans are based on lines of descent with the main clan families being the Darod, Dir, Issaq, Hawiye and Rahanweyn. There is no agreement on the sub-clan structure, with Somalis themselves disputing clan affiliations, further complicated by fluid sub-clan identity affiliations (see World Bank 2005 for alternative versions of clan structures). The stronger clans have tended to claim land owned by weaker clans and indigenous groups, often leading to their displacement, and in some instances enslavement. Competition for control of power and resources has significantly changed clan boundaries in many parts of the country, with new clans consoli-dating their position on occupied lands, which fuels further forms of conflict. Somalia's history shows that many of the factors that drive armed conflict have also played a role in managing, ending, or preventing war. For instance, clannism and clan cleavages are a source of conflict being used to divide Somalis, fuel fur-ther violence and clashes over resources and power, and to mobilise wider militia groups and obstruct attempts at reconciliation. But clan elders are also a primary source of conflict mediation; clan-based customary law serves as the basis for negotiated settlements, and clan-based blood-payment groups serve as a deterrent to armed violence. In short, Somalia has become a militarised society in which violence is the norm and guns an accepted form of conflict resolution. The back-ground to this current context is a history of Western colonialism in the region and conflict over land and political power.

Following French, Italian and British occupation and colonisation, Somalia became independent in 1960. Conflicts arising from disputes associated with the partitioning of territory in the region led to the Ogaden war in 1977/78 with Ethiopia, in which Somali forces intervened in support of Somali rebel fighters in a bid to liberate the Somali-inhabited region of the Ogaden. Somalia lost the war and suffered around 25,000 casualties. The second major armed conflict was the internal civil war between the Somali military and the Somali National Movement (SNM) for control of north-west Somalia. The SNM was formed in 1981 by some members of the Isaaq clan following the Ogaden War. Isaaq grievances deepened over the course of the 1980s, when the Barre regime placed the north-west under military control and used the military administration to crack down on the Isaaq and dispossess them of their businesses. The civil war mounted by the SNM began in May 1988 and produced catastrophe. Government forces committed atrocities against civilians (an estimated 50,000 to 60,000 Somalis died, mostly members of the Isaaq clan, which was the core support for the SNM); aerial bombardments levelled the city of Hargeysa; and 400,000 Somalis were forced to flee across the Ethiopian border as refugees, while another 400,000 were internally displaced. These atrocities fuelled Isaaq demands for secession in what became the self-declared state of Somaliland in 1991. Further conflict between government forces and a growing number of clan-based liberation movements followed. The strongest of these movements included the United Somali Congress, USC (Hawiye clan), the Somali Patriotic Movement (Ogadeni clan), and the Somali Salvation Democratic Movement (Majerten clan) (World Bank 2005). Deteriorating conditions in the region have followed the removal of the Transitional Federal Government, with Ethiopian support. Conflict particularly between the Hawiye clan (anti-government) and the Darod clan, has led to the destruction of large parts of Mogadishu and flight by large sections of the local population. Somalian minorities such as the Bantu and other caste groups have been targets of violence by all sides and their marginalisation has increased their vulnerability (Lattimer 2008). Somali minorities comprise principally the 'African' Bantu/Jarir, who are mostly landless labourers; the Benadiri/Rer Hamar urban traders of Middle Eastern origin; and the smaller, dispersed Gaboye caste-based minorities. There are other smaller minorities, such as the Ashraf and Shikhal Muslim religious communities, Bajuni fishing people and remote hunter-gatherer groups. These groups are highly vulnerable as they fall outside Somalia's clan-based structure and live in extremely poor conditions with international relief frequently being stolen by stronger local clans, lacking protection from warlords and militias and suffering from rape, attack and abduction (Matheson 2008). The humanitarian situation is deteriorating further as systems of clan protection disintegrate and over 3 million people require aid and assistance (HRW 2009)

Burma/Myanmar

This country is under the control of a military junta which suppresses dissent, and continues to commit abuses of human rights with widespread use of forced labour, including that of children. Also the situation of political prisoners and detention conditions is appalling and this has been severely criticised (UN 2008). Burman dominance over Karen, Shan, Rakhine, Mon, Chin, Kachin and other minorities has been the source of considerable ethnic tension and has fuelled intermittent separatist rebellions. Attacks on areas with concentrations of ethnic minorities by the army since 2005 have led to extensive forced displacements, for example in Kayin State and other areas in eastern Myanmar (Mon, Shan and Kaya) and in northern Rakhine State. Between 1996 and 2005, over 2800 Kayin, Mon, Shan and Kaya villages have been burned down and/or relocated en masse, or otherwise abandoned as a result of military campaigns. In Kayin State over 18,000 people are estimated to have been displaced in eastern Myanmar, with 3000 having crossed the border to Thailand, since the beginning of 2006 because of the military campaign in Kayin State. There are reportedly a total of 540,000 internally displaced persons in eastern Myanmar with minimum prospects of return and resettlement (UN 2006). The Government does not recognise the existence of internally displaced persons within its borders and severely restricts access to them by United Nations agencies and other humanitarian actors. Human rights groups believe boys as young as 12 are recruited to fight against ethnic minority rebels. Human Rights Watch (HRW) (2002) estimated that there may be more than 70,000 child soldiers in the army who are often kidnapped without their parents' knowledge while on their way home from school. They are then brutalised and physically abused during their induction and basic training before being shipped off to fight in the country's ethnic minority areas. 'Child soldiers are sometimes forced to participate in human rights abuses, such as burning villages and using civilians for forced labour. Those who attempt to escape or desert are beaten, forcibly re-recruited or imprisoned' (HRW 15 Oct. 2002).

The approximately 7 million Karen people in Burma faced entrenched discrimination in state institutions, for example state education in schools in Karen areas, even where they are the majority of the population, is exclusively provided in the Burmese language, and government offices provide no access to services in Karen languages. Control of government jobs in Karen areas is increasingly a reserved domain for ethnic Burman/Burmese people. The approximately 8 million Mon people in Burma face continual army raids, which have been responsible for enforced labour, displacement, rape, murder and widespread land confiscation. As a result, there has been a mass exodus of Mon to Thailand. The Chin people are another group who have suffered a similar fate at the hands of the Burmese army (HRW 2009).

One of the world's most persecuted people are the Rohingyas, a Muslim ethnic minority living in northern Rakhine State. Their position indicates the extent of persecution in this country. They have been regularly beaten by police, forced into slave labour, jailed for little or no reason and have no legal rights. They are unable to qualify for citizenship, unable to access medical and educational services, forbidden from marrying or travelling without permission and have no legal right to own land or property. Many have fled to escape persecution, ending up in refugee camps for decades, living illegally in surrounding areas or setting sail as 'Boat people' for other shores including Thailand, Bangladesh and Indonesia. In Thailand recent reports (BBC News 2009a) indicate that migrants and refugees who turn up on its shores have testified that they are being sent back to sea in boats without engines, their hands tied, left to their fate; many of these were Rohingya people from Burma. As one Rohingya man said recently, 'We have nothing in Burma. We are disabled people, like slaves. We can not work because our hands and feet are cut off. If we don't have permission to travel we are sent to jail. We are really like slaves there' (Thompson 2006).

Bangladesh – husband is missing – Thai military towed 250 men out to sea. Mohammad Iqbal Hossain's wife Nur Kahtun (C) and mother Asma Khatoon (L) cry at Fadanardal near Cox's Bazar, 30 January 2009. Iqbal was one of a 250-strong group of stateless Rohingya who left Bangladesh a month ago in a rickety wooden boat, lured by agents promising a job in Malaysia. Now his family is hoping he is one of those who survived brutal treatment at the hands of the Thai military who have admitted to towing hundreds of the Muslim boatpeople from Bangladesh and Myanmar far out in the Andaman Sea before cutting them adrift.
Source: © Rafiqur Rahman/Reuters/Corbis

Contemporary patterns of domination and mobilisation

The future racial and ethnic domination of minorities across the regions of the world is certain. The strength of ethnic nationalism in some of the Central Asian countries can be seen in the promotion of national language and dress, for example in Turkmenistan. This leads to the marginalisation of ethnic minorities, as is the case with the Uzbek community in Kazakhstan, Tajikistan and Kyrgyzstan, whereas in Uzbekistan dominance of the Uzbek language effectively bars many ethnic Tajiks from entry into higher education and public employment. A further common factor seen across all of Muslim-majority Central Asian countries is the continuous human rights violations of religious minorities as Christians in particular appear to suffer persecution, and in some cases violence, across almost every state (Eastwood and Mihlar 2008). The minority populations of the Americas continued to face significant patterns of domination, arising from socio-economic patterns established during colonisation. Here, the most disadvantaged and vulnerable continued to be those of African and indigenous origin who face territorial dispossession, socio-economic marginalisation and various forms of discrimination, together with limited access to political and other decision-making processes, inadequate basic services and restricted opportunities for self-determination (Bryan 2008). In Europe, Eric Witte identifies the parameters of a 'racial and ethnic crisis', and argues that:

> Yet in Europe, the ongoing marginalisation of many minority ethnic, linguistic and religious communities is challenged by perhaps the densest network of oversight organizations, monitoring mechanisms and legal infrastructure on any continent.

> (Witte 2008: 132)

The floundering failure of these institutions and mechanisms in the face of widespread domination and discrimination against minorities and migrants, such as the Roma, indicates the depth of the challenge that these groups face in their everyday lives and in their struggles for political mobilisation.

The case of indigenous peoples, such as the Sami in Finland, was finally officially recognised by the UN General Assembly in 2007, which adopted the UN Declaration on the Rights of Indigenous People. Four states voted against – Australia, Canada, New Zealand and the United States, which were concerned that this gave too much power to these groups over activities and operations occurring on their traditional territories including land and resources, intellectual property, redress, restitution, and prior and informed consent. Nevertheless, this and related moves towards greater inclusion have assisted in the mobilisation of indigenous groups in the Americas and elsewhere seeking recognition for their identity and claims and campaigning for material and political change. This process has shaped recent key election victories by pro-indigenous and minority candidates in Bolivia, Brazil, Ecuador and Venezuela. From Alaska to Argentina and Australia, formerly acquiescent indigenous groups such as the Mapuche in Chile's southern region and the Guarani in Brazil are now increasingly vocal about claiming ancestral lands which government and private industry are still seeking to appropriate and exploit (Bryan 2008). In Australia, aboriginal protest and claims for land rights have led to notable successes including legislation on land rights (1976 see below) and native title (1993). Native title involves recognition that there is a 'continued beneficial legal interest' in land held by local indigenous Australians which survives the acquisition of title to the land by the Crown.

Aboriginal Land Rights (Northern Territory) Act 1976

In 1962 Aboriginal people finally won voting rights for Commonwealth and Territory elections. Organised Aboriginal protest against poor living and working conditions on cattle stations began at Newcastle Waters in 1966 and continued at Wave Hill from 1968. In 1963 Yolngu people at Yirrkala sent petitions to Parliament to protest at the excision of more than 300 square kilometres of their land for bauxite mining. Their battle was lost in the Northern Territory Supreme Court decision in the Gove Land Rights case eight years later, with judgment against them.

Aboriginal protests continued and with growing public support, the McMahon Government reviewed Commonwealth policy, putting out a statement in January 1971 that retreated considerably from the direct assimilation policy. This statement acknowledged specifically that Aboriginal people 'should be encouraged and assisted to preserve and develop their own culture, language, traditions and arts so that these can become living elements in the diverse culture of Australian society'.

This document, signed by the Governor-General on 16 December 1976, established the basis upon which Aboriginal people in the Northern Territory could, for the first time, claim rights to land based on traditional occupation. This Act was the first Australian law which allowed a claim of title if claimants could provide evidence of their traditional association with land.

The Act contains notable inequities, for instance claims could be made to unalienated Crown land (until the terminating date of June 1997) only on the basis of 'traditional ownership', disadvantaging those most disrupted by European occupation who are least able to provide evidence of continuing traditional association. Nevertheless the Act was a milestone of Aboriginal advancement in Australia in the second half of the twentieth century.

Source: Documenting A Democracy website, copyright Commonwealth of Australia, 2005, http://www.foundingdocs.gov.au/ item.asp?dID=64, Reproduced courtesy of the National Archives of Australia – originally published in *Documenting a Democracy* at http://foundingdocs.gov.au/

Minority rights and minority subordination in China and Japan

These two sites were identified at the very beginning of this book as being places where early origins of the global formation of race could be traced, and the case of the domination of the Burakumin group in Japan and also the case of Tibet were specifically highlighted. These areas remain racially and ethnically stratified, with many different minorities being subject to a range of forms of subordination. Japan has traditionally considered itself to be ethnically homogeneous yet NGOs continue to claim that minorities face harsh discrimination and are deprived of their distinct cultures (Eastwood and Farar 2008). NGO activity included the collation of detailed survey evidence from a coalition of Ainu, Buraku and minority Korean women who worked together to research education, employment, social welfare, health status and exposure to violence, and related campaigning work.

Specification of the principles for the establishment of minority rights has been set out by the UN (1992). These include a claim for state protection and promotion of the national or ethnic, cultural, religious and linguistic identity of minorities, and recognition of their right to enjoy their own culture, to profess and practise their own religion, and to use their own language. External participation in political, social and economic life, and formation of internal minority associations and contacts between group members are also set out as key rights. The specific cultural practices of these minorities is to be fostered except where they are in violation of national law and contrary to international standards. Adequate opportunities to learn their mother tongue or to have instruction in their mother tongue, and to learn about the history, traditions, language and culture of the relevant minorities are also affirmed as key objectives. The minority rights approach, with its concern for the public and political recognition of difference, is broadly comparable to the forms of multi-culturalism advocated by theorists such as Will Kymlicka, Joseph Raz and Judith Sklar (Preece 2005).

China has over 100 million people belonging to many different minority ethnic groups, yet the superiority and dominance of Han culture and the inferiority of minority cultures, and their language, values and identity is conveyed through education. The Chinese government has resisted meaningful and inclusive political participation of minorities and there has been widespread international criticism of intolerance, with concern over the continuing violations of Tibetans' and Uyghurs' religious rights and Mongols' cultural rights (Eastwood and Farar 2008). As in Tibet, strategies of subjugation, forced assimilation and state-sanctioned 'ethnic swamping' which involves the resettlement of dominant Han Chinese into minority areas, accompanies discrimination in employment, social security, the use and teaching of minority languages, culture and housing. Discrimination against ethnic minority women was evident in the highly humiliating policy of forcible relocation of young and unmarried ethnic Uyghur women to work in factories in eastern China. Chinese modernisation necessarily involves racial and ethnic domination and the erosion of minorities' cultures, values, practices and identities. It also appears that technological, economic and political process in many regions of the world is inextricably bound up with processes of minority marginalisation and racial and ethnic domination. Lastly, it is also important to recognise that there are 'minorities within minorities' and forms of discrimination, for example against women, may be highly significant within minority groups themselves (Eisenberg and Spinner-Halev 2005).

The global racial crisis

The concept of a global racial crisis was spelt out above. This section seeks to provide a meta-analysis of the key arguments presented in this book and examines their implications for the future of the world. Science illustrates this crisis, as explored in Chapter 2. Science has been a key terrain for the elaboration of both excessively detailed systems of racial hierarchies and racial categories, i.e. the invention and promotion of racial 'truths'. It has also been the terrain on which there has been the most through-going rebuttal of the race idea and related systems of racial violence, for example in Nazi Germany. Racial systems of classification have been elaborated in scientific contexts and political imperatives to challenge such racial science developed. Current debates in both the US and the UK over the validity and status of the race idea has established ongoing ambivalence and conflict over whether or not it should be systematically and consistently rejected. Genetics and genomics illustrate both the rapid advance in our knowledge and understanding of human differentiation and the inability to move beyond racial categorisation. But it is clear that racial and ethnic conflicts are not natural or primordial, and that cultural and ethnic groups cannot be defined by biology or kinship; they are socially constructed. Genomics indicates the mixed historical origins of population groups and challenges fictitious notions of common biological descent. This makes any claim to 'purity' in the protection and formation of cultural, ethnic or racial identity devoid of a scientific basis.

The importance of analysing intersectionality, racialisation and the race/ethnicity nation complex were highlighted in Chapter 3, which identified the central contribution of William Du Bois, Anna Cooper, Max Weber and Robert Park, and also in the UK John Rex and Michael Banton, to the development of this field of study. It showed the importance of examining both the inter-relationships between race, gender, class, ethnicity and nation and the logic of racialisation. Whether examining racism and ethnicity in inter-war Hawai'i or post-war Britain, the ways in which these factors are mobilised in specific contexts needs careful scrutiny. Over-generalisation of both the nature of these situations and the processes and prospects for social change have been shown to be problematic for all these scholars. The durability, dynamics and resurgence of both racial and ethnic conflict and segregation has often been under-estimated. However, collectively these contributions have built and shaped a coherent field of intellectual and political endeavour. The desire to interrogate, understand and challenge the highly varied forms of racial and ethnic exclusion examined in the work of this core group has driven this output, and it continues to motivate the rapidly expanding ranks of social researchers in this field.

The foundational understanding of ethnicity provided by Max Weber provided the basis for moving on to examine contemporary debates and evidence. For Weber, ethnic groups are those which have a belief in common descent arising from either collective memories of colonisation and migration, collective customs, physical similarities or all three. Also ethnic groups are marked out by a range of dimensions of ethnicity including common language, the ritual regulation of life and shared religious beliefs. The scale and significance of ethnicity and related conflict across the globe is of major social significance, as it is the 'leading source of violence in international affairs' (Esman 2004: 26). In considering the 'state of the art' of ethnicity research it was clear that we still have much to learn, particularly from the comparative analysis of national and regional contexts. Separated typologies of ethnicity, post-war migration flows and regional racisms have been developed in this field of social science but often with unequal weight being given to each of these processes. There is considerable scope here for synthesising these approaches and building a global account. The terrible contemporary power of these processes is also evident across the globe. The link between undocumented migration and contemporary patterns of slavery is well researched and examples from Australia, Japan and China were used to illustrate the evidence of human trafficking. The increasing levels of conflict and hostility between Israel and Palestine focussed on the Gaza Strip illustrate the transition from a complex cosmopolitan order into segregating, ethno-racially divided sets of communities with expulsions, exiles and evictions central to this process. If the prospects for the creation of peace and a Palestinian state free from racial domination seem poor, the prospects for the resurrection of a Tibetan state free from Chinese racial domination seem even worse.

The impact of Chinese ideologies of national and racial superiority is most tellingly felt in Tibet where migration, settlement and occupation are used as weapons of racial domination, together with entrenched hostility to ethnic, cultural, linguistic and religious difference. The central importance of understanding the linkages between racism, migration and ethnicity is also necessary even where there have been many decades of initiatives aimed at addressing these issues. The problems the UK still faces 40 years after the first race relations legislation was passed include high levels of ethno-racial inequality and segregation, rising right-wing extremism and mass evidence of racial hostility and violence. We are part of a world where there are complex, diverse conflicts in super-diverse contexts. The construction of racial, ethnic, national and cultural hostility and its expression through racism, xenophobia, intolerance, discrimination, conflict and violence has been seen to be dynamic and complex. Also rapidly changing cultural environments, resulting from increasingly complex migration flows, claims for recognition of ethnic and cultural identities and expanding international networks of production and consumption are producing super-diverse contexts in which these conflicts play out.

The nature of Europe's racial crisis was explored in Chapters 6 and 7. Improving theory, greater understanding and better evidence of racist violence and related 'human waste', on the one hand, accompanies deepening 'structural' racism and European racial stratification on the other. This is a central contradiction in the post-colonial era and is evident within the European politics of race. The establishment of the European Monitoring Centre for Racism and Xenophobia (EUMC) in Vienna in 1997/98, which subsequently became the FRA, and the implementation of systematic surveillance of patterns and trends in racism and xenophobia across the expanding number of EU member states represents a significant advance in understanding. But this has been accompanied by deepening structural racism and associated violence across this region. There is a crisis in strategies to tackle racist violence where legislation, techniques and approaches increasingly proliferate in the face of highly durable and resurgent patterns of attack and murder. The location of the Roma at the bottom of racial and ethnic hierarchies in Europe further illustrates this crisis. Forms of both direct, indirect and structural discrimination were examined in a variety of contexts including housing and education. It is clear that despite a move away from the study of racial discrimination, for example in UK social science which had established a definitive track record of studies in the 1970s and 1980s, the strength and importance of these practices remains a highly durable and significant feature of the lives of minorities and migrants across Europe whether looking for a job, finding somewhere to live, trying to secure quality education or going shopping or to a nightclub. It was found that ethnic minorities in Europe are generally living in comparatively poor housing conditions which contribute to entrenched patterns of social and economic inequality. They are also subject to persistent, extensive and varied forms of ethnic, racist and national discrimination. The situation is complex and dynamic in terms of location, tenure and ethnicity. Within some minority groups, households are moving out of inner city areas into suburban and rural locations, while other poorer households are increasingly concentrated in inner city areas. Across and between migrant and minority ethnic groups there are substantial differences in housing conditions, tenure patterns, and the extent of discrimination and hostility experienced. Nonetheless, housing disadvantage is widespread, and often severe. Apartheid-like patterns of Roma/non-Roma segregation in schooling particularly in Central and Eastern Europe indicate the severity of contemporary racial divisions. The complete lack of schooling for many Roma children and massive dropout rates expose the failure of state institutions and are also indicative of high levels of widespread anti-Roma racism. In response to persistent exclusions and persecution many Roma/Gypsy/Traveller groups together with their allies have led a process of political mobilisation which has had some notable successes within the EU.

The contradictory tendencies evident in media representation were examined in Chapter 8. In the UK, minority ethnic perceptions of news content fitted closely with the definition of institutional racism used in the Stephen Lawrence Inquiry, these included perceptions of racial and ethnic bias against them, an inappropriate service for people from differing cultural and ethnic groups, and prejudice, ignorance, thoughtlessness and racist stereotyping which disadvantages minority ethnic people. It is also important to recognise the ways in which news media can contribute in the widest sense to an anti-racist, inclusive, humanitarian project. There has been some evidence of declining media, political and social hostility to both settled minority ethnic groups and new migrant groups which provide the conditions for the creation of a climate of greater trust in which more open discussion and debate of sensitive issues affecting minority ethnic groups in the news can fruitfully take place. These more progressive social spaces are continually subject to the swift remembering, reinvention and restatement of hostile messages, as seen in Russia, America and Europe in the first decade of this century. The strength of white backlash culture (Gabriel 1998) and racial and ethnically constructed forms of political nationalism must never be under-estimated, and the strength of repeated linkages between violence, crime, race and migration remain the most worrying aspects of contemporary news coverage. Global systems of communication appear to have reawakened nationalist, political myths and old fears of the Other, rather than contributing to enlightened public understanding (Brinks *et al.* 2006). The focus on political myths and conspiracy theories, and the use of communications media to promote these, is one of many tendencies in this arena. This does not undermine the radical case that exposing and challenging journalistic and media practices which buttress xenophobia, hatred and nationalist myths is a vital and urgent contemporary task.

Conclusion

The future prospects for the sociological analysis of racism, ethnicity and migration are good, in that they will increasingly provide new evidence and advances in our understanding of the ways in which the world works. Critical intellectual endeavour is a key force in moving towards the creation of a post-racial, post-ethnic world. A central danger has been to under-estimate the power and durability of these three social forces, and to under-estimate the opportunities for intervention and change. Our task as social scientists is to stay alert to their complexity and dynamics and continue to build our awareness and understanding of how they operate. A range of different agendas for liberation and emancipation have been identified in this book, including anti-slavery, anti-colonial and anti-racist reflexivities. A range of contemporary terrains on which opposition to racial and ethnic divisions has been built have been identified including indigenous people's rights, minority rights, anti-discrimination and racism reduction agendas, and also media representation and cosmopolitanism. Overall, the future prospects for racial and ethnic conflict, discrimination, killing, violence, immiseration and marginalisation of minorities are poor, and in many instances they may get worse. These twin trends indicate the nature of the global crisis we face.

End of chapter activity

Current international political debate on the shape of contemporary global racism and forms of anti-racist intervention can be explored on: www.un.org/durbanreview2009/index.shtml. This site supports the Durban Review Conference, held in Geneva, Switzerland, 20–24 April 2009, which evaluates progress towards the goals set by the World Conference against Racism, Racial Discrimination, Xenophobia and Related Intolerance in Durban, South Africa, in 2001. The Review Conference will serve as a catalyst to fulfilling the promises of the Durban Declaration and Plan of Action agreed at the 2001 World Conference through reinvigorated actions, initiatives and practical solutions, illuminating the way toward equality for every individual and group in all regions and countries of the world. The disruption to the conference caused by the Iranian President's virulently anti-semitic speech indicates the need for greater pessimism over the future prospects for international action in this field.

Further reading

Winant, H. (2006) 'Race and racism: towards a global future', *Ethnic and Racial Studies*, 29, 5, pp. 986–1003. This discussion piece provides a stimulating overview of some key trends in current forms of racism and anti-racism.

Lattimer, M. (2008) 'Peoples under threat', in Minority Rights Group (eds) *State of the World's Minorities*, London: MRG. This piece provides a useful global summary of minorities under threat of violence and genocide.

References

Ali, S. (2003) *Mixed-race, Post-race: gender, new ethnicities and cultural practices*, London: Macmillan.

Balibar, É. (2003) *We, the People of Europe? Reflections on Transnational Citizenship*, trans. J. Swenson, Princeton: Princeton University Press.

Bell, D. A. (2008) *Silent Covenants; Brown v. Board of Education and the unfulfilled hopes for racial reform*, Oxford: Oxford University Press.

Bestman, C. L. (1999) *Unravelling Somalia: race, violence and the legacy of slavery*, Philadelphia: University of Pennsylvania Press.

BBC News (2009a) *Thailand's deadly treatment of migrants*, 17 Jan., http://news.bbc.co.uk/2/hi/south_asia/7834075.stm

BBC News (2009b) *Somalia Country Profile*, http://news.bbc.co.uk/1/hi/world/africa/country_profiles/1072592.stm.

Brah, Avtar (1996) *Cartographies of Diaspora: Contesting Identities*, London: Routledge.

Brinks, J. H., Rock, S. and Timms, E. (eds) (2006) *Nationalist Myths and Modern Media, contested identities in the age of globalisation*, London: Tauris Academic Studies.

Bryan, M. (2008) 'Americas', in Minority Rights Group (eds) *State of the World's Minorities*, London: MRG.

Calhoun, C. (2004) 'Is it time to be post-national?', in S. May, T. Modood, and J. Squires (eds) *Ethnicity, Nationalism and Minority Rights*, Cambridge: Cambridge University Press.

Castro, F. with Ramonet, I. (2007) *My Life*, London: Penguin.

Collins, P. H. (2005) *Black Sexual Politics: African Americans, gender and new racism*, London: Routledge.

Dainotto, R. (2007) *Europe (in Theory)*, Durham, NC: Duke University Press.

Eastwood, E. and Mihlar, F. (2008) *Asia*, London: MRG.

Eisenberg, A. and Spinner-Halev, J. (2005) *Minorities within Minorities*, Cambridge; Cambridge University Press.

ERIO (European Roma Information Office) (2009) *Recommendations of the European Roma Information Office (ERIO)to the Czech EU-Presidency on the Social* Inclusion of Roma, Brussels: ERIO.

Esman, M. J. (2004) *An Introduction to Ethnic Conflict*, Cambridge: Polity.

Essed, P. (1991) *Understanding Everyday Racism*, Newbury Park, CA: Sage.

Gabriel, J. (1998) *Whitewash, Racialised Politics and the Media*, London: Routledge.

Gikandi, S. (1996) *Maps of Englishness*, New York: Columbia University Press.

Gilroy, P. (2000) *Against Race, imagining political culture beyond the colour line*, Harvard: Harvard University Press

Gilroy, Paul (2004) *After Empire: melancholia or convivial cultures*, Abingdon: Routledge.

Goldberg, D. T. (2002) *The Racial State*, Oxford: Blackwell.

Goldberg, D. T. (2008) *The Threat of Race*, Oxford: Blackwell.

Habermas, J. (1998*) Inclusion of the Other*, Cambridge, MA: MIT Press.

Harff, B. (2003) 'Assessing risks of genocide and political mass murder since 1955', *Amercian Political Science Review*, 97, pp. 57–73.

Hatch, A. (2008) 'Critical race theory', in *Blackwell Encyclopedia of Sociology Online*, www.sociologyencyclopedia.com.

Huggan, G. and Law, I. (eds) (2009) *Racism, Postcolonialism, Europe*, Liverpool: Liverpool University Press.

Human Rights Watch (HRW) (2002) *My Gun Was As Tall Me, child soldiers in Burma*, New York: HRW.

Human Rights Watch (HRW) (2009) *World Report*, New York: HRW.

Keith, M. (2005) *After the Cosmopolitan? Multicultural cities and the future of racism*, London: Routledge.

Lattimer, M. (2008) 'Peoples under threat', in Minority Rights Group (eds) *State of the World's Minorities*, London: MRG.

Lentin, A. (2004) *Racism and Anti-Racism in Europe*, London: Pluto.

Loomba, A. (2005) *Colonialism/Postcolonialism*, London: Routledge.

Marable, M. (2000) *How Capitalism Underdeveloped Black America: problems in race, political economy and society*, Boston: South End Press.

Matheson, I. (2008) 'Africa', in Minority Rights Group (eds) *State of the World's Minorities*, London: MRG.

Matsuda, M., Lawrence III, C., Delgado, R. and Crenshaw, K. (1993) *Words that Wound: critical race theory, assaultive speech and the First Amendment*, Boulder, CO: Westview Press.

May, S., Modood, T. and Squires, J. (eds) (2004) *Ethnicity, Nationalism and Minority Rights*, Cambridge: Cambridge University Press.

Miles, R. (1993) *Racism after 'Race Relations'*, London: Routledge.

Minority Rights Group (2008) *State of the World's Minorities*, London: MRG.

Nayak, A. (2006) 'After race: ethnography, race and post-race theory', *Ethnic and Racial Studies*, 29, 3, pp. 411–430.

Pajaczkowska, C. and Young, L. (1992) 'Racism, Representation and Psychoanalysis', in Donald, J. and Rattansi, A. (eds) *'Race', Culture and Difference*, London: Sage/Open University.

Preece, J. J. (2005) *Minority Rights*, Cambridge: Polity.

Prose, F. (2008) 'Literature for a post-racial world', *Washington Post*, 14 Dec.

St Louis, B. (2002) 'Post-race/post-politics? Activist-intellectualism and the reification of race' *Ethnic and Racial Studies*, 25, 4, pp. 652–75.

Thompson, M. (2006) 'Burma's forgotten Rohinyga', BBC News, http://news.bbc.co.uk/2/hi/asia-pacific/4793924.stm.

United Nations (1992) *Minorities, Fact Sheet, No. 18*, www.unhchr.ch/html/menu6/2/fs18.htm.

United Nations (2008) *Report of the Special Rapporteur on the Situation of Human Rights in Myanmar*, United Nations, http://daccessdds.un.org/doc/UNDOC/GEN/G08/140/62/PDF/G0814062.pdf?OpenElement.

Winant, H. (2006) 'Race and racism: towards a global future', *Ethnic and Racial Studies*, 29, 5, pp. 986–1003.

Witte, E. (2008) 'Europe', in Minority Rights Group (eds) *State of the World's Minorities*, London: MRG.

World Bank (2005) *Conflict in Somalia: drivers and dynamics*, Washington, DC: World Bank.

Index